LAS VEGAS LEGENDS

WHAT HAPPENED
IN VEGAS...

BY
GREG NIEMANN

Las Vegas Legends:
What Happened in Vegas...

Sunbelt Publications, Inc.
© 2011 by Greg Niemann
All rights reserved. First edition 2011

Project management by Deborah Young
Edited by Leah Cooper
Cover and book design by Leah Cooper
Printed in the United States of America by United Graphics, Inc.

Sunbelt Publications, Inc.
P.O. Box 191126
San Diego, CA 92159-1126
(619) 258-4911, fax: (619) 258-4916
www.sunbeltbooks.com

Adventures in the Natural History and Cultural Heritage of the Southwest
A series edited by Lowell Lindsay

15 14 13 12 11   5 4 3 2 1

Library of Congress Catalogue-in-Publication Data

Neimann, Greg.
  Las Vegas legends : what happened in Vegas... / by Greg Neimann. -- 1st
ed.
      p. cm.
  Includes bibliographical references and index.
  ISBN 978-0-932653-98-7 (softcover)
  1. Las Vegas (Nev.)--History--Anecdotes. 2. Las Vegas (Nev.)--Social life
and customs--Anecdotes. 3. City and town life--Nevada--Las
Vegas--History--Anecdotes. 4. Las Vegas (Nev.)--Social
conditions--Anecdotes. 5. Las Vegas (Nev.)--Biography--Anecdotes. 6.
Legends--Nevada--Las Vegas. I. Title.
  F849.L35N45 2011
  979.3'135--dc23
                              2011029110

All photographs are by the author unless noted or in public domain.

CONTENTS

Acknowledgements to:

— Entertainer Wayne Newton, "Mr. Las Vegas," for his time, gracious assistance, and direct input regarding his years in Las Vegas and his vision for the Las Vegas of the future. A big "thank you" to Leah Koza, Mr. Newton's assistant.

— Author Jack Holder, Past President of the Outdoor Writers Association of California, for his prompt, yet thorough read of the manuscript and his few suggestions that were "right on the mark."

— Eugene Moehring, Ph.D., Professor of History, UNLV, author of several books, including *Las Vegas: A Centennial History*, and *Resort City in the Sunbelt: Las Vegas, 1930-2000*. Dr. Moehring found time to thoroughly read the manuscript and get it back to me in an incredibly short time. His corrections, numerous ideas and suggestions, background stories, and penchant for detail all were outstanding and very, very helpful.

— Las Vegas resident Dennis Hallett, retired corporate manager, for his reading of the manuscript and his numerous recommendations that made the book that much better.

— Lt. Dennis Larsen (Ret.), Las Vegas Metropolitan Police Department, 50-year Las Vegas resident, 36-year cop, and Field Training Coordinator. His suggestions after reading the manuscript resulted in incredible personal input from someone who was there.

— Officer Bob Holland, Las Vegas Metropolitan Police Department, President of Metropolitan Police Museum Association of Nevada;

— University of Nevada Las Vegas, Special Collections; Peter Michel, Director, Kelli Luchs, Archivist.

— Lost City Museum, State of Nevada Department of Cultural Affairs, Overton, Nevada; Kathryne Olson, Director.

— Eldorado Canyon Mine Tours, Tony and Bobbie Werly. They've added a historical element for tourists at my sister's former Techatticup home.

— Little A'le'Inn, owner Pat Travis, Rachel, Nevada. She breathed life into a fascinating story about her mysterious area.

— Gamblers Anonymous, Unity Club, 900 E. Karen, Las Vegas. While you didn't know why I was there, I admire you.

— Many people answered questions or pointed me in the right direction, including Erik Pappa, Clark County Director of Public Communications; Mark Hall-Patton, Clark County Museum; Marcus Martin, Public Information Officer, LVMPD; Jace Radke, Public Information Officer, City of Las Vegas; Adam Harrison and Todd Benevidez, Gold and Silver Pawn Shop; clerks at EZ Pawn Shops (Various locations); the gracious librarians at the Las Vegas-Clark County Library; and Friends of Classic Las Vegas, a group of people who care about their city.

— To the great team at Sunbelt Publications, from Publisher Diana Lindsay for suggesting the book and lighting the fire to talented Senior Editor Jennifer Redmond and most helpful Project Manager Debi Young. Thanks also to designer Leah Cooper of Armadillo Creative who made these pages come to life.

— To my wife Leila who again had to juggle our retirement activities and travel around my engrossment in yet another project.

Dedication

To my siblings: Brothers Fritz, Joe, Tom, and Jim Niemann, sisters Camilla Collins, Barbara Ireland, and Mary Evans, and the family of our recently deceased brother Matt Niemann.

PROLOGUE

Las Vegas Centennial

THE CENTURY'S LARGEST CITY

The City of Las Vegas, Nevada chalked up its Centennial on March 16, 2011. On that date in 1911, then-Governor Tasker Oddie signed the charter granting cityhood to the growing town established by a railroad auction on May 15, 1905.

Because that railroad auction was the genesis of Las Vegas, in 2005 the city sponsored a major year-long Centennial fanfare to celebrate. No matter that Las Vegas "jumped the gun" a bit celebrating cityhood six years early, but hey, "they did it their way." That non-conformist Las Vegas mindset exemplifies the spirit of a city that has been swimming against the current for 100 years.

And what a 100 years it's been! By year 2000, Las Vegas was the most populous American city founded in the twentieth century. Beginning with an estimated population of approximately 945 in 1911, the Las Vegas population had roughly doubled every decade of the 1900s!

By 2010, the city's population soared over 600,000 (607,876), and with the surrounding adjacent area of mostly unincorporated communities, Las Vegas is pushing two million (1,951,000).

The name "Las Vegas" is often applied to those nearby unincorporated areas, most notably Paradise and Winchester that encompass the famed Las Vegas Strip. The entire southern Clark County has exploded with people. Consider that in 1911, Clark County, which had two years earlier split from Lincoln County, represented only 4.1% of Nevada's population. Today the county is home to approximately 75% of all Nevadans!

During its first 100 years, Las Vegas has become internationally renowned as a major resort city for gambling, entertainment, shopping, and dining. With daring, greed, an innate sense of what people want, and a willingness to provide it, the city has gambled and out-wrestled contenders to rightfully claim the title "The Entertainment Capital of the World."

The city's history is like no other. Mormon settlers, miners, ranchers, railroad people, and pioneers established the area, but the advent of gambling created a city the likes of which has been unseen in modern times. Even early on, Nevada encouraged visitors with relaxed divorce and marriage regulations causing many more to flock to the sparkling new lights of Las Vegas.

Casinos started dotting the desert floor like wildflowers after a storm and with them came hopeful gamblers and predatory owners who kept improving their methods to draw them in, entertain them, and keep them there. They added floor shows, big name entertainers, lounge shows, bright lights, drinks, food, nightclubs, and tolerance. In fact, the city's tolerance, especially for all sorts of adult entertainment, has also earned Las Vegas the title of "Sin City," a sobriquet mostly worn with pride.

For decades thousands of people have moved into Las Vegas and surrounding areas each month, almost all seeking some type of opportunity. Up until the recession that began in 2008, construction jobs had been plentiful; the hotels and casinos also have insatiable manpower needs. The massive CityCenter (which opened in 2010) alone needed 12,000 permanent employees at completion.

Unfortunately, the flip side of that is when CityCenter was completed, 3,600 construction workers were idled with no big projects in sight. The faltering economy dealt the fast-growth Las Vegas a devastating blow.

As the city reached its 2011 Centennial, it was struggling. With unemployment climbing as high as 13.8%, Las Vegas unfortunately earned the lamentable title of foreclosure capital of the country, six times worse than the national average.

The unprecedented growth seemed to be taking a breather, waiting for things to catch up. Hoping to lure more needed tourists, and their money, survival tactics have been employed, including offers of wildly discounted hotel room rates.

Some indicators have been suggesting that the dark clouds have begun to yield to blue sky. Clark County jobs grew by 7,400 from January to February 2010, compared to a loss of 18,000 jobs the previous month. In April 2010 it was announced that March home sales were up 32.8% over the previous month. Yet, by the end of 2010, Las Vegas found its fragile economy among the worst of 150 worldwide metropolitan areas. Without diversification, Las Vegas was bouncing back slower than most other places. Future and sustained growth depends on tourists, and there are plenty of places for them to play, stay, and—hopefully—spend! There are so many hotel rooms in Las Vegas (148,000) that if a person were to spend one night in each room it would take him about 400 years. Of the world's 25 largest hotels, 19 are on or near the Las Vegas Strip. Away from the hotels, there is a lot to the city that the casual visitor does not see, a city of families and homes and neighborhoods. The Clark County School District is the nation's fifth largest with 314,000 students (K-12). Las Vegas is home to the 20,000-student University of Nevada, Las Vegas (UNLV). There's a University of Nevada Medical School and other private colleges.

But it's the brash, the outrageous, the scandals, and the real or imagined legends and myths that have always been the focus of the Las Vegas spotlight.

The early history of Las Vegas is fascinating. It is unique and paved the way for all that followed. Millions of visitors through the years have departed for home following pleasurable days, memorable nights, fond memories, and their own titillating stories about "What Happened in Vegas..."

Chapter 1

The Meadows

A small spring and creek along The Old Spanish Trail began to attract Indians and a few travelers. Mormons came, built a fort, and made a stab at establishing a community in that place called The Meadows (*las vegas*).

Then came ranchers, miners, renegade Indians, and other characters who became the nucleus of southern Nevada. What would become the city of Las Vegas was a wide-open place, like a page out of a Wild West novel.

The Old Spanish Trail

Visitors to The Meadows

G litter Gulch without the glitter? No high rises, no casinos, no streets or sidewalks? Up to the mid-1800s the largest American city born in the twentieth century was merely a small oasis created by abundant artesian spring water.

For centuries, Indians (Southern Paiutes) often rested by the springs along their Paiute Trail, one of several trade routes they used crisscrossing the American Southwest. From underground aquifers near today's downtown Las Vegas, year-round water flowed in a small creek for several miles before vanishing into the sand.

Some of the Paiutes remained in the valley, spending time at the springs and creek to hunt and gather food. Cottonwood trees, willows and tules lined the banks, and a hardy desert grass carpeted the nearby valley floor.

The Paiutes, however, were not the first occupants.

It seems the Las Vegas valley has long been a busy place. After the last ice age ended about 9700 b. c., prehistoric animals roamed the former lush and verdant area. Proof of this was uncovered relatively recently, when construction workers in 1993 uncovered the remains of a Columbian Mammoth which paleontologists date to be 8,000 to 15,000 years old.

Decades before the discovery, in 1925-26, archeologist Mark Harrington, who went on to become curator of the Southwest Museum in Los Angeles, led expeditions into Nevada's Moapa Valley and the Muddy River to the north, and to Tule Springs just

Map of the Old Spanish Trail
(courtesy National Park Service)

outside Las Vegas. Along with bones of Ice Age sloths (9700-6500 B. C.), they uncovered early pueblo pottery, human bones, and artifacts.

In initially excavating 46 pueblo ruins, they determined that more than one human culture occupied the sites, including earlier basket makers, and later pottery makers, the first human inhabitants confirmed to date back to at least 900-400 B.C.

The desert winds caused billowing sandstorms which constantly took habitat from those early dwellers, especially to the north. By the nineteenth century only the springs near downtown Las Vegas remained attractive to receive tired and thirsty visitors along the Paiute Trail. Some 1,500-2,000 Paiute Indians were living in the area when outsiders arrived.

Until 1829, the original route of the Old Spanish Trail from Santa Fe to Los Angeles went far to the north of Las Vegas, skirting the impassable Grand and Glen Canyons. Then during winter 1828-29, New Mexico merchant Antonio Armijo had organized a California-bound trading party of 60 men and 100 mules. He'd long traded with the Southern Paiutes and most likely learned of a new, more southern, route from them.

Armijo sent a group of scouts ahead and they reached the Las Vegas Valley area around Christmas Day, 1828. All had returned to the main party by New Year's except Rafael Rivera, a young Mexican scout. Rivera, who is credited with being the first known non-Indian to visit the current Las Vegas area, finally rejoined the Armijo party on January 7, 1829 and thence led the group into the valley where they camped at the springs.

Knowledge of the abundant artesian water spread and soon Spanish traders and gold seekers began stopping at what they began calling "Las Vegas," which means "The Meadows" in Spanish. Due to word of mouth, the route became heavily traveled by caravans using the Old Spanish Trail. The route meandered a bit as scouts developed shortcuts for various reasons, such as hostile Indians, better water, etc. In time, that Old Spanish Trail that came through Las Vegas became the main trade route between Santa Fe and Los Angeles, and evolved into what was variously known as the Salt Lake Road, The Mormon Trail, the California Road and eventually U.S. Highway 91, and later yet, Interstate-15.

John C. Fremont
The Map of 1845

The historical trailblazer and one-time presidential candidate John C. Fremont was the man who put Las Vegas on the map, literally. Fremont was born in Savannah, Georgia in 1813 to a Frenchman and a young Virginia aristocrat. His mother, at age 17, was forced to marry a 62-year-old man. About

15 years later she was discovered having an affair with her French tutor, one Charles Fremón. Their child was John C. Fremont (The "T" was added later). Young Fremont went on to become a member of the U.S. Topographical Corps and helped map the upper Mississippi and Missouri rivers.

Fremont married Jessie, the daughter of powerful Senator Thomas Hart Benton (D.–MO), who was one of the leading advocates of western expansion. Fremont began leading expeditions to the West, and met and hired the remarkable but illiterate guide Kit Carson. Carson, who could not write, amazingly still spoke French, Spanish, English, and several Indian dialects and sign languages.

COL. FREMONT
PLANTING THE AMERICAN STANDARD ON THE ROCKY MOUNTAINS.

The press loved to follow the explorations of John C. Fremont

Fremont's trips to the west were successes and widely reported in the Eastern media. It was in 1844, when Fremont was heading south from Sutter's Fort, California to pick up the original Old Spanish Trail that he stumbled across Las Vegas quite by accident.

In April while stopping to slaughter and dry some animals along the intermittent Mojave River, they were approached by two Mexicans, a man, Andreas Fuentes, and an 11-year-old boy, Pablo Hernandez. The pair related that their small party of six was herding horses from Los Angeles toward Santa Fe when they were attacked by about 100 Indians. Running from arrows, Fuentes and the boy were the only ones to escape. The others in their party were Fuentes' wife, Hernandez' parents, and another man.

The Mexicans led Fremont back over their route, to the scene which was near today's Tecopa by the California-Nevada border. They found a sickening sight, the men's bodies naked, mutilated and pierced with arrows, and the women gone.

Later, Senator Benton's family adopted the boy, and Fuentes joined the Fremont expeditions.

Detoured off the main route, Fuentes then guided Fremont through Las Vegas, which they reached on May 3, 1844.

Fremont described his arrival: "After a day's journey of 18 miles, in a northeasterly direction, we encamped in the midst of another very large basin, at a camping ground called *Las Vegas*, a term which the Spaniards use to signify fertile or marshy plains, in contradistinction to *llanos*, which they apply to dry and sterile plains. Two narrow streams of clear water, four or five feet deep,

9

gush suddenly with a quick current, from two singularly large springs; these, and other waters of the basin, pass out in a gap to the eastward. The taste of the water is good, but rather too warm to be agreeable; the temperature being 71 in the one and 73 in the other. They, however, afford a delightful bathing place."

Fremont's 1845 report made the springs at Las Vegas very important. His report contained a map of the area mentioning Las Vegas. The map was so reliable and popular that Congress printed 20,000 copies.

The map rendered Las Vegas a primary stop and wagon trains considered it indispensable. If a group of emigrants did *not* have that map, that fact was mentioned in diaries and journals. Many travelers on their way to Los Angeles thus found water and a place to rest along the way at the springs in *The Meadows.*

While his map led thousands overland, Fremont himself went on to more grandiose endeavors, including leading the Bear Flag Rebellion against Mexico, thus being instrumental in the U.S. acquiring California.

Democrats sought to back Fremont for president, but he refused to endorse the Fugitive Slave Act, which would have forced escaped slaves back to their former slave masters. So he became the first candidate of the new Republican Party. He lost to James Buchanan, carrying only 11 states to Buchanan's 19. Later President Abraham Lincoln appointed Fremont commanding general of the Department of the West. He then served as governor of Arizona Territory from 1878 to 1881.

Fremont died in 1890. About him, his mentor Senator Benton said, "From the ashes of his campfire have sprung cities."

That is certainly prophetic when one considers Las Vegas. Fremont helped open up the West and his name is everywhere, on streets, towns, cities, schools and mountains. His map definitely gave Las Vegas early importance, and his adventurous spirit lingers on.

The Mormon Fort
Under Latter-Day Blessings

While the John C. Fremont report helped the expansionists better understand the West, it also helped establish the Mormon Road route for wagon freight traffic and emigration between Salt Lake City and Los Angeles.

During the years 1848-50, the majority of miners and opportunists headed for the California Gold Rush along the Old Spanish Trail. The Mormon Road part of that trail (From Salt Lake City through Las Vegas) was the only road open in winter, and the Mormons and their settlements were instrumental in developing and protecting it. Any supplies or goods from abroad, including fresh Mormon converts from elsewhere, traveled from Los Angeles-area ports to Utah along that route. Even things from California, like fruit tree cuttings, went that way.

More settlements were needed and missionaries were called upon to colonize remote locations along the Mormon Road between Utah and Southern California. Along with protection, the Mormons wanted the line of settlements to offer services and lodging for travelers. Thus they established a mission in San Bernardino, California.

The decision to establish a mission in the Las Vegas Valley (then New Mexico Territory) was made in early 1855 by Brigham Young, leader of the Church of Jesus Christ of Latter-day Saints (the Mormons) in Salt Lake City. He selected 30 men, and under the leadership of William Bringhurst they departed Utah in April with 40 wagons and ox teams, 15 cows and several riding horses.

The Mormons' purpose in Las Vegas was manifold. They were to raise crops, instruct the local Paiutes (there were about 1,500 in the area) in farming and hygiene, build a fort and settlement, establish a safe halfway station for protecting travelers and establishing trade on the Mormon Road, set up a post office, and explore the country where they even hoped to locate and mine minerals and ores. Of utmost importance to the missionaries, however, was to attempt to convert the local Paiutes to their faith.

After a 30-day sojourn from Salt Lake City, the last 55 miles through a waterless desert, the group arrived at the Las Vegas springs on June 14, 1855. They chose to "establish a camp near a creek running through some meadow land."

The creek was bordered on both sides by extensive mesquite growth that stretched about a half mile from the banks. The growth extended in a wide band the entire length of the flowing creek which then flowed into the sand at the eastern edge of the valley.

The men got to work right away laying out the areas for the fort and farming lots. Each man was given 2½ acres of land plus ¼ acre for a garden. They cleared the land for planting and built fences to corral the animals. The mission soon consisted of an adobe wall enclosure measuring 150 square feet with fortifications on the southeast and northwest corners. A corral measuring 150 x 132 feet was built on the north side. The walls were two feet thick at the bottom and tapered to one foot thick at the top. Residences were built inside the fort, and by November the families who were to stay for the winter had been moved into more comfortable quarters.

The Mormons eagerly looked forward to interaction with the Indians, whom they considered to be Lamanites, or descendents of ancient Israelites. They not only had considerable contact with the Indians, but according to the journal of missionary George Washington Bean, they utilized the locals to help them: "The weather was hot and the natives were very shy at first, but good treatment won them over in time, so that we used them for much of our labor. We taught them to be honest, truthful, and industrious, and also to be peaceful, and to some extent we taught them gospel principles. During the summer most of the adults were baptized and in many ways showed great improvement. They herded our cows and the stock belonging to the emigrants passing through to California. They took care of our land and irrigated our crops. They also assisted in making adobes…"

It was initially called The Bringhurst Mission because there was already a "Las Vegas" in the New Mexico Territory to which the new mission belonged. Monthly mail service was soon offered with the Post Office legal address: "Bringhurst Post Office, Las Vegas County, New Mexico."

All did not function smoothly at the mission. Men had to work in heavy garments on hot days that got up to and surpassed 110 degrees. They planted a variety of crops such as corn, melons, and oats, which did well at first, but high alkalinity in the soil and a severe frost ruined most of the crops.

Then too, the fiery Bringhurst pushed the men hard. Missionaries became discontented, not only over their leader's strict leadership, but also from their homesickness. There were also problems between the Mormons and the Paiutes regarding property rights. Out of the 1,500 Paiutes in the area, there were never more than 103 who joined the Mission. A drought exacerbated the meager food harvesting and many of the Paiutes took to raiding the fields.

Bringhurst's harsh punishment of shackling a young Indian boy all night for stealing corn pitted the formerly docile Indians against the missionaries.

The Mormons built a school, and in August the first child, Zilpha Fuller, daughter of Elijah Fuller's third wife Ellen Fuller, was born at the fort, becoming the first non-Indian born in Las Vegas.

Eleven homesick missionaries secured permission in November to return to Utah. So additional missionaries with families were sent to Las Vegas in February 1856. The 23 men, 14 women, and 15 children who came to the fort brought a new directive: instructing missionaries to grow cotton, to mine for lead, and to further advance the cause of religion.

Mormons Abandon Area
Silver Bullets

I n looking to follow the new edict and enrich the church's coffers, several Mormon missionaries continued to prospect for ore in the nearby mountains and desert. In April 1856, an Indian led them to a mountain about 35 miles southwest of Las Vegas, where lead ore was discovered high above on some cliffs.

The lead discovery seemed exciting at first, but it created new problems. Mormon President Brigham Young sent Nathaniel V. Jones to Las Vegas with orders to remove men from the mission to work the mine. Bringhurst didn't take the usurping of his power too well and according to one witness, "there was a great storm between them calling each other anything but gentlemen."

Jones took miners to the location, which he named Potosi after his Wisconsin boyhood home. In retaliation, Bringhurst childishly refused him supplies from the Mormon Fort. Miffed, Jones went back to Utah ("I'm telling Mom!") and returned with a letter from President Young that "disfellowshipped" Bringhurst from the church. Dispirited, the former disciplinarian departed for California. Some years later, Bringhurst was brought back into the good graces of the church, but he never attained another leadership position.

Getting the lead out was not easy for Jones. They built a smelter 700 feet below the mine and packed ore down by mule. Along with insufficient water for strip mining, it turns out the bullets the Mormons made from the lead were of poor quality. The high zinc content in the ore made the bullets too brittle. The Mormon mining attempt at Potosi ended in January 1857 and Potosi became the first abandoned mine of hundreds in what would become the "silver" state of Nevada.

The remaining Las Vegas missionaries were demoralized and wanted to return to Utah. In addition to questionable and argumentative leadership, there were uneasy feelings between them and the American Indians.

Brigham Young came to their rescue and in a February 1857 letter, informed them that they were free to close down the mission and return to Salt Lake. By mid-1857 only a handful of missionaries remained voluntarily. The Mormon Fort and mission became nearly deserted. The mission activities continued until September 1858 when, following a stolen harvest raid from non-converted Indians, the decision was made to totally disband and return home. The fort was left to deteriorate.

While not a total failure, the Mormon Fort was the beginning of non-Indian development in the Las Vegas area. The Indians themselves were in several ways better off following their interaction with the missionaries. Then too, the buildings and irrigation ditches, while inadequate for the sheer numbers of occupants and anticipated Indian converts at the time, later served others quite well.

The Mormon arrivals into southern Nevada in 1855 also brought different attitudes toward land use and ownership. Traditional Indian culture promoted the use and sharing of available resources without regard to ownership. The Mormon missionaries taking the water did not totally exhaust the supply, but the Indians learned that they were last in the pecking order. Soon they discovered that their existing small native farms would be displaced by white ranch and farm owners.

Indeed, by 1873, only 18 years after the arrival of the Mormons in the Las Vegas Valley, many Southern Paiute native inhabitants had been banished to the Moapa Reservation on the Muddy River to the north. Those Indians who remained off the reservation were tolerated only as long as they provided manual labor for area ranchers.

Water became more than subsistence for the small groups of early inhabitants. The precious water was corralled, harnessed, and irrigated for large farms and orchards where crops could be sold and exported. The springs of Las Vegas in effect were no longer earmarked for the gardens and camps of the Southern Paiutes who had lived in the area, but for large ranches and commerce.

O.D. Gass Rebuilds Fort
SETTLER ESTABLISHES WAY STATION

Octavius Decatur Gass, a Scotch-Irishman from Ohio, had attempted numerous ventures, including mining at Eldorado Canyon along the Colorado River, before he settled in Las Vegas. After looking over the ruins of the Old Mormon Fort at Las Vegas, O. D. Gass got an idea. He thought that perhaps supplying gold seekers and other travelers to the area with goods might beat prospecting, so he acquired the old fort site in 1865.

With assistance from a couple of mining buddies, Nathaniel Lewis and Lewis Cole, Gass set about restoring and improving the Mormon Fort to build the "Los" Vegas Ranch. (While grammatically incorrect Spanish, the term "Los" Vegas was used for years to avoid confusion with Las Vegas, New Mexico.)

They used part of the existing foundation and walls to build the ranch house near where the Las Vegas springs bubbled up from the ground and formed a small creek. (Today the fort and ranch remains are at the intersection of Las Vegas Boulevard North and Washington Avenue and are open to visitors.)

He and his buddies built a way station with a store and blacksmith shop for travelers of the Mormon/Old Spanish Trail. They also began to supply fresh food to nearby mining settlements. Gass then astutely began to buy out other landholders of surrounding acreage and the ranch was extended to 640 acres, with Gass himself holding 160 acres. By 1872, he had bought out his partners and owned it outright.

He raised livestock, and the ranch produced grain, vegetables, melons, and beans. He generally used produce to pay his Southern Paiute Indian ranch hands. He established orchards which produced peaches, figs, and apricots. His vineyard raised enough grapes to make a rudimentary wine, a big hit for many a thirsty traveler.

Gass' journals, which have survived, record the busy existence of ranching, planting, weeding, harvesting, laying up, storing, marketing produce, and repairing fences and ditches, as well as providing supplies and lodging for travelers and prospectors on their way to the mines or to Southern California and back. He even had a Chinese cook, Lee, who prepared meals for the travelers.

As Gass had hoped, it became an important way station between Utah and the Los Angeles area. Unfortunately there weren't always that many travelers. Many of his regular customers were another contingent of Mormons from St. Thomas some 60 miles to the north.

An old acquaintance of Gass' from Ohio, Conrad Kiel, started another ranch, the second in the Las Vegas Valley, just a couple of miles north of him, at the site of the old "Indian Farm." (Kiel Ranch is in today's North Las Vegas, near the corner of Carey Avenue and Losee Road.)

In 1872, Gass married Mary Virginia Simpson, a niece of President Ulysses S. Grant, who had settled in St. Thomas, Utah the previous year. Together at the Las Vegas Ranch they sired six children.

By 1877, at age 50, Gass had expanded his enterprise to 960 acres, was employing more than 30 men, several Indian women, and Lee the cook. But behind that apparent success, Gass was in debt, having been assessed two years' back taxes by the state of Nevada. (In 1866, Nevada assumed its current boundaries, acquiring the Las Vegas area from New Mexico.). Making that debt more onerous, he lost his many regular St. Thomas Mormon customers. They had learned from an 1870 survey that they were in Nevada and not

Remains of Old Mormon Fort became ranch where town began

Utah, so they refused to pay the Nevada taxes and moved back to Utah.

Gass had been trying to sell his marginally profitable ranch for years. He even mortgaged it in 1874 to a neighbor, William Knapp, for $3,000. Then in 1879 he borrowed $5,000 in gold at 2.5% interest from Archibald Stewart, a prosperous rancher and businessman from Pioche, Nevada.

In 1881, due apparently to a failed crop, Gass realized he could not repay the loan from Stewart and lost control of the ranch to him. Some historians surmise that Gass possibly planned to "walk from the ranch" after the "loan" from Stewart as he could not find a buyer and wanted to get out from under it. That would make the owner of the very first Las Vegas area ranch the precursor to all those homeowners today who "walk away" from "upside down" bank loans. Today's homeowners can point to history for an example of their understandable but questionable decision.

Hoping also to get a better education for their children elsewhere, the Gass family left in 1881 for California with their personal possessions and 1,500 head of cattle. Gass died in Redlands in 1924, and by that time his once-modest ranch on the site of the original Mormon Fort had become the center of a burgeoning town.

Archibald Stewart and his wife Helen then took over the "Los" Vegas Rancho. It was later called the Las Vegas Ranch or the Stewart Ranch.

Years later, in 1902, Helen Stewart, who had been living in the ranch house, sold the property along with the water rights to the San Pedro, Los Angeles & Salt Lake Railroad. That original ranch house built by Mr. Gass served a number of purposes through the years until it met the same fate that befell other Las Vegas buildings that would dare survive the ravages of time. It was demolished in 1966.

But from the ashes of a campfire once enjoyed by John C. Fremont, and the fort built by the Mormons, and the ranching endeavor of O.D. Gass, the city of Las Vegas would spring.

From the Fort to the Rancho
Feuding Ranchers

Archibald Stewart took over the isolated Las Vegas Ranch in 1881 after Octavius D. Gass had defaulted on the $5,000 loan against it. Stewart, of Scottish descent, was actually born in Ireland. He married Helen Jane Wiser in Stockton, California in 1873 and they moved to Lincoln County (Pioche) Nevada, where Stewart had become a successful businessman. He operated a freight business, a wood cutting business, a cattle ranch, and a butcher shop.

By 1881, Stewart and Helen had three children: William James, Hiram Richard, and Flora (Tiza) Eliza Jane. In 1882, Archibald moved the family to his new Las Vegas Valley ranch intending to sell it, but he stayed on and another daughter, Evaline La Vega, was later born there.

It turns out Stewart's business acumen came into play and he turned the combination ranch/way station into a successful operation. He began selling supplies, beef, vegetables, fruit and even decent wine to the miners of the mining camps throughout southern Nevada. The Las Vegas Ranch's grapevines could produce up to 600 gallons of wine in a good year, and prospectors from Eldorado Canyon lapped it up when they came for a little R&R.

Archibald Stewart's success and his life came to an abrupt end in July 1884. When Archibald was away from the ranch, a ranch hand went to Helen Stewart, announced he was quitting, and demanded to be paid immediately. Not familiar with the books, and not knowing how much he was owed, she told him that he would have to return after Archibald came home. At that, the disgruntled ranch hand, Schyler Henry, got upset and threatened and insulted Helen Stewart. She never repeated exactly what he had said, but told her husband about it, admitting that Henry had a "black-hearted slanderer's tongue."

That was enough for Archibald Stewart. He learned that Schyler Henry had headed for the nearby Kiel Ranch, run by O.D. Gass's old associate Conrad Kiel and his sons, Edwin and William. The ranch had developed notoriety for its blatant lawlessness, and its offering sanctuary for any men who had stumbled that way. Outlaws and other ne'er-do-wells had made the Kiel Ranch their hangout. Even the Kiel boys were considered drunks and low-lifes. Jack Longstreet, a mean and quick-tempered outlaw who had one ear cut off at an early age, spent time there. So did Hank Parrish.

The Old Fort on No. Las Vegas Blvd. (at Washington)

Hank Parrish was a perfect example of the lawlessness of the West in the 1880s. He shot and killed a fellow miner named Taylor in Eldorado Canyon. Then, in a poker game he shot both Jim Greenwood and N. Clark. Clark was hit in the groin and recovered and Parrish left Greenwood for dead.

In 1883, someone stole two of Archibald Stewart's horses. The rancher tracked the horses and found them, along with some stolen cattle belonging to an acquaintance's, at a place familiar to Parrish. He knew Parrish was the culprit but could not prove it. Undaunted, Parrish later sent word to Stewart that he planned to kill him, which could have set the scene at the Kiel Ranch.

Less than a year later, on July 13, 1884, Stewart prepared to confront the man who had just insulted his wife. After a quick dinner at home, he saddled his horse, grabbed his rifle and headed for the Kiel Ranch. Not only was Schyler Henry there along with the Kiels, but so was Parrish. A brief firefight left Schyler Henry with two flesh wounds and Archibald Stewart lying dead with wounds to the head and chest. Hank Parrish fled before authorities finally arrived; later, because of a lack of impartial eyewitnesses, a jury declined to indict Conrad Kiel and Schyler, who also participated. No one is positive to this day who actually killed Stewart, but Helen Stewart long maintained the whole incident with Henry was a ruse to lure Stewart to the Kiel Ranch and his death.

The lack of civility of neighboring rancher Conrad Kiel can best be seen in the cursory and rude note he sent with a rider to Helen Stewart immediately after the killing. It read: "Mrs. Sturd send a team and take Mr. Sturd away he is dead. C. Kiel." Helen Stewart described the pain in her journal: "I left my little children with Mr. Frazier and went as fast as a horse could carry me. The man that killed my husband ran as I approached as I got to the corner of the house I said O where is he O where is he and the Old Man Kiel and Hank Parrish said here he is and lifting a blanket showed me the lifeless form of my husband. I knelt down beside him took his hand placed my hand upon his heart and looked upon his face."

The agony of losing her husband never left her. But, with four children and pregnant with her fifth (Archibald Jr.), Helen Stewart would go on alone and become the first important woman in Las Vegas history. As for Hank Parrish, for other crimes his was the first legal hanging in Ely, Nevada. He was executed on December 13, 1890, accused of from eight to 20 murders, even though he admitted to only three, plus a "few other SOBs he shot and didn't die." While it did not bring her husband back, it gave Helen a little satisfaction. She made a note of his hanging in her journal and double underlined the words.

The saga did not quite end with Parrish's execution. A decade later, in October 1900, Edwin and William Kiel, the two sons of Conrad, were found murdered, shot to death, at the Kiel ranch. At first, it was thought that they had a drunken argument that resulted in some sort of murder-suicide. Years later, their bodies were exhumed and it appears that initial verdict was ruled out. They were shot by a different weapon. It was definitely murder. No one ever learned who killed them, but many have suspected that it was Archibald and Helen's eldest son, William, who had always held a grudge. He was among the group who discovered the bodies. Another Western mystery shrouds the infamy of Las Vegas.

Helen J. Stewart
THE FIRST LADY OF LAS VEGAS

Archibald Stewart had failed to leave a will, and probate ensued. His widow Helen received 50% of the Las Vegas Ranch and control of it, with their five children splitting the other 50%. Helen had to quickly learn to operate the ranch, at least until it could be sold. From 1887 to 1889 she had prospective buyers look at the ranch but did not receive a viable offer.

Rather than selling, she decided to keep it and even began buying nearby acreage. By 1890, she had become the largest landowner in Lincoln County, which at that time included present-day Clark County. Helen was not ignorant to business and was one of few educated women of the era. Born in Illinois in 1854, she moved with her family to California and attended Yolo College in the Sacramento area.

Helen yearned to be a city girl, with culture and society, but thus far that dream had eluded her. She enjoyed the brief time she and Archibald had living in Pioche proper rather than their ranch north of town. Then she

Helen Stewart
(courtesy Nevada State Museum & Historical Society)

moved to the Las Vegas Ranch, which was farther yet from civilization. At least there Helen enjoyed meeting the women of the teams and emigrants that traveled through.

For Helen, as she grew in the area, the area grew into a town.

Helen became extremely proficient as a rancher and a business woman. She was appointed the first postmaster of "Los Vegas" in 1893. The name continued to be spelled "Los" until 1903 when it officially became Las Vegas.

Concerned about her children's education, she hired an Oxford-trained tutor. After he died, she sent her three youngest to Los Angeles so they could attend school. Bad fortune visited Helen once again in 1899, when Archibald Jr. died after falling from his own horse while out chasing some wild ones. Helen took the devastating news of the death of her youngest very hard, but continued to operate the ranch. As a new century was about to unfold, progress was extending to the far western reaches of the country in the form of the railroad. Rumors abounded as to exact routes, and which properties would be needed. It turns out they wanted the Las Vegas Ranch, and in 1902 Helen sold the ranch to the San Pedro, Los Angeles & Salt Lake Railroad. The $55,000

price tag did not include 40 acres, the family cemetery, and an allotment of water from the Las Vegas Creek. From that contract, signed for the railroad by Montana Senator William A. Clark, sprang the modern metropolis of Las Vegas.

The four remaining Stewart children deeded their interest in the ranch to their mother for $1 "with love and affection." As the original ranch house was on the old Mormon settlement and went to the railroad, Helen had a new house built across the street from the old ranch. Part of that house is now the interpretive center of the Old Mormon Fort. Helen lived there the rest of her life.

In 1903, Helen remarried a longtime friend and employee Frank Roger Stewart (no relation to Archibald). Helen Stewart had always had a great relationship with the local Paiute Indians. (In fact, a loyal Indian girl named Nipe is buried in the family plot.) So in 1911 when the government decided to establish a reservation in or near Las Vegas, Helen Stewart donated the 10 acres, which in later years became known as "The Colony."

She befriended many Paiute women over the years and learned their oral history and much of the meanings and life stories behind their basket designs. Her collection of over 550 Indian baskets was considered one of the West's finest.

Much to her delight, the town of Las Vegas grew into a city. She became the foremost authority on the area and helped organize the Nevada Historical Society. She helped found Christ Episcopal Church, and in 1915, was the first woman on the Clark County School Board, and the following year the first woman to sit on a jury.

Helen J. Stewart, historian, rancher, businesswoman, the indomitable woman who many called the "First Lady of Nevada," died from cancer on March 6, 1926. All Las Vegas businesses closed for the day and people came from all over the West to pay homage. Shortly before she died, she was about to turn her basket collection over to the State of Nevada, but did not get the chance. Her heirs sold most of the collection to the Harvey House hotels that were operated by the railroads.

Surprisingly, the nucleus of her ranch continued as a ranch even after a tent city to build the railroad grew up around it. The town became a city that grew in every direction and today, the Old Mormon Fort that became the Las Vegas Ranch occupies only a small plot of land at Las Vegas Boulevard North and Washington Avenue. Today, while millions of visitors gamble and play a short distance away, only a few stragglers and small groups tour the historic place where it all began, where a strong-willed woman kept the dreams of her family alive.

Miners Come to Nevada
Seeking El Dorado

My sister Camilla and her husband Bill Collins were not the first to seek their El Dorado in southern Nevada. "El Dorado" ("The Golden One" in Spanish) is a legend, a place, a person, an elusive dream. Take your pick.

Bill and Camilla gave up on what they considered the Los Angeles rat race to relocate in Nevada's remote Eldorado Canyon, where they lived for over 20 years. They found their solace among the multi-hued rock cliffs, mines and hills where for almost 200 years many others had sought their fortunes.

They lived in and around the little hamlet of Nelson, where the dirt road from Searchlight met the narrow paved one from Boulder City. I knew both roads intimately, often arriving on one and leaving on the other. It's still remote (south of Boulder City for 13 miles on Highway 95, then State Route 165 for about 11 miles to Nelson). You can continue down Eldorado Canyon past the Techatticup Mine to Lake Mohave.

For a number of years in the early 1970s, Bill and Camilla were the only occupants at Techatticup and the curators of the mine there. They lived in a wide trailer at the time, and also used the old weathered-wood mining buildings for storage and family gatherings.

Las Vegas Review-Journal writer Ray Chessan became their friend and featured them in one of his Sunday columns. The photo of my sister defiantly sitting in front of the old mine's "No Trespassing" sign holding a rifle smacked of the Old West at its best.

In those days only a few looky-loos stopped along their way to the landing at Lake Mohave, but back in its glory days it was quite a bustling place.

In 1775 the first Spaniards arrived looking for gold. So optimistic were they that they established a small settlement on the river they called Eldorado. However, while the area had a lot of gold, they did not find any, only silver—and small amounts at that—so they moved on.

At the height of western gold euphoria in the 1850s, other prospectors made their way into the Eldorado Canyon. Unlike the early Spaniards, they did find gold and began mining it in earnest. By 1858 word was out. A large vein was found in 1861 and several miners formed the Techatticup (Paiute word for "hungry.") Mine. Keeping with the mysteries and folklore of the West, several shady deals were made to form the mining company. The mine was later even part of a portfolio owned by Senator George Hearst of California (1886-1891), the father of publishing magnate William Randolph Hearst.

Mines began proliferating throughout Nevada's richest gold mining district. The Techatticup was joined by the Duncan, Gettysburg, Gold Bug,

Golden Empire, Solar, and Wall Street mines, along with many small claims. Over 5,000 miners at various times were working the canyon, and lawlessness reigned.

Claim jumping, feuds, disagreements, and fights over gold, and over women were so common that killings were an almost daily occurrence. Plus, the large Techatticup Mine itself had labor and ownership disputes and became as notorious as the surrounding area. The law refused to even go near the place.

The Techatticup became the most successful in the area, mining millions of dollars in gold, silver, copper and lead over the next 70 years, remaining active until about 1945. As the gold played out in one tunnel, they just carved a new one, leaving dozens of tunnels some 500 feet below the upper entrance. In almost 100 years of mining, the entire Nelson District yielded more than $500 million in ore.

Extracted ore was transported to Nelson's Landing along the Colorado River, where the area's first mill, a 10-stamp, steam-driven mill, was constructed. Then it was shipped by steamboat to Yuma, and thence overland to San Francisco. Supplies for the camps along the canyon also arrived from the river steamboats. Miners who left the canyon often headed first to recuperate at the small ranches in the Las Vegas Valley.

Lawlessness in Eldorado Canyon was pervasive. Many of the miners were Civil War veterans and deserters—some blue, some gray—who continued their animosities in the remote mining district. Federal troops even had to be brought in by steamboat to quell the riotous miners and curtail the bloodshed.

Finally, in 1867 a military post was established in Eldorado Canyon to protect the steamboat traffic and to keep an eye on the local Indians who were beginning to raid the canyon. Eventually, better overland routes eliminated the need for the steamboats.

If the white miners killing each other didn't create enough bloodshed, there were at least two renegade Indians who lived in or near Eldorado Canyon. One was said to have killed five area settlers. In the early 1900s an Indian named Queho, reportedly Nevada's first serial killer, was said to have murdered 23 people.

In the early 1900s Nelson's Landing was one of the largest ports along the Colorado River. It became an important landing for bootlegged liquor during the prohibition days, and later an important ferrying point for Hoover Dam workers.

When the dam was completed, the area became a major tourist site for fishing and tours of the dam. Before long, Nelson's Landing prospered as a resort, where boats, bait, gasoline, food, and cabins were provided. After Davis Dam downriver was completed in the mid-1950s, Lake Mohave began to fill up. The lake drowned the old stamp-mill site, the steamboat landing, and the remains of the original Eldorado Camp.

A small marina and dock was built on the site where the Eldorado Canyon wash empties into the Colorado River, and with a contingent of mobile homes and trailers, the "landing" became the area's social hub. I caught some huge trout off the dock where my sister kept a boat. We all drank many a beer in the restaurant.

I was, therefore, quite numb following a distressing telephone call from her in September 1974. It was a flash flood, what they call a "100-year flood." It had been raining and Bill and Camilla were getting dressed to head down to the marina for an evening's socializing. Bill noticed it was really raining hard and called his friend, the landing's proprietor, on the phone to advise him of the tremendous downpour which later was calculated to be about three inches of rain in about 30 minutes.

His buddy went outside to check the security of the mobile homes when he looked up to see a huge, at least 12-foot, wall of muddy water come roaring down the canyon. Later estimates even placed the water at 30 feet high in places. He barely had time to scramble halfway up the cliff before the water rushed by to tragi-

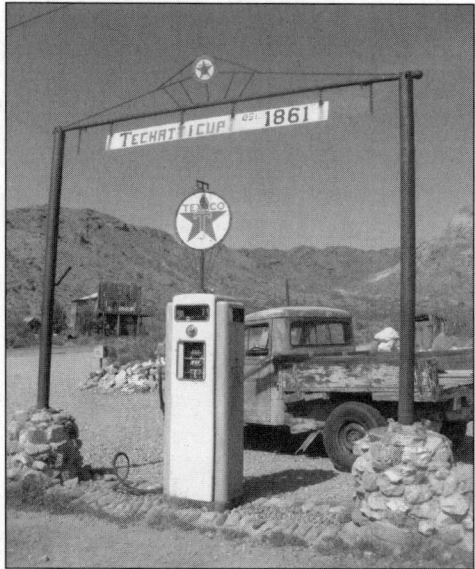

Artifacts at Techatticup Mine,
Eldorado Canyon

cally eliminate the entire settlement. Gone were the restaurant, marina shop, dock, boats, 20 mobile homes, 50 cars, and most tragic, the lives of nine of my sister's closest friends.

There's a plaque on the nearby hillside now commemorating the loss. It still leaves my legs weak when I stop to read it.

Later Bill and Camilla moved to "downtown" Nelson and then on out of state. Their years in Eldorado Canyon left an indelible impression on me. I hiked, I explored, and I found a little gold. I learned from my sister's friends, active miners Jim Harris and P.G. Harrison, how they worked their rudimentary Nelson mill and slowly added to their meager holdings. They never struck it rich but never considered abandoning their rustic lifestyle along with their hopes and dreams. The Eldorado Canyon is an excellent example of the Wild West and its hearty miners.

For many years after my sister left guarding the Techatticup Mine, it sat vacant before it was purchased in 1995, along with 51 surrounding acres, by

Tony and Bobbie Werly. They restored and preserved some buildings, gathered Old Western artifacts from around the state, and now offer mine tours and canoe and kayak rentals. Vegas visitors can transport themselves back to a rougher and more authentic Old West than one finds on the Strip.

The famous mine has now been featured in two movies, both starring Kurt Russell. *Breakdown* was partially filmed there and released in 1997. Then *3000 Miles to Graceland*, also with Kevin Costner and Courtney Cox, in 2001, had several scenes filmed in the area. In fact, some props, including the crashed airplane, are still at the site.

I remember partying hearty at the old Twin Gables restaurant/bar in downtown Nelson, but even it is no longer operating. In fact, Nelson itself is no more than a ghost town, with fewer than two dozen people living amid the old weathered sheds and small corrugated metal dwellings.

Yet, in the 1880s when Las Vegas could only boast a couple of ranchos, Nelson and the Eldorado Canyon had a bigger population than the entire Las Vegas Valley.

My sister and her husband moved there for its remoteness, and they too discovered that the Eldorado Canyon was still capable of taking lives long after the desperadoes had gone. Nevada, a desert state that has settled where the water is, has found that valuable water can be both a friend and a foe.

The Legend of Queho
Settlers Feared Renegade Indian

The life of renegade Indian Queho (Kay-ho) is full of legend and supposition. History isn't even sure who he was. Western lore has offered numerous accounts through the years, but they only all agree on one salient fact—he was a killer!

How many people he killed is up for speculation as he was often given credit, if one can call it that, for almost every unsolved murder committed in southern Nevada during the early part of the twentieth century.

There are numerous accounts even as to his tribal affiliation. He's been called a Cocopah, Mojave, Chemehuevi or Paiute. Most accounts contend he was of "mixed blood," his mother a Cocopah and his father rumored to have been a Mexican miner, a white soldier, or even a neighboring Paiute.

Queho was born around 1880 near Nelson in Eldorado Canyon and his mother died shortly after giving birth. It is said that he was born with a club foot, although some accounts speculate that he may have broken his foot or leg later in life. Either way, his deformity was easy to track.

The clubfoot from birth version is most likely, as that, along with his mixed blood, would have made him an outcast by the local tribe. Queho was raised on a reservation near Las Vegas and from boyhood worked as a ranch laborer or helped out in some of the nearby mining camps. He was considered sullen, moody, and quick-tempered.

Stories of his troubles with the law soon crept out. It is said that he shot his half-brother, another outlaw Indian, in the back on Cottonwood Island. While not proven, it is said he was involved in the death of another Indian in 1897.

But it was years later that his notoriety took on a new and more violent nature. In November 1910, Queho was the main suspect in the slaying of Indian Harry Bismark during a brawl on the Las Vegas reservation. Queho went on the run and allegedly murdered two Paiute Indians when he stole their horses in his escape.

Before heading out, he stopped for supplies in Las Vegas and got into an argument with merchant Hy Von. Wielding a pick handle, Queho broke both the man's arms and fractured his skull. From there he fled to Nelson and the many rocky nooks and crannies of Eldorado Canyon, where he eluded a small posse.

Queho went to nearby Searchlight and was hired by a woodcutter named J.M. Woodworth, who set him to work cutting trees on Timber Mountain. Somehow, Woodworth angered Queho, (one account says it was over pay) and he reacted by grabbing a piece of timber and fatally bashing in Woodworth's skull. Another account says Queho shot Woodworth. A posse was formed under the leadership of Deputy Sheriff Howe. At the Woodworth killing site they found the distinctive print left by Queho's clubfoot. The tracks led the posse down the Eldorado Canyon to the Gold Bug mine.

At the mine, Howe and his posse found the body of L.W. "Doc" Gilbert, the watchman, who had been shot in the back. They noted that his special deputy badge No. 896 had been ripped from his shirt and taken. The trail continued down Eldorado Canyon toward the Colorado River, where the crippled Indian eluded them.

Nevada State Police Sergeant Newgard, called in to continue the search, went to Eldorado Canyon with several Indian trackers and two experienced hunters. Occasionally they uncovered the characteristic clubfoot track, but they could not find the renegade Indian. They returned to Las Vegas in February, 1911.

Over the next few years, the Queho legend continued to grow, and his name struck the fear of the "bogeyman" into the hearts of all. Throughout the area, Queho was blamed for missing cattle, unexplained thefts, and mysterious murders. Lone prospectors and sheepherders were found dead in isolated areas. In those cases, the victims' shoes and food supplies were usually stolen, something Queho would have done. Fear and rumors ran rampant along the river.

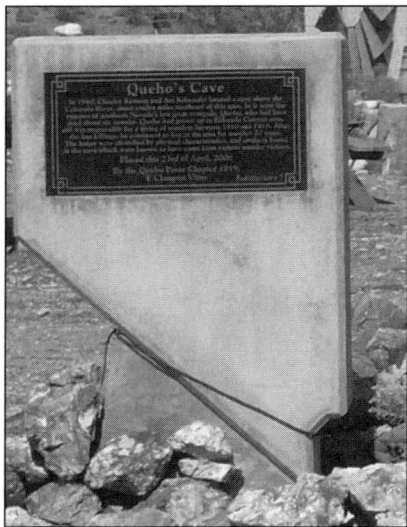

Queho marker in Eldorado Canyon

In 1913, local newspapers blamed Queho for the death of a 100-year-old blind Indian known as Canyon Charlie. Charlie's few provisions and food were missing, so some thought Queho did it. Others, however, doubted that Queho was responsible as Charlie was his friend and confidant. A few months later two more miners working claims at Jenny Springs were found shot in the back and their provisions stolen. These murders, too, were blamed on the illustrious outlaw. An Indian woman found dead a short time later was also blamed on the renegade.

As the hysteria grew, so did the rewards until $2,000 was offered for his capture, "Dead or Alive." The Searchlight Bulletin fanned the flames of discontent by advocating and reminding all that "A good Indian is a dead Indian."

In January 1919, two prospectors named William Hancock and Eather Taylor were found shot dead near their camp on the Muddy River. They were robbed of their shoes. Queho was immediately the prime suspect. About a week later, on January 21, 1919, an Eldorado Canyon miner's wife, Maude Douglas, was awakened in the night by a noise in the kitchen at the rear of the cabin. When her husband heard a shotgun blast, he found her shot in the chest. Next to her body were canned goods piled up as if they were in the process of being taken. When authorities arrived at the cabin near the Techatticup Mine, they attributed the murder to Queho as they allegedly found his footprints around the cabin. Though a four-year-old boy in Maude's care said that the woman had been killed by her husband, no one listened, immediately resuming the chase for the elusive Indian renegade once again.

In March 1919, the reward for Queho's capture was increased to $3,000, with Arizona officials, Clark County, and private individuals adding to Nevada's $2,000. Southern Nevada Sheriff Sam Gay ordered Deputy Frank Wait to round up a posse and hire the best trackers to once and for all kill or capture Queho. The intensive manhunt lasted almost two months, and all they found were two more skeletons that they attributed to Queho as well. The fugitive status of Queho was abetted, not only by fellow Indians, but a few whites as well, including Murl Emery, the legendary Colorado River ferry operator at Nelson's landing. Emery saw him "many times," came to like him, and developed a "leave him alone" attitude. Emery himself lived to old age in nearby

Nelson, where even into the 1970s, in the "live and let live" West, the townspeople treated the crusty old man as the unofficial "Mayor of Nelson."

But the renegade Queho had vanished, although there were alleged sightings over the years, including someone reporting seeing him walking down Fremont Street in February 1930.

For years Queho was not seen nor heard from and settlers were sleeping better.

Then, on February 18, 1940, prospectors Charley Kenyon and brothers Art and Ed Schroeder found the remains of a dead Indian in a shallow cave high up the riverbank, about 10 miles south of Hoover Dam and upriver from Eldorado Canyon. The mummified body of an Indian male who had apparently died of a rattlesnake bite was found along with a Winchester 30/30 rifle, clothing, cooking utensils, tools, and a "special Deputy badge, No. 896." Blasting caps and dynamite that could only have been taken from the dam site found in the cave indicated he was alive at least until the early 1930s.

A few days later on February 21, 1940, the headlines in the *Las Vegas Review-Journal* read "Body of Indian Found."

Queho's remains were taken to a funeral home in Las Vegas and Charles Kenyon, who had first found the body, demanded the reward. After the 20-plus-year-old rewards were ignored, Kenyon demanded possession of the body.

Then some Indians came forward claiming to be Queho's heirs. Meanwhile the body sat in the Palm Funeral Home and continued to amass storage fees for three long years. When the due bill was presented, both Kenyon and the Indians decided it wasn't so important after all. It turns out that Queho's most ardent pursuer, Frank Wait, paid the bill and gave the remains and artifacts to the Las Vegas Elks Club, who put the body on display, even propping him up for a ride in one of the Las Vegas Helldorado parades. The Elks even built a glass case and recreated a "cave" to exhibit the body and artifacts where they remained until the early 1950s.

Sometime later, Queho's remains were found discarded in a wash that had been used as a dump. Then there was private ownership of the remains for years. Finally, on November 6, 1975, Queho's body was finally interred on a private ranch at Cathedral Canyon near Pahrump, Nevada.

Queho was credited with the deaths of 23 people, becoming the state's first mass murderer. According to writer Ray Chessan, "Just how many people Queho killed, and under what circumstances, will probably never be known. During the course of his career, he was accused of practically every murder committed in the vicinity of Eldorado Canyon…"

Senator Harry Reid (D.-NV) devoted an entire chapter to Queho in his 1998 book, *Searchlight, The Camp That Didn't Fail*. He noted that his grandparents, John and Harriet Reid, had an encounter with the Indian in October 1910, when he galloped toward them with a Winchester rifle in his saddle.

They exchanged greetings, then went on their respective ways. They realized later that it was Queho coming down from Timber Mountain where a murder had just occurred.

The reign of terror and uneasiness generated by Queho's deliberate and vicious murders made him a legend. Time distorts reality and there are people who give him "cult status," and envision him as a Robin Hood, or a Ché, or a Pancho Villa, or even the violent mobsters who later came to Las Vegas to begin their own nefarious legends.

Chapter 2

From a Settlement to a City

Railroad tycoons raced to build a train through Nevada, with a station in Las Vegas. In 1905, the railroad then auctioned off lots which created the town.

Along with attendant challenges, the village grew and in six years achieved cityhood on March 16, 1911. The construction of a dam in nearby Boulder Canyon in 1931 provided an impetus to the growth of the area.

Senator William Andrews Clark
Tycoons Bring the Railroad

Clark County, Nevada got its name from someone who never lived in the state, but is the person most responsible for bringing the railroad and the ensuing growth to the Las Vegas Valley.

A shrewd and ambitious businessman, William Andrews Clark was born in Pennsylvania, taught school for a while and studied law before he headed west. A complex man, he was a northerner who fought for the South during the Civil War.

After making a few mining claims in Montana, he realized the best way to get rich was to provide needed supplies and materials. He made trips to Salt Lake City where he returned to the mines laden with whatever would sell the best. He sold cases of eggs, many of which even froze, for $3.00 a dozen. When the miners ran out of tobacco, he brought back a wagon full for another handsome profit.

Gold dust became an impractical exchange commodity for the miners, so Clark bought dust from them for cash, again tilting the scales in his favor. It was hard for the miners to extract the gold from some of the quartz layers, so the enterprising Clark bought numerous quartz claims, and acquired a mill to process the ore, and reaped even greater profits. Clark was married but, by 1878, his wife and their children moved to Europe to live. Clark visited each winter until she died in 1893. Meanwhile, the enterprising Clark took on a mistress who bore him two children. His most notable Montana coup was in buying up all the water rights in an area where George Hearst and Marcus Daly discovered the biggest copper seam ever found at Anaconda. Thus, without water Daly and Hearst (the father of publisher William Randolph Hearst) begrudgingly had to pay Clark to run their own mine.

The Nevada county's namesake became wealthy but not very well liked. Even so, in 1893 he ran against Daly for a Montana U.S. Senate seat, but neither could win a majority from the state legislators who in those days elected the senators.

The ambitious Clark tried again for the Senate seat in 1898, and that time a masked gunman attempted to steal a ballot box. The precinct raid left one worker dead and another wounded. No one knew who ordered the raid, but about 95% of the votes in that pivotal box were for Clark's opponent, Daly.

Undaunted, Clark kept trying. In 1901, he was caught offering $30,000 to four Montana state legislators for their votes. That blatant abuse of justice created the impetus for the U.S. Government to ensure future U. S. senators would be elected by popular vote. Finally, in 1901, Clark won his coveted seat by promising all sorts of benefits to the miners' union. Most of those promises were not kept.

Sniffing out opportunities like an animal honing in on prey, Clark wanted to build a railroad from Montana (and his holdings) to the seaport in the Los Angeles area. He knew too that Los Angeles wanted a rail link to Salt Lake City. Striking fast, Clark and his younger brother J. Ross Clark bought the Los Angeles Terminal Railroad with its harbor property at San Pedro. They created

William Clark and youngest daughters, Andree and Huguette, 1917

a new railroad company to run from San Pedro across Nevada to Salt Lake City and called it the San Pedro, Los Angeles & Salt Lake Railroad.

Southern Nevada became an important midway location. As early as 1890 railroad developers had determined the Las Vegas Valley would make an ideal supply stop and town. In addition, gold, silver, and other precious metals were being discovered throughout the state: Eldorado Canyon, Tonopah, Goldfield, and the Bullfrog district. Better transportation was needed to capitalize on and market those ore deposits. Also Southern California was becoming an agricultural center with a need for a more efficient transportation system. J. Ross Clark himself lived in Los Angeles and was heavily invested in the sugar beet industry. He realized the need to move Southern California produce to eastern markets, and also of the potential of the Pacific port at Los Angeles-San Pedro. The Clarks were not the only ones who saw the value of the route across Nevada. Primary among competitors was E. H. (Edward Henry) Harriman, a ruthless and wealthy businessman who had rebuilt the bankrupt Union Pacific Railroad. He had become a director of the Union Pacific in 1897, the following year chairman of the executive committee, and in 1903, president. He too envisioned moving freight: ore from the mines, supplies to the mining camps and towns, and California fruit to Salt Lake and the eastern markets.

Harriman and the Union Pacific (U.P.), and his chief competitor, Collis Huntington and the Southern Pacific Railroad (S.P.), both fought to establish a terminus in Southern California. While they were dickering and trying to cut a deal, Montana Senator William Clark had already struck and acquired the terminus.

To counter Clark's new railroad, Harriman quickly extended his Oregon Short Line (Part of U.P.) south into Nevada hoping to meet the Union Pacific in California. The Clark brothers fought back, and two competing grading teams were racing against each other. There were even skirmishes where the men fought each other with shovels. Finally they made a compromise deal in which Harriman acquired half of Clark's railroad and let Clark finish the line; The Union Pacific then absorbed the Salt Lake Route.

Helen Stewart of the Las Vegas Ranch was a beneficiary of the competition. First she bargained with Harriman and the Oregon Short Line, then drove a hard bargain and sold the ranch in 1902 for $55,000 to Senator William Clark for his San Pedro, Los Angeles & Salt Lake Railroad. Work on the first railroad grade into Las Vegas began in the summer of 1904. A tent town called "Las Vegas" grew around the old Stewart Ranch, soon offering saloons, stores and boarding houses. By October 1904, the San Pedro, Los Angeles & Salt Lake Railroad was connected with the eastern track. The final spike was driven in on January 30, 1905, about four miles from Jean, Nevada.

Clark's San Pedro, Los Angeles & Salt Lake Railroad made its inaugural run from California through Las Vegas and on to the East on January 20, 1905, before the railroad was absorbed by the Union Pacific. Harriman and the Clarks charged high rates for their railroad, even to businessmen who wanted to build spurs off the line, which were normally heavily discounted. The Interstate Commerce Commission looked into it and the ensuing testimony help break Harriman's railroad trust. The Union Pacific bought out the Clarks' interest in their railroad in 1921. J. Ross Clark remained active in Las Vegas affairs until his 1927 death.

Senator William A. Clark left Montana in 1907 and moved to New York where he built an incredibly ostentatious 100-room mansion on Park Avenue. Clark bought quarries and a brass foundry to ensure the highest quality material. He fitted his castle with original paintings and tapestries from Europe. He died there in 1925 at the age of 86. His monstrous mansion was razed by the city three years later. His estate left a bundle to his mistress and all of his children. The youngest, Huguette, died an eccentric recluse in May 2011 at 104, leaving over $500 million to charity and her longtime nurse.

Without the railroad, Las Vegas with its springs and small creeks fit for limited agriculture, would most likely have failed as a town. But as a railroad supply stop on a major east-west rail line, Las Vegas survived. Railroad employees arrived with their families, machine shops were constructed, and there was even an ice house for refrigerating produce from California.

The economic dependence of Las Vegas on the Union Pacific created strong local support of national railroad strikes and strikers for years. Las Vegans were vocal enough with sporadic acts of violence during the Railroad Strike of 1922 that there were rumors the U.P. planned to relocate the machine shops and supply depots to the Nevada town of Caliente, which it later did.

But the railroad kept its station and yards in Las Vegas, and the Union Pacific Rail Station was for years at the end of Fremont Street.

I often visited the little park around the old station as it held a memory for me. In early 1961, I was partying in Los Angeles and a buddy said, "Let's go to Vegas. I know a girl up there who's in a show." Within the hour, we were roaring across the desert in my old Ford in the middle of the night.

All he had was her phone number and at that late hour nobody answered. We didn't have a lot of money, so we looked for a place to sleep. There at the end of Fremont Street was a small park which encircled the old stucco train station. Like a couple of bums, Wayne and I spent the remainder of the cold night trying to get comfortable on park benches there. That day we got in touch with his friend and her roommate, both dancers at the newly opened Aku Aku Lounge in the glamorous Stardust Resort & Casino on the Strip. I was grateful; I don't think I could have endured another night shivering on that unforgiving bench.

The park is gone now, replaced in 1971 with the big new Union Plaza Hotel & Casino (now Plaza Hotel & Casino). The train begat the town of casinos, and its influence is not forgotten.

Railroad Sells Lots
AUCTION LAYS OUT TOWN

The newly created San Pedro, Los Angeles & Salt Lake Railroad assigned engineer Walter Bracken to help pick a route between Salt Lake City and the Pacific coast. His party arrived in Las Vegas in 1901 and went to work. A map drawn by A. Russell Crowell in 1902 shows their proposed route to the south of the old Emigrant Trail and throughout the Las Vegas Valley.

Bracken decided that the Las Vegas Ranch, already a well-known rest stop with rights to plentiful water, would be ideal for a way station. Its location and water made it a logical choice to develop a community where engines could be serviced, and where train crews and other support personnel could be housed.

After dealing with Helen J. Stewart for the railroad, Bracken took possession of the old ranch and in 1904 became the postmaster of the new "town" himself, even though the post office was a tent which also served as his living quarters. As the railroad's man on the scene, he got involved in everything. He surveyed and helped develop the plan for a new town site. He offered free lots to any denomination that would establish a church. He set aside the land for a city library and even for a future county courthouse, anticipating a new county would be split from Lincoln County, which had its county seat in Pioche.

But another surveyor, J.T. McWilliams, who had been in the area for several years, had some ideas of his own. He had been hired earlier by the Clarks to survey the large Stewart ranch. Seeing it looked like a good thing, for himself he bought 80 acres of land west of the railroad right of way directly from Stewart, and began to lay out his own orderly town site. He advertised and sold many lots during the winter 1904-1905.

In a December 26, 1904 letter, Bracken informed J. Ross Clark thusly:

"Dear Sir—Our old (?) friend McWilliams is here and has staked out a town site on the north half of south west fourth of sec. 27— (N2 of 5.W4 — Sec. 27) and is selling lots there. I am reliably informed that he has already sold to some saloon men. By looking on your map you will see just how his land lies with reference to the ranch and your railroad terminals. Yours truly, JKW Bracken."

Senator William A. Clark and his brother bristled at this perceived intrusion, and with Bracken's help quickly laid out their town. Engineer E. G. Tilton was hired and under pressure from the Clarks made a 400'=1" blueprint of the proposed Las Vegas town site. Most of the lots would be 300 by 400 feet and, with a 20-foot alley, were subdivided into lots 25 x 140 feet.

The Clarks also quickly formed the Las Vegas Land & Water Company and J. Ross Clark even warned that all water in the area was controlled by the railroad and would be unavailable to McWilliams' upstart town. In ads, the Clarks insinuated that the competition would be an instant slum, and endeavored to steer prospective buyers away from him.

McWilliams became the founder of what would become "West Las Vegas," with his town site boundaries: Bonanza Road, Washington Avenue, A Street and H Street. From 1904 to May 1905 the "Westside" boomed with the valley's first businesses and the most people. The boom was short lived however, as the Clarks were successful in its sudden demise by withholding water. The "Old Town" Westside has been a poor stepchild ever since.

It turns out McWilliams wasn't the only fly in the ointment for the Clarks. A former Fred S. Harvey Santa Fe railroad chef, Pete Buol, came to Las Vegas in 1901. He later recalled, "...when I got here there was no town, only the two old ranches, the Stewart and Kiel, and a couple of tents." Buol realized that Goldfield, the state's biggest town up north, was too expensive, and he liked the opportunity in Las Vegas. He bought land adjacent to what would become the official railroad town site, subdivided it, and had his lots for sale a full two months before the railroad did.

As the railroad had claimed the rights to the Las Vegas springs, Buol secured rights to other areas with springs. He formed the Vegas Artesian Water Syndicate and began drilling for wells throughout the area. He was successful, and not being dependent on the town water was able to establish a fine residential neighborhood.

McWilliams was not as lucky. For their "official" town, the Clarks advertised lots at specific prices, and accepted applications and down payments, implying sales on a first-come, first-served basis. But at the last moment, with buyers on the scene ready to build, J. Ross Clark received a telegram from W.H. Bancroft, who represented the Harriman interests in the partnership. It seems that E. H. Harriman wanted to further exploit this unexpected demand by selling the lots at auction, instead of the advertised prices. J. Ross Clark wired back that to do so would be impossible, as deposits had been accepted on most lots. Bancroft answered tersely, "Auction or nothing. Bancroft." So deposits were returned and the railroad announced that its lots would be sold at auction only and set the date as May 15, 1905. They offered special passenger rates for those traveling by rail to the auction ($16 and less from Los Angeles, $20 from Salt Lake City, to be rebated if the ticket holders actually purchased a lot).

People also went to the Las Vegas auction via covered wagon, buckboard, and horseback. Auction prices went from $150.00 to $750.00 for corner lots, and from $100.00 to $500.00 for inside lots. When the auctioneer opened bidding for the lots, more than 1,000 people stood at the original railroad yards at the corner of Fremont and Main Streets, downtown Las Vegas, hoping to be successful. Many were land speculators from California. Others just wanted their own land, but all participated in the birth of a great American city. Thus the railroad led to the founding of Las Vegas on May 15, 1905. That one day, the San Pedro, Los Angeles & Salt Lake Railroad, owned by Montana Senator William Andrews Clark, sold over 600 lots out of 1,200 available. It has been reported that the total value of the lots from that first day totaled $265,000.

The auction site became the Union Pacific Railroad depot, which was built the following year. In 1971, the old depot was torn down to become the Union Plaza Hotel & Casino. Freight and Amtrak passenger trains used the depot site at the hotel as a terminal until 1997—the only railroad station in the world so affiliated with a hotel-casino.

Las Vegas train depot (circa 1924)

By the end of 1905 Las Vegas boasted a few hotels, stores, a saloon, and about 600 residents. There were a few initial distinctions. Block 16, between First Street and Second Street (now Casino Center Boulevard), and between Ogden Street and Stewart Street, was designated as the drinking and party block, an anything-goes red-light district. Block 17 (same block as the Lady Luck Hotel & Casino), to the rear between Second and Third, was designated for "non-white" residents.

After Las Vegas was established, spring water from the original ranch was diverted into the town's water system, and the creek that had earlier served the Indians, Mormons and ranchers finally dried up.

The Clarks tried to diversify the economy, employing men to prospect for gypsum and other minerals. They helped establish the Home Building & Loan Association in 1905, and also the First State Bank.

Senator William A. Clark did not easily forget enemies, and his former surveyor J. T. McWilliams was a thorn in his side. McWilliams had previously claimed about 1,300 acres for timber in the Spring Mountains. In 1906, following the Las Vegas town site competition, McWilliams found his mountain permits were revoked by some "powerful Washington politicians."

But McWilliams was not to be dismayed. He wired President Teddy Roosevelt, no lover of the big railroads, and within four days his claims were revalidated.

Then Clark and the railroad accidentally built an icehouse on what actually turned out to be part of McWilliams' property. McWilliams demanded payment for the lot, but the railroad just moved the project elsewhere.

It went like that for years. Even once-neutral Walter Bracken, as a railroader, also became a bitter enemy of McWilliams. McWilliams, though snubbed by the town's hierarchy and society because of his conflict with the railroad, nevertheless continued to make a presence in Las Vegas and produced many fine maps of the entire area. But he was clearly swimming upstream by himself.

Once, around 1914, McWilliams was beaten up very badly and his perpetrator was only fined $50.00. Then he caught the railroad dumping the machine shop cesspool into McWilliams' Old Town (or what the railroad called Ragtown) water supply. After that they restricted water going into McWilliams' Old Town. Finally in 1926 after many pleas from residents, and a deterioration of the west side, Old Town was allowed to receive city water. Regardless, the bitter feud continued until McWilliams died in 1941.

Even though McWilliams and Buol also sold property to prospective homeowners, it was the big railroad auction that really created the town. Those people who bought lots on that heady auction day in May 1905 were really at the beginning of something big, whether they realized it at the time or not. As the town prospered, many of them wore their heritage on their sleeve, and for generations proudly proclaimed that they were among the first of the Las Vegas settlers.

The Village of Las Vegas
TAMING THE Wild WEST

That first wave of settlers stood there in the desert after the gavel fell, many wondering what they would do, clutching pieces of paper that declared them lot-holders in a town yet to be built. In true Western spirit they went right to work and a small town resembling a cowboy movie set sprung up on dusty lots up and down the streets near the rail yards. One settler, a Minnesota-born businessman from California, C. P. "Pop" Squires, had a better idea of the challenges and opportunities than most, and was about to commence on his destiny. He had earlier learned of the Las Vegas town site plan from J. Ross Clark and had made a previous inspection tour with him.

They had formed a partnership with a couple of other men, put up $1,250 each, and then borrowed $25,000 to establish a bank, hotel, real estate firm, lumberyard, and anything else they could think of to get the town up and running.

Squires had learned from his previous visit there was virtually nothing there before the auction. On that trip they stayed in the hamlet's only lodging, a large tent owned by a character named James Ladd, where for $1, a visitor could share a bunk with another man.

"Pop" and his wife Delphine, later affectionately called "Mom," took the new train from Los Angeles, paying $13.65 each. Pop recalled, "…the train bumped slowly along and at last came to a stop near an old passenger coach on a little spur, on which was nailed a piece of board, on which was painted the magic name "Las Vegas.""

Squires bought several lots at the auction, including one at Fremont and Fourth Streets where he built his own home.

Since no infrastructure was yet in place, the townspeople realized they needed a number of things: a viable water system, adequate sewage, generators, power poles, telegraph and telephones, a school, a newspaper, a church, and most importantly, law and order.

Several of the town leaders, especially Squires, started addressing these problems. Believe it or not, in that first year three newspapers came into being, two of them short-lived. Squires took over the most viable, the *Las Vegas Age*, which he published until 1940 when, at age 75, he finally sold it to retire.

The *Age* immediately began feeding the townspeople the "goings on" in their new settlement, much of it "soft news" such as comings and goings, but it gave them a sense of community.

The following about an important new business is from a 1905 issue: "The Kuhn Mercantile company's big store opposite the depot site is rapidly becoming a veritable emporium. During the past week an ice cream and cold drink department has been added, and in one corner the First State Bank has established temporary quarters. The post office adjoining contributes to make this one of the busiest stores in the valley."

It may have been the busiest, but many of the boisterous railroad workers and miners who came to town bypassed Kuhn Mercantile to head straight for Ogden Street and Block 16 where they partied and spent their hard-earned pay.

Other newcomers, however, had a different calling and in 1905 the first United Methodist Church of Las Vegas was formed. The first school in Las Vegas initially opened in a tent for about 20 children; that tent soon became a courtroom. In the summer, the townspeople selected a three-member school board with a very limited budget. A small four-room building initially called the Salt Lake Hotel was bought, moved, and renovated for $700.

Not ready until October 2, 1905, it finally opened with two teachers and between 50-60 students, and was growing. With no city government to levy taxes, the school went broke and closed on March 30, 1906. By fall 1906, thanks to a fattened treasury, it reopened and grew so much the city had to build another small schoolhouse next door, and hire a third teacher. On January 13, 1906, the town's first and oldest regular hotel, the Hotel Nevada, opened in downtown Las Vegas at 129 E. Fremont St., at the corner of Main Street across from the train depot. Initial room and board rates were $1 per day. In 1955 after a couple of name changes, that first hotel became the Golden Gate Hotel & Casino and it is still in existence; it has offered signature shrimp cocktails at bargain prices for over 50 years.

Telephones came to Las Vegas in 1907 when the first telephone wires were strung on Fremont Street, with the city's first phone going to the Hotel Nevada.

As a newspaperman, Pop Squires got involved in a number of civic endeavors. He served on the finance committee for the group advocating that the southern half of Lincoln County break away and form its own county. On July 1, 1909 with the blessing of the state legislature, Clark County, named for the railroad man who held the auction, Montana Senator William A. Clark, came into being.

The town of Searchlight to the south also wanted to break away from Lincoln County and was disappointed it did not get the county seat. Searchlight residents reconciled that at least Las Vegas was only half the distance to Lincoln County's seat, the far-away town of Pioche.

While E. H. Harriman and Senator William Clark had earlier squabbled over the railroad rights, a man named Ed Clark (no relation) was elected treasurer of Lincoln County. His transferring of the county funds to Las Vegas helped tip the scales for the new county. Ed Clark promptly became treasurer of the new county and also director of the bank where the county funds remained, the First State Bank.

An important factor in the law and order of early Las Vegas was housed in the formidable form of 6'2", 260-pound Sheriff Sam Gay. Gay had been a bouncer at the rough and tumble Arizona Club in the notorious Block 16. Lincoln County Sheriff Jake Johnson liked his style and made him Las Vegas night watchman, and later town constable. Then under Lincoln County Sheriff Orrin K. Smith, Gay was appointed deputy sheriff for the southern half of Lincoln County. When it became Clark County, Gay was first a deputy and then ran for the job of sheriff. Sam Gay became the county's second sheriff in 1911, a job he held until 1930 when he stepped down at age 70.

Gay was the right man to try to tame the bustling and bawdy new settlement built for a train stop. He later described early Las Vegas this way, "From 1905 to 1910, Las Vegas was a rough and tumble Western town. Five men dead for breakfast one Sunday morning and 10 men wounded…"

Sam Gay was as tough as the men he tried to control and had earned so much respect some voters traveled many miles on Election Day just to vote for him. He was the law and order of early Las Vegas.

Another successful lot bidder on auction day was Ed Von Tobel, who was shrewd enough, and broke enough, to wait until the end of the auction when the prices dropped. He and his buddy Jake Beckley ended up buying adjoining $100 lots for almost nothing, especially considering their train fare rebate. Von Tobel ended up developing a hardware store and lumber yard, which he worked successfully until he died in 1967.

Then there was big Jim Cashman who arrived in Las Vegas in 1904 at age 19. He washed dishes and waited tables in the tent town camp that was springing up to build the railroad. He later got involved in everything, hauling, running a type of rural taxi service, and speculating in real estate. Cashman owned the area's first automobile and also southern Nevada's first automobile dealership, which he located in Searchlight. What is probably the most far-reaching of Cashman's contributions was changing the Los Angeles to Las Vegas highway to run through Jean, Nevada and Baker, California. The main road had previously gone through Searchlight. Cashman became a Clark County commissioner in 1920 and he worked with officials from San Bernardino County to help build a new, more direct road. It opened in 1927 and for over 80 years that road (Highway 91, now I-15), has whisked millions of Southern Californians, along with their hopes and dreams, to the enchanting and fabulous city of Las Vegas.

As Sam Gay had indicated, Las Vegas was becoming a wide-open town during its first few years of infancy. Gambling was first legalized in Nevada in 1869 when the state legislature overrode a governor's veto. The state was full of rowdy and free-spending miners to whom gambling was more than a vice; it was a very important past-time. During Las Vegas' early years, gambling, bars, and prostitution were confined to Blocks 16 and 17 just a short distance off Fremont Street. While the town's wide-open iniquities were localized, that did not prevent detractors.

The turn of the century was also the era of virulent anti-vice attitudes and a broad-based temperance movement. In 1901 Carrie Nation became a household name for attacking Kansas saloons with an ax. It was this type of pressure, from churches, educational leaders, women's groups and reformists, that forced many states to outlaw gambling and prostitution.

Nevada didn't even bother with restricting prostitution at that time, and became the last Western state to outlaw gambling. The anti-gambling law took effect on October 1, 1910. The Nevada law was so strict, it was illegal even for miners to flip a coin for a drink. That law didn't set well with them. Needless to say, the miners did not waste time setting up underground games. In fact, the ban was enforced for only three weeks before the law decided to just look the other way. Many Nevada saloons continued to openly offer illegal gambling in their back rooms.

Upon Governor Tasker Oddie's recommendation, and under great pressure from Reno club owners, the 1915 Legislature somewhat relaxed this prohibition by permitting nickel slot machines and certain social games, like bridge or whist, provided the play was for drinks, cigars or small prizes valued less than $2.00. By 1919, more and more card rooms that offered games were being locally licensed. In addition, there were a large number of clubs with illegal games as well.

The miners, railroad workers and other laborers who insisted on gambling had no idea how their tenacity would spawn the greatest gambling city on the face of the planet. But it did.

Las Vegas Cityhood — 1911
A City is Born

All sorts of setbacks cropped up against the hardy settlers, the extremes in weather among them. That second winter, in December 1906, a snow storm blanketed the town, causing chaos and forcing stage coaches to arrive hours late. The *Las Vegas Age* reported one old prospector said he'd only seen such a storm about two times over the past 40 years.

A few months later, in February 1907, it rained so hard that flash floods washed out the railroad tracks near Caliente to the north, isolating Las Vegas from points east. Shortly thereafter, the railroad town was cut off from the south when track washed away near Barstow, California.

Isolated, food became scarce and the saloons ran out of beer. Undaunted, the boozers just shifted to drinking locally distilled whiskey. The situation became so dire that on March 7, the *Las Vegas Age* reported, "The last ham and eggs were eaten yesterday, and the chickens in town are hiding in the sage brush."

In 1907 there was a national, long-lasting financial panic and Las Vegas businessmen were having problems getting loans. As many had their savings tied up in the fledgling town, they had nowhere to go and just weathered through it, grateful that the railroad men were spending a little money.

Then there were fires. In 1910, a fire burned the Overland Hotel, and another fire that same year burned the old school. On July 4, 1910, Las Vegans laid a cornerstone for a new school on a two-block parcel of land bounded by Fourth and Fifth streets, and by Bridger and Clark streets, donated by the railroad's Las Vegas Land & Water Co. But that fall, before the new 14-classroom two-story school was completed, a fire burned the original two school buildings down. Until the new school opened in 1911, the children split classes between a church and part of an old rooming house.

Another flood in 1910 in roughly the same area as the 1907 flood wiped out 100 miles of railroad track and the powerful floodwaters carried away most of a train, leaving at least one flat car miles away. Despite the setbacks, the town slowly grew. The mission-style Lincoln Hotel was built across from the railroad depot in 1910 at 307 S. Main St. It catered to railroad passengers and employees. Later called the Victory Hotel, the two-story building still stands.

Early Fremont Street. Overland Hotel on left burned in 1910 *(Thanks to As We Knew It and Classic Las Vegas)*

The railroad also built 64 bungalow-style cottages to house its workers. The cinder block buildings of four to five rooms were located from Clark to Garces Streets, and from Second to Fourth Streets. A handful of them remain and can still be seen along the 600 block of Casino Center Drive. With the growth, residents sought to control their own destiny. In late 1910, Pop Squires and three other leading citizens drafted a Las Vegas city charter and got it into the state legislature. Nevada at the time had a total population of 81,875, of whom a little over 1,000 lived in Las Vegas.

City Charter Signed

The March 11, 1911 issue of the *Las Vegas Age* was proud to announce under the headline "Incorporation Assured" that the charter had passed the lower house of the legislature and was then in the senate, with passage assured. In pointing out the immediate significance, the story added, "This will be of great advantage to the city, enabling us to get a sewerage system…our streets should be rolled and graded and sidewalks laid, which will add to the attractiveness of Las Vegas as a place of residence and investment."

Governor Tasker L. Oddie signed the charter on March 16, 1911, and Las Vegas became an incorporated city. The original city boundaries were from Garces Street to Stewart Street, and from Main Street to Fifth Street. In granting cityhood, Governor Oddie prophetically proclaimed, "I wish to convey through you to the people of Las Vegas my hearty congratulations on what they have accomplished and my sincere wish that they may continue to prosper and reap the rewards they so richly deserve. I have firm faith in the

43

future greatness of your city." The city of Las Vegas, until 1944, operated under a "commission" form of government with each commissioner having administrative control over certain operating departments of the city. For mayor, Peter Buol ran against Bill Hawkins and Buol won by "about 10 votes," he recalled later. He was paid $15 a month for performing this civic duty, serving as the first Las Vegas mayor until May 1913, when Hawkins replaced him. Buol went on to the Nevada Assembly, and after one year, was elected to the Nevada State Senate.

Leaders emerged in every profession to help nurture the new city. Dr. Royce (Roy) Martin from the Midwest began his modest Las Vegas medical practice in an 8' by 10' tent at Stewart Avenue and Third Street. He visited patients all over Clark County and was an early advocate of changing the road to Los Angeles from going through Searchlight to its present route.

Contractor E. W. Griffith, who had been hired by the railroad to build a roundhouse, bought two lots at the famous May 15 auction. He built his home at Fremont and Second Street, a corner later dominated by the Golden Nugget Hotel & Casino. His son, Robert Griffith, who as a teenager accompanied his father at the auction, became a civil engineer and later helped bring air service to Las Vegas. Robert Griffith had become the community's postmaster after Pop Squires retired from that job on January 1, 1925. In that capacity Griffith helped the federal government make Las Vegas a stop on the airmail route, and even had to prepare an air strip.

Pop Squires, who some historians called the "Father of Las Vegas," got involved in a project that would ensure continued prosperity for Las Vegas and all of southern Nevada. It was an organization called the League of the Southwest with representatives from western states. The California and Nevada representatives met in Los Angeles in April 1920 to discuss the possible merit of harnessing the mighty Colorado River by building a dam! Squires was excited about the project and reported the idea to Nevada Governor Emmett Boyle, who was very interested. The governor then gave broad powers to Squires to explore this dam possibility. Squires selected three other Las Vegans (James Cashman, E.W. Griffith, and Dr. Roy Martin) to also serve as Nevada delegates.

At the League meeting there were stalemates, with numerous ideas and caveats thrown out, including some fearing that a dam might flood the Grand Canyon. After two days and no resolution in sight, Idaho Governor D. W. Davis asked Squires to draft something, anything. After working late into the night on it, the resolution drafted by Squires was accepted and adopted the next day with very few minor changes. In essence it called for a high dam to be constructed across the Colorado River at or near Boulder Canyon. It was finally a direction and a start, but at another meeting it was pointed out that an interstate project of this dimension required a multi-state compact to be formed, agreed upon, and then presented to the U.S Congress for further review and approvals. It was not going to be the hasty project the "can do" guys from the new city of Las Vegas had envisioned.

But they were not to be denied. The dam would be built, thanks to the vision of then-U.S. Secretary of Commerce and later President Herbert Hoover. Even as a young engineering student, Hoover had dreamed of a high dam in the area.

The Massive Hoover Dam
HARNESSING THE COLORADO RIVER

In January 1921, legislatures in the seven western states started working on a multi-state compact necessary for the large project of building a high dam on the Colorado River.

The Colorado River Commission was formed in January 1922 with a representative from each of the states (Arizona, California, Colorado, Nevada, New Mexico, Utah, and Wyoming) and one from the Federal Government. The federal representative was Herbert Hoover, then serving as Commerce Secretary under President Warren Harding. Hoover met with the state governors to work out equitable apportioning of Colorado River water for their states' use. The resulting Colorado River Compact, signed on November 24, 1922, basically divided the river basin into upper and lower regions; the states within each region would decide how their water would be divided. Known as the Hoover Compromise, this arrangement removed existing concerns and hurdles and allowed for the Boulder Dam Project to be built.

This huge dam was massive in scope and was slated to provide water for irrigation, for flood control, and for hydroelectric-power generation. On December 21, 1928, President Calvin Coolidge signed the bill approving the project. That was a big day in Las Vegas history. All of the businesses closed to celebrate—excepting those that sold alcohol, of course. They all knew that their city had been given an impetus to keep it growing.

Pop Squires and the other delegates on the League were not the only Las Vegas proponents of the dam. Throughout much of the 1920s, it had become a hot topic. In fact, the Las Vegas Rotary Club even published a newsletter called *The Boulder Dam* to report on progress.

Albert Scott (A.S.) Henderson, a pioneer resident, former teacher and attorney, was a member of the Nevada state legislature from 1921 to 1923, and Nevada state senator from 1927 to 1929 and 1931 to 1933. During this time, Henderson was instrumental in writing much of the legislation concerning Boulder Dam.

Henderson later became Clark County district attorney and Las Vegas city attorney. He was an advisor to the Colorado River Commission and was involved in many intense battles over water, power, and revenue rights over the years. In 1946 he was appointed a district judge, and kept getting reelected until he retired in 1960.

Ed Clark, another Las Vegas dam proponent, served on the Interstate Commerce Commission that finally persuaded Congress to build it. After years of anticipation, he personally benefited greatly from the boom that followed. He had earlier bought out his bank partners, becoming sole owner of the First State Bank. In 1924 he became president of the local power company, which became the first utility to distribute electricity from the new dam. For 16 years his company provided all the local power needs.

Nevada Governor James Scrugham (1923-1926) was a northern Nevadan who spent so much of his career working on the Colorado River project, he was accused of placing too much importance on southern Nevada. As state engineer before becoming governor, he was long a dam proponent. He chaired the state's Colorado River Commission in 1922 which helped that multi-state pact. In 1927 after his tenure as governor, and because of his knowledge of the Boulder Dam project, he was appointed special advisor to the U.S. Secretary of Interior and helped see it to completion.

The initial appropriation for construction of the dam was made in July 1930, by which time Herbert Hoover was President. Early plans called for the dam to be built in Boulder Canyon, so the project was known as the Boulder Canyon project. The dam site was eventually moved eight miles down river to Black Canyon, but everyone still referred to it as the Boulder Canyon project.

Bids were solicited for the construction of the incredible engineering project and, on March 4, 1931, the winning bid of $48,890,955, was awarded to a private enterprise called Six Companies, Inc. That the figure was only about $24,000 higher than the expected cost worked up by the Federal Bureau of Reclamation engineers is testimony to the astuteness of one man—Frank Crowe.

Crowe was a U.S. Bureau of Reclamation civil engineer who had completed several western projects, including dams in Idaho, Washington and Wyoming. He was well familiar with the Boulder Dam project. Back in 1919, he and his boss, Commissioner Arthur Powell Davis, together drew up a cost estimate for a dam farther down river. Crowe also worked on that dam's preliminary design, which would be built much later and named Davis Dam after the Commissioner.

Crowe was hoping to oversee the Boulder Canyon project. But in 1925, the government changed its methods, and would use private construction firms rather than the government to build dams. Knowing his only chance was to go private, Crowe quit the government and joined the private construction firm of Morrison-Knudsen. He then persuaded his boss, president Harry Morrison, to form the Six Companies and bid on the project.

Six Companies, Inc. was a joint venture with Morrison-Knudsen of Boise, Idaho; Utah Construction of Ogden, Utah; Pacific Bridge Company of Portland, Oregon; Henry J. Kaiser & W.A. Bechtel Company of Oakland, California; J.F. Shea Company of Portland, Oregon; and MacDonald & Kahn Ltd. of Los Angeles, California. W.A. Bechtel was named president, and Frank Crowe, who had previously pioneered many of the techniques used to build the dam, was named construction superintendent.

A new town for the workers was also supposed to be built. But the onset of the Depression caused the dam's construction to be accelerated to quickly create jobs. Thus the new town, Boulder City, was not ready when the first dam workers arrived at the site in March 1931. Boulder City only consisted of a rail yard and a makeshift camp. Crowe, frustrated with the lack of progress and overly-elaborate plans of an urban designer, grabbed a roll of drawing paper and sketched out a town. Construction commenced within a week, but during that first summer, workers and their families were cramped in a temporary camp called Ragtown.

Discontent with living quarters and dangerous working conditions at the dam site led to a strike on August 8, 1931. Crowe told the *Las Vegas Age* at the time that it was mostly a few agitators responsible and that they would be happy to get rid of them. Not messing around, Six Companies identified the men perceived to be union agitators, sent in strike-breakers with guns and clubs and physically threw the miscreants out of town.

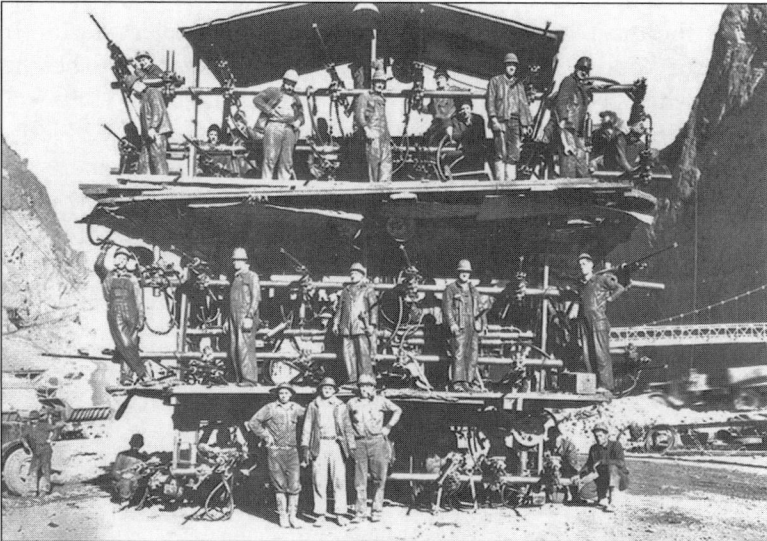

Jumbo Rig, Hoover Dam, 24-30 drills able to operate at the same time
(courtesy of the Bureau of Reclamation)

While the strike was squashed, the necessity of speeding up the construction of Boulder City became obvious, and by early 1932 the tents of Ragtown were vacated. While Boulder City became a nice place to live, workers had to go to Las Vegas to blow their paychecks. Gambling, drinking alcohol, and prostitution were not permitted in Boulder City during the period of construction. In fact, to this day gambling is illegal in Boulder City.

Construction of the gravity-arch dam was on a giant scale. Walls had to be blasted and reinforced. Four 56-foot diameter diversion tunnels had to be dug and lined with three-foot-thick concrete. Enough concrete to pave a two-lane road from San Francisco to New York was used in the dam, mostly poured in slabs to facilitate curing and drying. There were 112 deaths associated with the five-year project, mostly in the dangerous construction, but some of these were heat strokes, heart attacks, or not directly related to the project. Hoover Dam was completed and turned over to the government on February 29, 1936, two full years ahead of schedule, and has been managed by the Bureau of Reclamation ever since. It was renamed Hoover Dam in recognition of the efforts of President Herbert Hoover.

When completed, it was both the world's largest electric-power generating station and the world's largest concrete structure. Control of water was the primary concern in the building of the dam. Power generation allowed the dam project to be self sustaining: repaying the 50-year construction loan, and continuing to pay for the multi-million dollar yearly maintenance budget. The lake created by the dam, Lake Mead, has a surface area of 157,900 acres, backing up 110 miles behind the dam. The Lake Mead Recreational Area, which includes dam visitors, has developed into the fifth busiest National Park Service area.

One of the most important benefits of the dam project during its construction turned out to be the employment opportunities. In the height of the Depression, when people across the country were struggling to find work, that huge dam built in the narrow Black Canyon created up to 5,128 jobs at one time. All told, 21,000 men worked on the dam over the five years.

That Depression-era project not only helped the nearby new city of Las Vegas with employment opportunities, but the workers also got the city started as a good place to spend money. That never changed.

Chapter 3

Las Vegas' Destiny

A combination of factors provided Las Vegas with employment and growth while much of the country suffered in the Great Depression: construction at Hoover Dam, the railroad, liberal divorce laws, and the introduction of legalized gambling.

The first casinos were located along Fremont Street downtown; shortly several enterprising businessmen began to establish hotel casinos on the road to Hoover Dam, and south of town, on the road to Los Angeles.

More than anything, the 1931 legalization of gambling created the destiny of Las Vegas.

Making It Legal

Beating the Depression

While much of the country suffered in the 1930s, Las Vegas escaped the worst of the economic hardships created by the Great Depression. The young city even thrived, chiefly because of four main factors: 1) the railroad; 2) the dam in Boulder Canyon; 3) liberal divorce laws; and 4) legalized gambling.

Individually, or together, they attracted people to Las Vegas and southern Nevada. Las Vegas was growing with the beginnings of a permanent city. Fremont Street was paved in 1925. In 1926, the first commercial flight arrived. In 1928 future mayor Ernie Cragin and William Pike opened the first indoor movie theater, the El Portal Theatre on Fremont Street. In 1929, a new newspaper, the *Las Vegas Review-Journal*, began its long service to the community. And also that year, the new Las Vegas High School opened.

The Railroad

The Union Pacific Railroad had been a big part of that development as it offered steady employment in the important Las Vegas station. In 1930 it connected Las Vegas with Boulder City. Soon the economy spawned by the railroad would be boosted by other forces—firstly, Hoover (Boulder) Dam.

Hoover (Boulder) Dam

Thousands came to Las Vegas hoping to get a job at the dam site 30 miles away. It has been reported that over 40,000 job aspirants flocked to Las Vegas, "The Gateway to Boulder Dam," hoping to secure one of the more than 5,000 jobs available. In 1930 there were only 5,165 permanent Las Vegas residents, and about 8,500 in the area. Yet, during the difficult 1930s, Las Vegas city grew from 5,165 to 8,422 (1940), with the area population approaching 14,000.

Haven for Divorces

Another unlikely factor in Nevada's growth was in abetting the break-up of marriages. Divorce became a uniquely Nevada business. The inviolate institution of marriage saw more and more people wanting out. By the early twentieth century, divorce statutes in most states were so strict, couples either headed for one of four states (Arkansas, Idaho, Nevada or Wyoming) where more lenient laws were in place, or they stayed in an unhappy marriage—not only making their own lives miserable but others whom their rancor influenced as well.

From early statehood days in 1864, Nevada had set the residency require-ment at six months and allowed seven grounds for divorce. Compare that to New York's one legal ground—only adultery—and that had to be proven in court. Plus New York and most states had long residency periods. South Carolina did not even allow for a divorce at that time. People realized that Nevada provided the best option, and at first much of that activity was centered around the northern city of Reno. Later, University of Nevada, Reno history professor William D. Rowley acknowledged, "Reno by 1910 was known as the divorce capital…A divorce capital with a residency requirement willing to be shortened to beat out the competition and bring in the famous divorces Reno has become known for.…"

Nevada adjusted its laws to exploit the divorce phenomenon, but not with-out some initial opposition. In 1913, reformers convinced the legislature to raise the residency requirement to one year like most of the other states, and the legislators complied. But the backlash was instant. Many business owners howled and in 1915, the law was changed back to six months.

One famous Nevada divorce during this time was all it took for others to follow. In February 1920 film star Mary Pickford began a six-month residence, living at the Campbell Ranch in Genoa, near Carson City. Divorce papers were subsequently filed in the Douglas County seat, and the famous 27-year-old silent-film star won her divorce against actor-husband Owen Moore.

The rush was on, and the divorce business income for Nevada became so lucrative they even lowered the six month residency requirement—in 1927 to three months, and in 1931 to just *six weeks*, the nation's shortest by a long shot. Back then, State Senator Harry Heidtman also drafted the law that allows the parties to have divorce records sealed from the public, adding further appeal to the liberal Nevada law.

The results were instant and staggering. In 1926 the Nevada courts granted 1,021 divorces. In 1927, when the residency requirement was lowered to three months, the figure almost doubled to 1,953. The 1930 divorces numbered 2,609, and in 1931 when the six-week requirement was the law, the number of divorces almost doubled again to 5,260.

The money Nevada reaped in attorney fees and from profits in hotels, casinos, restaurants, and merchants was in the millions. The divorce racket put Nevada on the map, because along with the income, there was notoriety—a mystique—for being America's divorce capital. Nevada's celebrity divorces soon fed the nation's gossip mongers. Mary Pickford's divorce started a whole chain of them. There were Mrs. Clark Gable, Mrs. Nelson Rockefeller, Cornelius Vanderbilt Jr., Jack Dempsey, and Estelle Taylor, just to name a few.

Early on, the city of Reno was the divorce capital, but Las Vegas eventually nudged the northern city aside and took prominence. One famous tongue-wagging Las Vegas divorce was when crooner Eddie Fisher divorced Debbie Reynolds to marry the actress Elizabeth Taylor in 1959.

By the time "no fault" divorces became the law in most of the United States during the 1970s, Nevada had made millions and had achieved renown as a "divorce haven."

Gambling Made Legal

1931 was a banner year for Nevada. Not only were divorce residency laws shortened and construction begun on Boulder Dam, but the Nevada Legislature passed a law that virtually created the Las Vegas of today. The law legalized the gambling that had been going on all the time in the back rooms of saloons across the state.

An innocuous 29-year-old Nevada freshman Assemblyman Phil Tobin authored Assembly Bill 98 to re-legalize casino gambling. He was a northern Nevada rancher who didn't gamble and had never visited Las Vegas. He was approached by Las Vegas businessmen and was obviously influenced, ergo the legislation. However, he justified his legislation, saying he sincerely felt that the legalization of the rampant illegal gambling might generate the needed taxes for public schools.

The timing was right. The onset of the Great Depression, the state's diminished mining output, along with a slump in the state's agriculture production, helped sway the legislature. The lawmakers were reluctant to enact a sales or income tax, nor did they want to raise property taxes. The bill was passed and signed into law by Nevada Governor Fred Balzar on March 19, 1931. Gambling was legal!

Tobin and many of the legislators actually anticipated gambling merely to be a short-term fix until the state's economic base widened to include less cyclical industries. But Nevada has never seriously considered changing that law back, and today, 80 years later, more than 43% of the state's general fund is a direct result of gambling tax revenue, and more than 34% of that goes for public education.

In a late life interview, Tobin, considered by some the "father of modern Nevada gambling," somewhat-ruefully admitted, "I don't think it's right allowing these one-armed bandits in every supermarket…and restaurant in the state."

But the maverick state of Nevada had not only survived the Depression—it had created its destiny.

The First Casinos
DOWNTOWN BECOMES GAMBLING MECCA

The genesis of gambling in Las Vegas was downtown, along Fremont Street where the town began. By the time gambling was legalized in 1931, downtown already sported a few hotels, bars, and card rooms which offered minimal and restricted games. There were also illegal games in some places.

Arizona Club

By 1931, the Arizona Club on First Street in the wide-open Block 16 had already opened (1905) and closed (1912). The erstwhile fancy club was the swankiest place in town before it merged with a bordello/saloon in 1912.

Hotel Nevada/Golden Gate

A few older places were still around in 1931 to exploit the new legalized gambling. The Hotel Nevada on East Fremont Street opened in 1906 and is today the oldest continually operated hotel downtown, now known as the Golden Gate Hotel & Casino. When gambling initially became legal, the Hotel Nevada became the Sal Sagev (Las Vegas spelled backwards), and continued to operate under that name until 1955 when some San Francisco businessmen bought it and named it the Golden Gate after their home city. With only 106 hotel rooms, some of them original, the Golden Gate is still an icon. It originated and continues to sell the famous shrimp cocktail.

Boulder Club

Then there was the Boulder Club which opened in 1929 at 118 E. Fremont. It was originally a small, one-story club that became part of Binion's Horseshoe Club in 1960.

Northern Club — First License

The Hotel Nevada and the Boulder Club were already downtown entities when gambling became legalized, but it was the competing Northern Club that snagged the state's first casino license—and it went to a woman.

Mayme Stocker, her husband Oscar, and their three sons, Clarence, Harold and Lester, had years earlier (September 2, 1920) opened the Northern Club at 15 E. Fremont St. It was reputedly a soda fountain, but the limited gambling then allowed by law had been available there from the start.

Harold Stocker later reported that there were five games legal in the 1920s: stud, draw, lowball poker, 500, and bridge. No other gambling was allowed, and Harold recalled that their very tough sheriff Sam Gay made sure everything was on the up and up.

Oscar and the sons worked for the railroad which had restrictions against what types of businesses their employees could engage in. Thus, it fell to Mayme to operate the whole thing, at least on paper. Mayme's son Lester tried several times from 1925 to 1931 to encourage legislators to legalize gambling. Frustrated, in 1930 he held a meeting with other downtown club owners, businessmen, and city officials. He requested some money to "spread around," to get state officials seriously interested. They came up with $10,000 and went to Carson City to "spread it around." They got a legislator from up north, Phil Tobin, to introduce the history-changing bill. While his name was on the bill, Tobin later insisted that all he got out of it was "three bottles of scotch."

Regardless, the bill passed and shortly thereafter Mayme Stocker applied for, and on March 20, 1931 received, the state's first license to operate a casino.

Mayme's son Lester died in 1934, her husband Oscar died in 1941, and in 1945, Mayme Stocker leased the club to Wilbur Clark, who changed it to the Monte Carlo Club, and then went on to become a major Las Vegas developer. Mayme's son Clarence continued to operate the Northern Hotel above Clark's casino.

Las Vegas Club

In 1931 former WWI biplane pilot and mining ore assayer J. Kell Houssels Sr. invested $6,000 to become a part owner of a small legal card club on Fremont Street called the Smokehouse. He got one of the first casino licenses, remodeled for slot machines and table games, and changed the name to the Las Vegas Club Hotel & Casino.

Fremont Street, 1940s

Houssels also later had an interest in the Boulder Club down the street. Ten years later he established the El Cortez Hotel & Casino, and by the 1940s was seemingly into everything.

The Meadows

People began to build away from downtown. Tony Cornero, a California floating casino operator and convicted felon, went to Vegas in 1931 and got his brother to get a license to open a casino. Called The Meadows, it was along the highway to Boulder City at Charleston Blvd. They had actually started construction on the project, planning to offer back room activities before gambling was legalized. The hotel only had 30 rooms but a Labor Day 1931 fire gutted the rooms. The casino continued to operate, catering to locals but closed after the Hoover Dam was completed.

From Hotel Apache to Binion's

Downtown Fremont Street was literally becoming "Glitter Gulch." Most of the casinos were Western in decor and ambiance. One-armed bandit slot machines, sawdust-covered floors, honky-tonk pianos, and dealers in Western garb lured gamblers and tourists in from the brightly-lit street.

Neon was beginning to define the town. The Hotel Apache (1932-1944) at 124 E. Fremont displayed the city's first neon sign and had the first elevator. That hotel was later bought by Tony Cornero, who named it the S. S. Rex (1945-46) after his floating casino. It then became the Eldorado Club (1947-51) before it was bought by Benny Binion in 1951, who called it Binion's Horseshoe Club (1951-2004). It is now called Binion's Gambling Hall & Hotel (2004—). Throughout the name changes, the casino grew and added more bright lights and neon. High stakes gambling, poker tournaments, and an open display of $1 million (100 $10,000 bills) in a glass frame brought huge crowds downtown.

Nevada Club/Silver Club/Frontier

Among other Fremont Street casinos that sprang to action during the 1930s were the Nevada Club (1932-1969), the Silver Club (1934-1956), and the Frontier Club, (1935—1953). In 1945, while getting a toehold in Las Vegas, Benjamin "Bugsy" Siegel bought some shares in the Frontier Club. It later became the Lucky Strike Club.

The 1940s added to the success of Glitter Gulch with more casinos, more hotels, more neon, brighter lights, more gaming tables, and more gamblers. The constant clicking of silver dollars vied with the clanging of bells and whistles reminding all that jackpots are there for the taking.

El Cortez Hotel & Casino

In 1941, J. Kell Houssels Sr., who had earlier opened the Las Vegas Club, built the El Cortez Hotel & Casino in partnership with John Grayson and Marion Hicks. It is a few blocks from the heart of downtown (600 E. Fremont Street) yet had always been very popular with locals. Still operating, today it is one of the oldest casinos in town. In December 1945, Houssels and partners sold the El Cortez to a group with ties to organized crime, including Moe Sedway, Gus Greenbaum, Dave Berman, Meyer Lansky, and Benjamin "Bugsy" Siegel. In early 1946, at the group's request,

Historic El Cortez Hotel

Houssels and Ray Salmon of Utah leased the El Cortez back and made major expansions including adding a four-story wing. Jackie Gaughan bought the El Cortez in 1963 and constructed an additional tower. He still lives there today.

Golden Nugget Hotel & Casino

In 1946 the Golden Nugget Hotel & Casino (1946–) opened with 22,000 invited guests at 129 E. Fremont Street. It was designed to replicate the original Golden Nugget on San Francisco's Barbary Coast. It was the first casino to introduce a house dealer versus each poker player rotating the deal. The bright gold neon sign on the corner made it an integral part of Glitter Gulch. In 1973 Steve Wynn became a majority stockholder. In 1984 extensive remodeling made it the most luxurious, and with an added hotel tower (now 1,907 deluxe rooms and suites), the largest downtown hotel. The world's largest gold nugget, a 27.21 kilo monster, was put on display there in 1981.

Pioneer Club

Nothing was more iconic of the Glitter Gulch's Western heritage than Vegas Vic, the 40-foot neon cowboy at the entrance to the Pioneer Club, who waved his arm while his recorded voice blurted out "Howdy, pardner" every 15 minutes.

The Pioneer Club (1942–1995) took over a 1918 restaurant building on Fremont Street and for years was one of the most successful downtown casinos.

When the Fremont Street Experience opened in 1995, the Pioneer Club determined it couldn't compete with the larger casinos and closed. The building houses souvenir shops now, but a silent Vegas Vic is still guarding the entrance.

Fremont/Mint/California Club/Lady Luck/Four Queens

The 1950s and early 1960s saw the addition of the Fremont Hotel & Casino (1956), Mint Las Vegas (1961), California Hotel & Casino (1964), Lady Luck Hotel & Casino (1964), and the Four Queens Hotel & Casino (1966).

Downtown got an annual boost with the Elks-sponsored Helldorado Days celebration, a community-wide festival launched in 1935 to attract tourism by saluting Las Vegas' Western heritage. Helldorado Days was fun for the cowboys and wannabees alike.

Downtown has survived and is still growing, slowly shedding its Western image, having added more casinos, hotels, and tourist attractions every decade. But by the end of the 1940s, people were looking to another direction for the future of Las Vegas. They found it on the road to Los Angeles, now referred to as the "Strip."

The Early Las Vegas Strip
ON THE ROAD TO L.A.

Pair-O-Dice

There were two main reasons for growth on what would become the world-famous Las Vegas Strip. It was outside the city limits of Las Vegas, and it was on the road to and from Los Angeles, thus the first casinos one encountered coming from California.

The Pair-O-Dice was the very first nightclub on the four-mile Strip. In 1930, Las Vegans Frank and Angelina Detra bought land fronting the Los Angeles Highway (Highway 91) and opened the Pair-O-Dice later that year. Being outside the city limits and ostensibly farther from the arm of the law, as a private club only open nights, they offered illegal alcoholic drinks (it was during Prohibition), and illegal gambling. After March 1931 and the legalization of gambling, Las Vegas and Clark County set up licensing procedures for casino games, with most of the licenses going to Fremont Street venues.

While the Pair-O-Dice owners were waiting for license approval, in April the county issued a license to a competing nightclub, the smaller Red Rooster, about a mile farther south on Highway 91 (in front of today's Mirage). The Red Rooster had opened a year after the Pair-O-Dice, yet secured the first Strip casino license, but only by a couple of weeks. Pair-O-Dice became licensed on

May 5, 1931 and, broadened from the speakeasy-type club, opened its doors to the public at large. Run by manager Oscar E. Klawitter, the club offered roulette, craps, and blackjack. And when Prohibition was repealed in 1933, booze was legally served.

Pair-O-Dice also offered live bands, singers, dancing, and Italian food. Throughout that first decade on the Strip, it was far more successful than the Red Rooster.

In 1939, former Los Angeles police officer Guy McAfee bought the Pair-O-Dice, that original Strip nightclub, renovated it and renamed it the 91 Club for its location on US-91. He is also the guy who originally gave the Strip its name, copying the Sunset Strip.

El Rancho Vegas

In 1940 longtime Las Vegas businessmen Robert Griffith and James Cashman threw a teaser idea out to Thomas Hull, a Californian who owned and operated several hotels including the San Francisco Bellevue, Hollywood Roosevelt, and Mayfair in Los Angeles. Hull was also developing several "El Rancho" motor hotels in California (Fresno and Sacramento), and after listening to the Vegas businessmen, wondered about a possible Las Vegas location.

There's a story that says Hull's car broke down a few miles before Las Vegas on Highway 91, and after counting the number of cars that whizzed by, realized the highway location was a sound one. Whether true or not, after Cashman showed Hull lots closer to downtown, Hull said no and decided on the highway before town.

Hull bought a large lot on Highway 91 at the corner of present day Las Vegas Blvd. and Sahara Ave. It was in county territory just outside the city limits, thus saving Hull from higher city taxes.

He constructed the Strip's first resort, the El Rancho Vegas, blending a Spanish-style exterior with a Western, cowboy- type interior. Along with the casino was a lounge, steakhouse, a showroom, a huge Chuckwagon buffet, and the largest dining room in Las Vegas with 250 seats. A neon windmill on top of the casino and adjacent gas station beckoned motorists.

On April 3, 1941, the El Rancho opened on 57 acres of land. The resort was like a dude ranch and featured 63 guest rooms (mostly bungalows), later adding 47 more. The popular showroom was a first for Las Vegas and featured the El Rancho Starlets dancing to a live orchestra. Hull sold the El Rancho Vegas early on and there were several owners in the 1940s, including Wilbur Clark who later developed his signature Desert Inn and other Las Vegas properties. It was purchased by Beldon Katleman in the late-1940s.

Katleman improved the developing popular Las Vegas trend of using entertainment to promote the casino, signing such headliners as Joe E. Lewis for his showroom. Also showcased at the El Rancho Vegas were stars like Pearl

Bailey, Lita Baron, Milton Berle, Ben Blue, stripper Lili St. Cyr, Billy Daniels, singer Lena Horne, Guy Landis, Lenny Maxwell, Ann Southern, Sophie Tucker, and popular crooner Rudy Vallee.

Later, the resort hosted the weddings of Eydie Gorme and Steve Lawrence in 1957, and Paul Newman and Joanne Woodward in 1958.

Then disaster struck. Betty Grable and her husband, band leader Harry James, were on stage in the lounge on June 17, 1960, when a blaze erupted. Grable spotted the flames, grabbed her husband's hand and ran out a side door. No one was injured in the fire but all that was left of the main building was a charred shell.

The fire had apparently started in the kitchen. Katleman had originally planned to rebuild, but he never did, and the El Rancho Vegas, the Las Vegas Strip's first resort, was razed, leaving only an empty lot that soon had other resorts rise up around it.

The Last Frontier

The Hotel Last Frontier, the Strip's second full-fledged casino resort came into being when Texas theater developer R.E. Griffith and his architect nephew, William J. Moore, visited the El Rancho Vegas in 1941 and saw opportunity in the area. However, they wanted to be the very first resort for California travelers.

Their answer was the existing 91 Club, about one mile closer to Los Angeles than the El Rancho Vegas. They purchased the club and 35 acres of land around it for $1,000 an acre. While Moore was placed in charge, it was the mogul Griffith who was the driving force behind what became the Strip's second casino resort, the Last Frontier.

The sprawling resort was designed like an Old Western town and even had a Last Frontier Village, including the Little Church of the West, the city's first wedding chapel.

The Last Frontier, later known as the The First Frontier, and then just The Frontier, was an instant success following its October 1942 opening. Griffith died in November 1943, but Moore carried on. William Moore became the father of the junket when he began using airplanes to fly entertainers and gamblers to his resort. He initially booked flights with a small airline owned at the time by future casino mogul Kirk Kerkorian.

The Last Frontier immediately started booking big entertainment, something it became known for throughout its long history. Some of the celebrities to perform at the resort during the 1940s and '50s included the biggest names of the time: Sophie Tucker, Mandrake the Magician, Marx Brothers, Judy Garland, Ronald Reagan, Frank Sinatra, Sammy Davis, Jr., Eddie Albert & Margo accompanied by Jack Eastern, Jack Carter, Henny Youngman, Tommy Dorsey's band, and Josephine Baker.

In 1951, Moore sold the Last Frontier to Jake Kozloff, a mob-connected trucking and brewery company owner who optimistically later changed its name to "The New Frontier." Later owners also included Murray Randolph and Irv Leff, Los Angeles businessmen; and Maurice Friedman.

For a while even German munitions heiress and actress Vera Krupp had a partial ownership. All the while, the Frontier was associated with organized crime, and profits skimmed off the top cost owners so much they sold their interests.

The New Frontier became a real hard-luck operation. The casino closed down in 1957 and didn't re-open until 1959. Unfortunately, the Western theme was getting stale, especially as fancier and swankier resorts were being built along the Strip. Competition was taking the luster away from The New Frontier.

In 1967, the Frontier Operating Company was formed with some new blood to take over the lease. One of the owners was an aggressive 25-year old from the East Coast named Steve Wynn, who was hoping to learn the ropes of the casino business. The FBI however immediately investigated the new owners and found hidden ownership and mob affiliations. Apparently, Wynn himself was oblivious about his partners and walked away from the scandal unscathed. But the scandal hurt the hotel and The New Frontier was losing money.

Billionaire Howard Hughes bought the problematic casino in July 1967 for $14 million. He shortened the name to The Frontier, and the casino started turning a profit.

But the yo-yo problems of The Frontier continued. Casino operator Margaret Elardi bought The Frontier from Hughes, and in 1991 encountered problems with the Culinary Union, resulting in an arduous 61-month strike involving 550 union workers that crippled The Frontier.

Finally, in October 1997, Kansas businessman Phil Ruffin purchased The Frontier for $167 million and agreed to a five-year contract ending the strike. Ruffin changed the Las Vegas Strip's second resort's name back to The New Frontier.

Of course, by that time it was a far different Las Vegas Strip than when the Last Frontier was originally developed, and it was quite obviously out-classed by its more lustrous neighbors.

Fremont Street
Gambling in Glitter Gulch

South of town along the fabled Strip, casinos were being developed at a rapid pace. Yet, there was still plenty of activity going on downtown, along Fremont Street, throughout the heart of "Glitter Gulch" where the constant clinking of silver coins provided the background ambiance and glittering neon signs brightened the darkest night.

By 1954, Las Vegas was being visited annually by more than eight million tourists who dropped more than $200 million in slot machines and on the tables. More visitors were coming each year and developers and casino operators were anxious to help them part with their money. More and more casinos were being built to help them do just that.

Fremont — 1956

One big major addition to Downtown Las Vegas in the 1950s was the Fremont Hotel & Casino, which opened in May 1956 as the tallest building in the state of Nevada. It opened with 155 rooms and was expanded in 1963, at which time a parking structure was added. The Fremont is still one of the most viable casinos downtown.

Mint — 1957

The Mint Las Vegas at 100 E. Fremont St. was built in 1957 and sold to developer Del Webb in 1961. He added a 26-story hotel tower which made it taller than its neighboring Fremont, and thus the state's tallest building at the time. He sold the property in 1988 and it became part of Binion's Horseshoe Club. The hotel tower closed in late 2009.

California Club Hotel & Casino — 1964

The California Club, a block off Fremont (Ogden and Main), opened in 1964 as a smaller casino. Still open, now with 750 rooms, it also boasts a large sports book section and showroom. With package tours arriving regularly from Honolulu, it has a large and loyal Hawaiian clientele base.

Lady Luck — 1964

It was a tiny slot machine-only casino at Third and Ogden the first time I visited the Lady Luck Hotel & Casino in 1964 and I watched it grow over the years. Numerous expansions made it as dominant and viable as its neighbors.

Two large towers were added in the 1980s and some of the units were sold as time shares. In 2003 the 792 room hotel was renamed the Park Plaza but the hotel closed in 2006. Renovation has been planned and the new owners are hoping for an early 2012 reopening. For now, it remains closed; it has been called a "blight" by Mayor Oscar Goodman. Of course he would know; it's right across the street from city hall.

Four Queens — 1966

The Four Queens Hotel & Casino opened at the corner of Fremont and Third streets in 1966. For trivia buffs, the casino is named after the builder Ben Goffstein's four daughters: Faith, Hope, Benita, and Michele. Still open at that dominant corner, it now has almost 700 hotel rooms and a 33,000-square-foot casino with over 30 table games and 1,000 slot machines.

Plaza — 1971

Originally called the Union Plaza, referring to the Union Pacific railroad station and small park the casino replaced, the Plaza Hotel & Casino opened in July 1971 at 1 Main Street at the head of Fremont.

Developers included Las Vegas businessmen Sam Boyd, Howard Cannon and Jackie Gaughan. Now owned by the Tamares Group, the Plaza has 1,037 budget rooms and 80,000 square feet of gaming space.

Just Like Downtown

Seemingly unmindful of the extravagance and growth of the Strip casinos, for a long time Downtown Las Vegas did not miss a beat. There was always something going on to attract new waves of tourists, including the high-stakes, no-limit poker games initiated at Benny Binion's Horseshoe Casino.

The bright lights of Glitter Gulch were a beacon. In fact, author Ross Macdonald in his 1965 novel *Black Money* offered this description, "I took a cab to Fremont Street. The jostling neon colours of its signs made the few stars in the narrow sky look pale and embarrassed."

There were the expansions of both the Mint and Fremont along with the major rehabilitation that Steve Wynn did in upgrading the Golden Nugget to elevate it above its neighbors in luxury. For a time, it seemed there were two cores to that attractive place called Las Vegas. But Downtown Las Vegas still could not compete. In time the Strip resorts began to pull away with their newness, largeness, luxury, and entertainment, and Downtown Las Vegas floundered. For a couple of decades many tourists never even went downtown—some not even aware it existed. Rather than bury itself in an early grave, Downtown Las Vegas had to do something more to reinvent itself. It just took a while to do it.

CHAPTER 4

TENTACLES OF THE MOB

Opportunity, and an "open territory" declared by the "Syndicate" brought mobsters to Las Vegas from around the county.

They became owners, either overtly or covertly, and ran Las Vegas, skimming, intimidating, and ruling with a brutal fist.

"Bugsy" Siegel, Moe Dalitz, Tony Spilotro, and Frank Rosenthal are but a few of the memorable and colorful characters who left their imprint on Las Vegas during the days of mob rule.

Nevada Welcomes Opportunists
The Smell of Money

Prohibition in America (1919 to 1933) created untold opportunities for those willing to break the law and supply alcohol to a booze-deprived nation. The 18th Amendment dictated that all sales, manufacture, and transportation of alcohol were banned.

The National Prohibition Act set up by that amendment was extremely difficult to enforce and the government lacked the means to do it. Therefore bootlegging, the illegal production and distribution of liquor, became rampant, and underworld suppliers got stronger each year. It is estimated that in New York City alone, by 1925 there were over 30,000 illegal speakeasy clubs, all buying and selling smuggled or illegally manufactured alcohol.

By 1930 Chicago gangster Al Capone made millions of dollars through illegal alcohol sales, controlled all 10,000 Chicago speakeasies, and oversaw a huge bootlegging empire.

On December 5, 1933, the Twenty-First Amendment repealing the Eighteenth Amendment was ratified and alcohol was legal again. However, the effects of Prohibition lingered on. As rum-runners and bootleggers scrambled to figure out how to make money outside the black market, most states saw a need to clamp down on the widening crimes spawned by the wide-open Prohibition days, including illegal gambling. Except Nevada, that is.

Nevada legalized gambling in 1931 for several reasons, one being to bring out in the open what was already going on in saloons and back rooms across the state. Nevada wanted to avoid situations that the Prohibition days fostered: illegal activity, bootleggers, and bribed officials.

A selling factor for the state of Nevada was the gambling tax and license fee income. Initially, the licensing fees were split with 75% going to the county and 25% retained by the state. Fees were set up based on a casino's number of table games and slot machines. Gambling began in Nevada as a local answer to local concerns.

The fact that numerous other states took an opposite approach in the post-Prohibition days created enormous opportunity in Nevada. Elsewhere, supported by the federal government, states began cracking down on illegal casinos and gambling and sending operators to jail. In nearby Southern California, gamblers and gambling operators were being hit hard, with raids and vigorous enforcement by local, county, state and federal officials.

It didn't take long for the "Smell of Money" to waft far out of Nevada and begin to attract gamblers, and more important—those who would bank the action—those with casino gambling experience. Most of the early investors came from those states that had a lot of illegal gambling during Prohibition, places like California, New York, Chicago and Texas. Nevada was an attractive beacon for opportunists.

Creating the Syndicate
A United Front

Anticipating the repeal of Prohibition, several former competing East Coast crime families got together at a New Jersey conference in 1929 and formed a loose federation, or National Commission—called the Syndicate by the media. With the possible impending legalization of the black market in booze, a lot of gangsters and hoodlums would shift their "talents" in other directions: prostitution, drugs, numbers games, loan sharking, business shakedowns, gambling, and much more.

During the waning months of an East Coast gang war which left as many as 60 mobsters brutally murdered, some realized that they would survive better without internal warfare among them. They needed to establish territories and have the means to enforce them. United, their power could return even stronger than before.

The Syndicate confederation that was established at that May 1929 meeting in Atlantic City, N.J. was attended by leading underworld figures including Joe Adonis, Albert Anastasia, Al Capone, Frank Costello, Meyer Lansky, Charles "Lucky" Luciano, Dutch Shultz, and Abner "Longy" Zwillman.

That it was a multi-ethnic conference with both Jewish and Italian mobs was due to Luciano, who defied the old Mafia members and their Sicilian traditions. He felt that the Italians and Jews could make more money by working together.

Luciano emerged as the leader and was assisted by his longtime associate Meyer Lansky. The Syndicate set up a commission to divide up and regulate the country's markets and for the first time there was a lot of cooperation, even between the Jewish and Italian organizations. But that didn't stop individual animosities and grudges.

Luciano and Lansky were tough and mean and they rose to power by eliminating those in their way, including previous leader Salvatore Maranazo, who was mowed down in a volley of gunfire.

After his hostile takeover, astute businessman Luciano organized the Syndicate of organized crime. He shaped the old Mafia into a smoothly run national crime organization which was focused on the bottom line.

The Syndicate (often referred to as the Mafia, Mob, Families, or Organized Crime) became pervasive and nationwide. It was run by two dozen family bosses who controlled bootlegging, numbers, narcotics, prostitution, unions, and businesses in their respective areas. They got into everything and their influence and tentacles grew and corrupted everything from legitimate business, to politics and law enforcement. When Luciano went to prison for running a prostitution ring in 1936, Meyer Lansky took over as chairman even though Luciano still orchestrated Syndicate activities from a jail cell.

Mob leaders, from Joe Profaci in Brooklyn, to Joseph Vallone in Milwaukee, to Johnny Lazia in Kansas City, to Moe Dalitz in Cleveland, cooperated better among themselves as they carved up the country to grasp their ill-gotten gains.

California and the West were ripe pickings, and so was an emerging desert gambling town in Nevada called Las Vegas. Creating a major factor that defined decades of mob rule, they declared Las Vegas "open territory."

Tony Cornero
Ahead of the Mob

O ne of the first gangsters in Las Vegas, Tony Cornero, also known as Tony Stralla or "The Admiral," was born in Italy in 1900. He ended up in California and assisted Prohibition scofflaws by running booze. He had a small fleet of freighters, one of which, the *S. S. Lily*, could hold 4,000 cases of Canadian whiskey. With his ships anchored far off the Southern California coast, he used small, fast boats to transfer the illegal alcohol to deserted beaches.

Unfortunately, he got caught bootlegging and served time. His criminal record later included two bootlegging offenses and three murder attempts. However, by age 25 he was a millionaire. He began making booze, some 5,000 gallons a day. He was raided, but escaped due to a prior tip-off. Up in Nevada, all those honky-tonks and underground casinos that had been proliferating during the 1920s needed alcohol, so Cornero and his brothers Louis and Frank began to furnish the booze that kept the various Las Vegas saloons going.

At the time Cornero was not a member of any Syndicate family but still had connections. The Los Angeles mob was run by Jack Dragna and it was nowhere near as effective as its Eastern counterparts. In 1931 Cornero decided to include gambling among his many talents.

The Cornero brothers optioned a 30-acre site just outside the city limits of Las Vegas on Boulder Highway (Fremont and Charleston) and began to construct a casino. It was almost complete when gambling was legalized, so by getting a license they did not have to run an illegal joint.

Because Cornero was a felon, his brother had to apply for, and thus received, a gambling license, one of the first ever issued in Nevada. The Meadows was one of the earliest major hotel/casinos in the Las Vegas area and the most luxurious at that time. It had 30 rooms (all with bath), electric lights, and hot water at all hours. As the Meadows started making big money, Cornero began investing in other Las Vegas casinos.

It is reported that New York mobsters Charles "Lucky" Luciano, Meyer Lansky and Frank Costello demanded a cut of Cornero's action, and Cornero refused to comply. On Labor Day 1931, the Meadows was mysteriously set ablaze. Cornero gave up, sold his interests, and moved back to Los Angeles.

Flyer for Cornero's S.S. Rex ship

Cornero then developed a gambling ship, the *S.S. Rex*, which was anchored just off the coast of California, a 10-minute water taxi ride away. After years of fighting off authorities, Cornero lost the *Rex* to the government in a 1939 seizure.

He returned to Las Vegas, where he had always envisioned classy carpeted gambling joints. He leased the casino of the Apache Club on Fremont Street and nostalgically called it the *S.S. Rex*. After selling that, he returned again to California and opened another floating casino called the *S.S. Lux*.

Back in Vegas, Tony Cornero organized the

Stardust Company in 1954 and started construction of a casino resort that would be the largest in the world with over 1,000 rooms. But he never saw it completed.

Cornero survived one assassination attempt when he was shot in the stomach. In July 1955, Cornero suddenly dropped dead of an apparent heart attack while playing craps in the Desert Inn. It turns out the county coroner never did an autopsy, and some people wondered why. Stories circulated that he was poisoned so the mob could get control of the Stardust. Who knows? His death marked the end of another Las Vegas legend.

The Stardust would be finished by others—and yes, they would be mob connected.

Greed Feeds Greed
How the Mob Got In

Mob ownership of Las Vegas casinos became an insidious reality and remained so for many years. Behind the various and often murky layers of ownership lurked many people affiliated with organized crime. And they usually nudged aside the previous owners and virtually controlled the casinos. How did the mob get entrenched in the first place? It might surprise some people—but they were invited.

In a typical case of greed feeding greed, the casinos did whatever they could to attract and retain gamblers to their establishments. And the mobsters had something the casinos wanted. It all started with the wire service.

Continental Press Service, a wire service that served the entire country, transmitted immediate horse racing results from racetracks everywhere. Bookies and illegal betting operations across the country needed the service to stay in business and paid Continental, which had a lock on the business, for it. The service was established and run by a Chicagoan named James M. Ragen.

The Chicago mob, under Al Capone, developed the Trans-America wire service in direct competition to Continental to be offered to bookies and gambling establishments for a similar monthly fee.

To help sell the new service in the West, the Chicago outfit was aided by New Yorker Gus Greenbaum, whom they sent to Phoenix as early as 1928. Greenbaum's success in Arizona later helped him play a big role in Las Vegas casino development.

Meyer Lansky came into the mob with a couple of guys he grew up with, Moe Sedway and Benjamin "Bugsy" Siegel. Along with all sorts of mayhem and "protection" services, the three also performed murders on contract. Sedway and Siegel had thus also both advanced in mob power and importance.

In 1937, Lansky and the New York family sent Siegel to California to oversee Capone's lucrative new wire service and help set up gambling rackets with Los Angeles mobster Jack Dragna. Continuing the rising mobster spirit of cooperation, gangster Mickey Cohen was sent by the Cleveland mob to help Siegel.

Trans-America was doing well. Rather than risk broken limbs or worse, bookies rallied to sign up for the new wire service.

Lansky smelled opportunity in the West, Las Vegas in particular, and also wanted Siegel to cultivate that blossoming area. Siegel preferred the Hollywood life, so the Las Vegas market fell mostly to their old pal, Moe Sedway, a little guy with a long face and large nose.

Little Moe Sedway had found his niche and was very successful. For one, the competing Continental Press focused its efforts in California, totally disregarding that upstart desert town in Nevada. Second, in Las Vegas the whole thing had been legalized and the subscribers were legitimate licensed casinos. And third, the casinos really liked the horseracing books in house to help draw gambling customers for the slots and table games.

The casinos needed and wanted the wire service so much, they were pawns falling into the greedy hands of mobsters. In early 1942 Moe and Bugsy decided to restrict access to the wire service even for fee paying customers. They wanted more than the monthly fee—they wanted a piece of the action.

Bugsy Siegel, in support of Sedway, told the casinos that if they wanted the wire service they would have to give up all, or in some favored cases, only two thirds, of their bookmaking income. To keep the horseracing books in house, they agreed.

The casinos were even willing to give pieces of the overall action, casino ownership shares, to Sedway and his pals. Thus Moe Sedway, Bugsy Siegel, and Meyer Lansky became part owners of the El Cortez Hotel & Casino which opened in 1941, extending the tentacles of the mob into Las Vegas casino ownership.

In December 1945, Houssels and partners sold the majority ownership of the El Cortez to the group with ties to organized crime, including Dave Berman, Sedway, Greenbaum, Lansky, and Siegel. The El Cortez became the foothold of mob rule in Las Vegas for years to come.

Siegel, Sedway and Lansky also acquired interest in the Golden Nugget Hotel & Casino and the Fremont Hotel & Casino downtown in the same manner. By then, Siegel also controlled the Northern Club, and the horse books at the Golden Nugget and the Las Vegas Club. That year it is estimated that Bugsy Siegel's income from the Las Vegas bookmaking operations alone was $25,000 a month!

The mob was excited about the tremendous opportunities in Las Vegas and established a few ground rules to ensure a reciprocal relationship there for many years. To be taken seriously, they realized they had to get along amongst themselves. They reiterated they wanted Las Vegas to be "open," and they could all operate there. They wanted to be accepted into the social structure and assume a veneer of respectability. One rule to sidestep any possible law-enforcement or media scrutiny was to ensure than any contract killings take place outside of Las Vegas. That rule was mostly followed and later assassinations occurred elsewhere.

It wasn't long before the Trans-America Wire Service was in every single horse parlor in Las Vegas.

And James Ragen? Well, his refusal to sell Continental to the mob cost him plenty. Not only did he turn down their offer but he foolishly went to law enforcement with it, sealing his own fate. Someone in Chicago blasted him enough times with a shotgun to cut him in half, yet he survived only long enough to be poisoned with mercury in a hospital! The Chicago mob family, then under Tony Accardo, very shortly thereafter controlled both wire services.

Ben "Bugsy" Siegel and The Flamingo
MObsTER's MURdER JUMP-sTARTS VEGAS

The 1940s brought major changes for Las Vegas, but the most pivotal and far reaching was when the brutal assassination of a gangster casino operator focused the eyes of the world on that emerging gambling town in the desert. The scandalous murder of casino owner Benjamin "Bugsy" Siegel, even though it happened in California, became the catalyst that instantly made Las Vegas a tourist destination—and it has never looked back.

By the mid-1940s, Nevada was becoming attractive to a certain clientele because authorities in California had been cracking down on illegal gambling, booze running, and prostitution in the Los Angeles area. Many gangsters just moved their operations to neighboring Nevada. The gamblers followed.

The state of Nevada began to realize its potential and in 1946 levied gaming taxes on the casinos. The taxes did not hinder those who realized the powerful financial potential of regulated gambling. The Flamingo Las Vegas (originally called the Pink Flamingo Hotel & Casino) got its flamboyant start that same year.

Bugsy Siegel is credited with a lot of things, some real, some legend, but his involvement with the Pink Flamingo Hotel & Casino was capitalizing on the dream of another. Not that he didn't have his own dreams.

According to his selective service file, he was born Benjamin Siegel on February 28, 1906 in New York City. As a poor Jewish teenager growing up in Brooklyn, he, Moe Sedway and Meyer Lansky formed a mob that offered protection services, thefts, and an "elimination" service that was the forerunner to Murder, Inc.

In 1937, the East Coast families sent Siegel west, and even after the Las Vegas casinos gave pieces of the action to Siegel and his pals, Siegel still preferred Hollywood to Las Vegas.

Ben Siegel hated the nickname "Bugsy" given to him because of his violent and unpredictable behavior. In contrast to the aquiline-faced Lansky, Siegel had movie star good looks and let it go to his head. He started hanging around with actors, like Jean Harlow and George Raft. He became infatuated with Hollywood, and the mob didn't appreciate his rising public profile. He became a man they wanted to watch.

The Flamingo was started by Billy Wilkerson, who owned the famous Sunset Strip nightclub Ciro's in Hollywood and was one of the founders of *The Hollywood Reporter*. In 1945, he bought 33 acres on the west side of Highway 91 about one mile south of the Last Frontier. He hired George Vernon Russell to design a luxurious hotel resort much more upscale and European in concept than the "sawdust" and "Western" places that had defined the town.

Wilkerson had plenty of big ideas and plenty of underworld contacts, including Siegel. The Flamingo was to be his crowning glory, but he never completed the project. For numerous reasons, including his personal gambling habit which put him in a serious cash problem, Wilkerson was unable to continue. By then, Siegel and his associates, Sedway, Greenbaum, Lansky and Harry Rothberg, had sold their interest in the El Cortez and used their profits to buy into the Flamingo as silent partners. One of them had to take over Wilkerson's failing desert project.

Siegel, who knew Wilkerson and lived near him in Beverly Hills, was the obvious choice, but Siegel wanted no part in any operation that took him back to Nevada permanently. It meant forsaking Beverly Hills and the playboy life to endure not only the desert heat but the social isolation of Nevada. At Lansky's insistence, however, Siegel consented.

Through all this, the FBI kept tabs on Siegel, hoping to pin something on him. He was tried for murder once and acquitted. A July 18, 1946 personal memorandum to the Attorney General from FBI Director J. Edgar Hoover read: "In the course of the above investigation, we have ascertained that Benjamin "Bugsy" Siegel, notorious racketeer with underworld connection on the west and east coasts and Las Vegas, Nevada, will again visit the latter city within the next few days and reside at the Last Frontier Hotel there in suite 401. As previously pointed out, we are desirous of following Siegel's widespread activities and, therefore, are requesting authority to place a technical surveillance on his telephone at the Last Frontier Hotel which will be Las Vegas 1800."

Back in Vegas on June 20, 1946, Siegel formed the Nevada Project Corporation of California, naming himself president. He was also the largest principal stockholder in the operation, which defined everyone else merely as shareholders. From this point the Flamingo became Syndicate-run.

Siegel took control of the unfinished project but the job immediately ran over its initial $1 million budget and would exceed an incredible $6 million before finished.

Siegel fired Russell and others hired by Wilkerson. He began to micro-manage the construction details, driving the price up. Feeding his paranoia, he insisted that the Flamingo be built like a fortress. The thick concrete walls were reinforced with steel, and his personal top-floor suite became a maze of trap doors and escape hatches, one leading to a getaway car in his private garage. The hotel was a design disaster created by a common street hood who was vying for respectability.

Benjamin "Bugsy" Siegel *(City of Los Angeles file photo)*

There were also expensive amenities never before seen in Las Vegas. Siegel wanted to create a swanky, upscale resort capable of attracting the Hollywood celebrities. He insisted each bathroom of the 93-room hotel have its own sewer system (cost: $1,150,000); more toilets were ordered than needed (cost: $50,000); because of the plumbing alterations, the boiler room, now too small, had to be enlarged (cost: $113,000); and Siegel ordered a larger kitchen (cost: $29,000). He bought the finest carpets and fixtures; he made it a real resort with tennis courts and riding stables supplementing the large swimming pool.

During those months immediately after the end of World War II, materials were scarce but Siegel was able to get them through the black market, even though at higher prices.

Theft and pilferage at the Flamingo construction site was legendary. It has been reported that a lot of suppliers and other workers duped him and stole from him. It was said that some suppliers would drive through the front gates with materials, get them signed off and drive out the back to return the next day to "resell" them.

It was also reported that Siegel himself stole from his own project. It was alleged that his girlfriend Virginia Hill was making trips to Europe and depositing funds into a numbered account.

By early November 1946, the Syndicate was concerned and issued an ultimatum: provide accounting or forfeit funding. Producing a balance sheet was the last thing Siegel wanted to do. After the Syndicate's refusal of more help, Siegel tried to raise private funds. He sold nonexistent stock. Now in a hurry, Siegel doubled his work force, paying overtime and double-time. He hired Del Webb to finish the resort, which opened the door for Webb in Las Vegas. However, costs continued to rise, and by the end of November work was nearly finished.

Siegel moved up the opening from Wilkerson's original date of March 1, 1947 to the day after Christmas, 1946. Even though the 105-room hotel was not complete, the Pink Flamingo Hotel & Casino opened with comedian Jimmy Durante as headliner and was attended by a few Hollywood celebrities including George Raft, George Sanders, Sonny Tufts, and George Jessel.

Horrible weather in Los Angeles grounded flights and prevented many others from attending. As Las Vegas openings go, the Flamingo was a tremendous flop—construction was still going on in the background and locals who preferred the more comfortable western-type casinos shied away. To add insult, the casino immediately hit a bad luck streak and lost $300,000 at the tables before Siegel closed the Flamingo after only two weeks.

Regrouping before opening again, Siegel wanted to improve his image and hired a young Hank Greenspun, who would later publish the *Las Vegas Sun*, as a publicist to help extol his questionable virtues.

The Flamingo reopened on March 27, 1947 and immediately began turning a profit. Over the years, the Flamingo has been called the Pink Flamingo, the Fabulous Flamingo, the Flamingo Hilton and the Flamingo Las Vegas. Still open, today it boasts a 3,565-room hotel and a 78,000-square-foot casino. While the Flamingo would endure for over 60 years, Bugsy Siegel's days were numbered.

Siegel's execution was ordered. He should have known that deceiving the Syndicate and stealing from them would have signed his death warrant, even someone as powerful as he had become. He had yet to pay back money invested. He also rubbed the mobsters the wrong way by allowing his persona to become so public. When he was omitted from a high level Syndicate meeting in Havana, Cuba, he should have foreseen his future. He was apprehensive but remained positive as the Flamingo was beginning to bring in the money.

Siegel died like he lived however, violently. While his girlfriend Virginia Hill was in Europe on June 20, 1947, he was at her house in Beverly Hills, California. He and pal Al Smiley had just returned to the house from a late dinner and were on the couch when shots rang out.

According to FBI SAC Hood of the Los Angeles Division, "...The gun which killed Siegel was a .30 caliber carbine and that nine two-inch-long shells had been used....These shells hit him in the head and one went right through his eye and his eyelid was found about ten feet away from Siegel. The gun was fired about fourteen feet away from where Siegel was sitting and the killer rested the gun in the cross of one of the trellises by the window." No killer was ever caught or accused of the murder.

A media frenzy ensued, and speculation ran rampant. One FBI memo mentioned a speculation that "New York members of the mob instigated the killing of Siegel and same may have been precipitated by information furnished to the mob in New York by Virginia Hill, as to how Siegel had been double-crossing them." That was never proven, however.

What is Siegel's legacy? "I think what it shows more than anything else is the public's fascination with gangster-type characters," Flamingo Las Vegas publicity director Terry Lindberg said. "(His death) turned a man who was basically not a historical figure into somebody who was a lot larger than life." Others give Siegel a different type of credit. UNLV Public Administration Department Chairman William Thompson: "It's folklore, it's my-thology...His death let the world know we had casinos...It was im-portant that we turned the cor-ner and quit being just a cowboy town and became a resort town. He was responsible for that."

Las Vegas historian Frank Wright said, "His (Siegel's) death was a great advertisement for the city of Las Vegas, in a sense. It certainly brought attention to Las Vegas and created a sort of sense of illicit excitement about Las Vegas."

Bronze bust of Benjamin "Bugsy" Siegel at Flamingo Las Vegas

Casinos Line the Highway
THE STRIP WAXES GLAMOROUS

With the eyes of the world soon focused on that upstart gambling city in the desert, developers and businessmen from all walks of life hastened to get their "piece of the pie." They realized that casinos could mean big money, and that the Las Vegas Strip was the place to be. Over the decade following the Flamingo's debut, nine major casino/hotels would open on the Strip, offering entertainment and a type of class and elegance heretofore not seen in the casino industry. After the Flamingo, it seemed the mantra was "Bigger, better, and fancier."

Thunderbird Hotel — 1948

The fourth casino resort on the fabled Strip (After the El Rancho, Last Frontier, and Flamingo) was the Thunderbird Hotel, which opened in 1948. It was about a mile closer to downtown than the Flamingo, yet still in county territory, and across Highway 91 (The Strip would later be called Las Vegas Boulevard) from the El Rancho. El Cortez Hotel owners Marion Hicks and J.K. Houssels, and Nevada lieutenant governor Clifford A. Jones were early principals.

The Thunderbird boasted an Indian motif and was named for a Navajo icon. It was an early leader in attracting big name entertainment to Las Vegas, including Rosemary Clooney, Donald O'Connor, and Mel Torme. It also hosted the Folies Bergére. The Thunderbird became the Silverbird in 1977, and the El Rancho in 1982. In 1992 it closed and was imploded in 2000 to make way for a condominium complex.

Desert Inn — 1950 (See Moe Dalitz)

Wilbur Clark, at one time a San Diego hotel bellman and former owner of the El Rancho Vegas, parleyed his $1 million from the sale of that first hotel into the $4.5 million Wilbur Clark's Desert Inn. The Desert Inn was considered the most luxurious resort on the Strip when it opened in 1950. The mob, in the form of Moe Dalitz, quietly helped finance completion of the Desert Inn and Clark became beholden to their power.

When it opened, the hotel featured the highest unobstructed panoramic view of the Las Vegas Valley from the resort's *third-floor* Skyroom, where celebrities occasionally mingled with hotel guests. The adjacent Paradise Valley Golf Club on Desert Inn Road hosted many important golf tournaments, including the prestigious Tournament of Champions.

The Sahara — 1952

Opening a couple of months before the Sands, the Sahara Hotel & Casino was built just across the street (Now Sahara Avenue) from the city limits and across Highway 91 from the El Rancho Vegas. The Sahara added a 24-story tower in 1963 and a 27-story tower in 1987. Surviving almost six decades, the Sahara finally closed its doors on May 16, 2011. With an illustrious history of entertainers (The Beatles, Frank Sinatra, Dean Martin, Jerry Lewis, etc.), the Sahara Theater and legendary Congo Room welcomed generations of Vegas visitors. The iconic Sahara was also featured in the 1960 movie *Ocean's Eleven*.

Sands — 1952

The Sands Hotel & Casino, just south of the Desert Inn, opened in December 1952 and was the "in" place over the next 20 years. Visited by Presidents Harry Truman, John F. Kennedy and Lyndon Johnson, it was also the venue of the infamous "Rat Pack" gatherings. In fact, both Frank Sinatra and Dean Martin held ownership interests. Their pals (Sammy Davis Jr., Peter Lawford, and Joey Bishop) usually joined them for a night of ad-libbed hilarity.

The venerable Sands, even though an institution, was still susceptible to the "bigger and better" mind-set that defines Las Vegas and was imploded in 1996 to make room for today's Venetian Hotel.

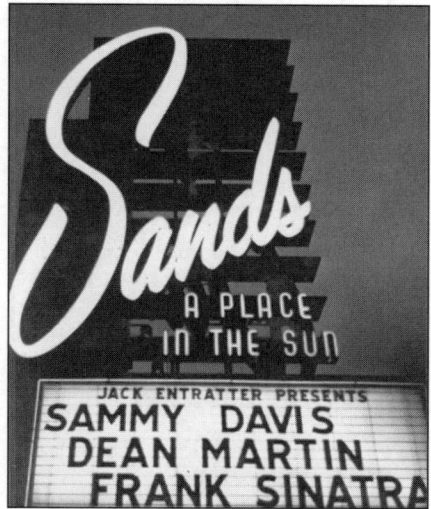

"Rat Pack" helped draw crowds at the Sands

Dunes — 1955

Initially criticized for being on the "wrong side" of Highway 91, the other side from arriving weekend traffic, the Las Vegas Dunes Hotel & Casino had problems right away making it appear the wags might have been right. Even a turbaned Frank Sinatra riding an elephant at the grand opening in May 1955 didn't seem to help, and after a brief closure, the Dunes was leased to the operators of the Sands who made it a go.

One-time Al Capone associate Major Riddle was called in and acquired controlling interest in 1956. He immediately got things going, including building a world-class golf course, adding a high-rise hotel, and bringing in top entertainment, including Minsky's Follies.

When it opened it was called the "ultimate carpet joint" as again the bar of Las Vegas opulence was raised a notch. The mid-Eastern desert theme was supported by a 35-foot Sultan gracing the hotel's entrance.

The Dunes was favored and visited by numerous celebrities (Cary Grant, Judy Garland, Betty Grable, Sir Lawrence Olivier, Telly Savalas, Liz Taylor), yet it was about the most "in-your-face" mob-run operation in town with dubious ownership and rampant skimming.

Steve Wynn bought the Dunes and surrounding area in 1992 for $75 million. In 1963 the Dunes was another implosion that tore down the old to make room for the new. Over 200,000 people witnessed the flamboyant detonation.

Many saw that particular implosion as a symbol of ending mob control over their city. On the site, Wynn erected the ultra-luxurious Bellagio Hotel with 3,933 rooms and suites.

Riviera — 1955

The first high-rise on the Las Vegas Strip was the nine-story Riviera Hotel & Casino which opened in 1955. It was originally built by a group of Miami investors who went broke with cost overruns ($10 million instead of $6M), so it emerged with changed ownership run by the mob.

Lee Liberace was the opening act and he performed at the Riviera for many years. Other big names also performed there. In 1973 the Riviera was acquired by Meshulum Riklis who insisted his wife Pia Zadora be a headliner. While Riklis did a lot of positive things (expanding the hotel and doubling the casino space), in many opinions his wife's act was not the best stratagem. The Riviera is still open, yet struggling to stay alive on a Strip full of newer and more popular resorts.

Hacienda — 1956

When the Hacienda Hotel & Casino opened in 1956, it was considered way out of town, the first hotel one came to driving from Los Angeles. Hacienda owner "Doc" Bayley formed Hacienda Airlines in 1957 and offered Southern Californians a package deal which included air transportation, room, and some casino chips. The Hacienda was later owned by Argent, and then by Circus Circus. Hacienda was a mainstay anchoring the southern end of the strip for 40 years, until it was imploded in 1996 to make way for the Mandalay Bay.

Tropicana — 1957

In April 1957 the Tropicana Las Vegas opened about midway between the Hacienda and the rest of the Strip, becoming the closest hotel to the McCarran International Airport. On numerous occasions I took an all-night free junket from Los Angeles in an older propeller airplane to play at the Tropicana, arriving about 11 p.m. and departing around 6 a.m. the next morning.

Towers were added in 1979 and 1986, creating 1,878 rooms. Today the intersection (Las Vegas Blvd. and Tropicana) with three other major hotels (Excalibur, New York New York, and MGM Grand) has the greatest number of hotel rooms of any intersection in the world, necessitating a four-way pedestrian overpass.

After several ownership changes, the Tropicana has still endured over a half century since it first graced the Strip. It's getting a little long in the tooth, with noticeable frayed carpeting and shopworn fixtures, especially in the earlier low-rise buildings.

Stardust — 1958

When the Stardust Resort & Casino opened in 1958 it was the world's largest resort motel and the biggest casino in Nevada. It was across from the Riviera and closer to downtown. Located on 63 acres, its main 32-story tower and much of the casino were added in 1991.

While the Stardust had an outer space theme, the Polynesian Aku Aku lounge had the first Las Vegas lounge show I had ever seen, at the ripe age of 21. The famed Stardust sign, surrounded by stars and stardust, was a Las Vegas icon and allegedly could be seen 60 miles away when lit up.

At its peak, the Stardust had 1,500 rooms and a 100,000-square-foot casino. It was run by the unsavory characters who inspired the movie "Casino." In March 2007, the Stardust became the shortest-lived casino to be imploded. It is the site of the under-construction, large new Echelon Place.

Why Not Annex the Strip?

The Las Vegas Strip through the years has become world renown. It is by itself a primary destination, its own entity, and feeds upon its own pulse and vibrancy. It is the very heart of fantasy and dreams. The money spent along Las Vegas Boulevard alone would be the envy of many small countries.

Even in its infancy, once the county's Las Vegas Strip started to take on its own economic base, the city of Las Vegas wanted some of the action.

There have been seemingly valid reasons for annexation through the years. For example, back in 1946 Las Vegas Mayor Ernie Cragin had all sorts of public improvements going on (new police station, street paving, sidewalks, public swimming pools, etc.). But he got shot down when he tried to annex the Strip to help pay for his programs. He felt that the few Strip resorts at that time fed off the fame of more established Fremont Street, and he had a good argument.

But nobody listened to him. Needing only 50% of the affected residents to block the annexation, the opposition got a mandate of more than 90% to oppose it. Later, Gus Greenbaum, the mobster who ran the Flamingo after Siegel was assassinated, led a successful campaign to make the community of Paradise, which included the Strip, an

Las Vegas Strip, 1960s *(photo courtesy Classic Las Vegas)*

unincorporated town. This meant the area could not be annexed without the approval of county commissioners. That pretty much cinched that, and while Cragin and successive mayors had to tap other sources to improve the city of Las Vegas, the Strip developers were able to escape from under a bigger tax umbrella, a situation that has continued to this day.

Today the Las Vegas Strip is in Clark County's unincorporated communities of Paradise and Winchester. Most tourists are not even aware that the Strip is not in Las Vegas, and could care less. They call it all Las Vegas. In several places in this book where it makes a difference, the distinction is pointed out; most often the term "Las Vegas" includes both.

The Strip is the Strip

By the early 1960s, the Strip developers had succeeded in elevating gambling, gaming, and show entertainment to new levels. Downtown were the cheap "sawdust joints." On the Strip were the "carpet joints." And they were classy.

By the mid-1960s there were 11 luxury casino/hotels along the four mile Strip: New Frontier, Flamingo, Thunderbird, Tropicana, Desert Inn, Sands, Sahara, Stardust, Riviera, Dunes and Hacienda. Even so, in most cases there was enough space between them that people usually drove to go from one to another.

Even early on, the casinos did their best to keep the gamblers in, and keep the gamblers gambling. There were no clocks or windows to remind anyone whether it was day or night, much less what time it was. There were no couches or chairs in which to relax, unless you wanted to sit at a gaming table.

Although it seems hard to believe today, during the 1950s and 1960s there was even a dress code. Though unwritten, dress expectations in the "carpet joints" on the Strip existed. There were many overt reminders, from a few looks of disdain to comments made about someone underdressed. You felt out of place at the more sedate Strip casinos without slacks and a jacket, or a dress. If you did not want to dress up, you stayed downtown where jeans, shorts and t-shirts were perfectly acceptable.

Downtown remained low key. That snobbish, almost superior, attitude on the Strip slowly changed, and was accelerated when the push was later made to make Las Vegas a family-oriented destination.

Morris "Moe" Dalitz
Looking for Respect

O
ne of the most successful mobsters making the transition from hoodlum to respectability in Las Vegas was Morris "Moe" Dalitz. Born
on Christmas Eve 1899 to Jewish-American parents, Dalitz was a
Michigan bootlegger who was even later referred to as "Mr. Las Vegas" for his
philanthropic efforts to improve the city.

Dalitz worked in his family's Ann Arbor laundry and later opened his own
businesses in Michigan and Cleveland. To keep workers in his laundries from
organizing, he hired local mob muscle. Then he got into bootlegging with the
1919 advent of Prohibition. He eventually ran the Cleveland Syndicate (the
Mayfield Road Gang), mostly Jewish-American gangsters known for their
violence and criminal ways. Dalitz ran truckloads of booze from Canada on
barges across the Great Lakes. He invested his profits and owned numerous
laundries and other companies in Michigan and Ohio. By the time Prohibition
ended, Dalitz also owned and operated several illegal casinos in the Ohio and
Kentucky areas.

As a laundry fleet owner, Dalitz established a relationship with a rising star
in the Brotherhood of Teamsters, one Jimmy Hoffa. After an impasse in Detroit
negotiations between the Teamsters local and the laundry owners. Dalitz allegedly bought out Hoffa, who sided with the owners to the consternation of the
local union negotiator. That friendship with Hoffa would later serve not only
Dalitz but the entire city of Las Vegas. Dalitz served as an Army officer during
WWII and returned to a country that was getting tough on illegal gambling.
He looked to Las Vegas and the time was right.

Wilbur Clark had invested the $1 million he made from the sale of the El
Rancho in 1949 into a new resort, the Desert Inn which was under construction. Clark ran out of money and Dalitz and three partners from his Cleveland
gang came to the rescue bankrolling the Desert Inn.

Originally called Wilbur Clark's Desert Inn, it eventually cost $4.5 mil-
lion, and opened in April 1950 as the Strip's fourth resort. Dalitz made major additions, including a country club which hosted major golf tournaments.
Wilbur Clark became the public persona of the Desert Inn while majority
owner Dalitz quietly remained in the background.

In 1958, after the death of Tony Cornero, Dalitz and associates, using millions in Teamster loans, took over the Stardust Resort & Casino from a group
led by Jake "The Barber" Factor. It was the first of what would be millions loaned
by the Teamsters Central States Pension Fund for Las Vegas investments.

Deciding it was time to get respectable, Dalitz also tapped his old Teamster
associate Jimmy Hoffa for a $1 million loan. This was not for a casino—it was

for the Dalitz-controlled Sunrise Hospital, the first major community gesture by a mobster. Hoffa cut a deal with his union members in Las Vegas, their employers, and Sunrise Hospital where a fund was established to provide medical services for union members. Dalitz would later secure Teamster funding for numerous civic improvements in Las Vegas: shopping malls, golf courses, and other important institutions. He was a frequent donor to the Las Vegas Public Library system along with other community organizations in Las Vegas. While under constant pressure from authorities for his close ties with other known mobsters, Dalitz paid his taxes and was never convicted of anything.

Dalitz owned the Desert Inn until 1967, when he sold it to the billionaire Howard Hughes. The last casino Dalitz owned was the Sundance Hotel & Casino on Fremont Street, later renamed Fitzgeralds Casino & Hotel.

Dalitz continued to be active in the Las Vegas community and in 1976 was named Humanitarian of the Year by the American Cancer Research Center, and in 1982 Dalitz received the "Torch of Liberty" award from the Anti-Defamation League. When he died in 1989, his will left substantial donations to numerous organizations.

Moe Dalitz was a complex man, by any measure an astute and successful businessmen. His lifelong association with crime parlayed him quickly into the big time. Yet he spent most of his life trying to shed that image and gain respectability; he achieved it better than any other mobster.

Central States Pension Fund
TEAMSTERS NATIONAL BANK

One of the most important persons in the development of Las Vegas did not live there. He invested there, and not even with his own money. James Riddle Hoffa, who seized control of the Brotherhood of Teamsters, Warehousemen, Chauffeurs and Helpers of America (Teamsters Union) in the 1950s, used the union's pension fund to bankroll millions of dollars of worth of low-interest loans to Las Vegas casino developers, many with ties to organized crime.

From 1958 to 1977, the Teamsters Union's Central States, Southeast, and Southwest Areas Pension Fund, based in Chicago, loaned almost $250 million that developers would have had a difficult time securing elsewhere. Former federal organized crime prosecutor Stan Hunterton said, "It got the town started, before banks would loan money, before Wall Street and public debt funds were available, that's where you got money to start building casinos."

Hoffa's relationship with the mobs kept him in power and he, in turn, allowed them to use the pension fund as their private bank. Of course, the mobs were given carte blanche to install their own casino employees, who were able to skim untold millions of dollars to keep them in power.

The Teamsters Pension Fund played a major role in the rapid expansion of Las Vegas' hotel-casino industry for two booming decades. In 1955, then-Teamster vice president Jimmy Hoffa negotiated the Teamsters' first centralized pension contract. The union assessed each employee $2 a month for the pension fund which accounted for approximately $10 million that first year. The fees were deposited into bank accounts meant to pay union retirees.

Hoffa hired Chicago mob figure Paul "Red" Dorfman to administer the fund, and he was succeeded by his stepson Allen Dorfman. According to retired FBI agent Joseph Yablonski, "When Jimmy Hoffa went to jail (for jury tampering), Allen Dorfman became the alter ego for Hoffa, and he was the one who controlled the Central States Pension Fund. Of course, he was controlled by the Chicago mob, and I think the guy who had the main contact with him was Joey 'The Clown' Lombardo."

Hoffa acted with impunity; he considered the pension fund as a bank to be used to invest in real estate loans and charged lower than market rate interest to his friends, allies, and mob associates. Hoffa's largesse also included kickbacks, usually a "finder's fee" of 10% of the loan amount.

The first Teamster money in Las Vegas came in 1958, one loan for $4 million for the Dunes Hotel & Casino which would be run by James "Jake" Gottlieb and Major A. Riddle. Another $250,000 went to *Las Vegas Sun* publisher Hank Greenspun to build the Paradise Valley Golf Course (now the Las Vegas National Golf Club).

The next year Hoffa's old friend, Morris "Moe" Dalitz, got $1 million to build the private Sunrise Hospital. The fund soon backed other loans to Dalitz for hotel-casinos he controlled: the Stardust ($6 million) in 1960, and Fremont ($4 million) in 1961.

Once the tap was turned on, the money flowed into Las Vegas. Other projects receiving initial or additional Teamster money included: the Desert Inn, Caesars Palace, the Landmark, the original Aladdin, Circus Circus, and the Four Queens.

By 1963, all Central States Pension Fund assets totaled $213 million, nearly two-thirds of it in real estate loans across the country, mainly in hotels, shopping centers, and commercial buildings, and much of it in Las Vegas.

Caesars Palace developer Jay Sarno received over $15 million in Teamster fund money to open that luxurious resort in 1966 and Circus Circus in 1968. While Sarno was the "front man," ownership of Caesars Palace was a veritable "who's who" of organized crime figures, including Tony Accardo and Sam Giancana of Chicago as well as members of East Coast families.

In 1967, with Hoffa off to prison, Allen Dorfman and the Pension Fund got help from a Teamster official named Roy Williams, who would later become president after Hoffa and Frank Fitzsimmons. Kansas City mob leader Nick Civella had considerable influence with Roy Williams, a former Kansas City truck driver. Civella, with his brother Carl "Cork" Civella, led the Kansas City family in several lucrative ventures into Las Vegas casinos with Teamster backing. By the mid-1970s, the Kansas City mob was involved in widespread skimming from several Las Vegas casinos purchased with Teamster loans approved by Roy Williams and other mob-friendly officials. Sharing in the undeclared Las Vegas skimming profits were the organized crime organizations in Chicago, Cleveland, and Milwaukee.

The largest Teamster loan to Las Vegas was in 1974 when mobsters Civella and Milwaukee's Frank Balistrieri convinced Allen Dorfman to lend $62.7 million to the Argent Corporation to purchase the Stardust and Fremont hotels. Argent was owned by young Allen R. Glick, hence the name A.R.G. ENTerprises. Of course the loan came with strings, and it meant the mob installing its own people to really run the casinos and ensure a vast skimming operation. Mobster Frank "Lefty" Rosenthal thus worked for Argent, but it was really the other way around and Glick later discovered who the boss really was.

Meanwhile, in 1971, President Richard Nixon pardoned Hoffa, but the former union leader disappeared in 1975 never to be seen again.

By 1977, the Teamster pension fund started by Hoffa had lent almost $240 million to Las Vegas, about a quarter of its total loans. That year the U.S. government forced the Teamsters Union to allow outside regulators to oversee their loans. The end result shut off the tap of easy cash to Las Vegas.

Las Vegas, however, had already grown and expanded far beyond what would have been possible without the union money. It came with strings though and it would be many years before Las Vegas ownership would escape the grasp of organized crime.

Under Mob Control
KEEpiNq It IN The FAMiLy

After Benjamin "Bugsy" Siegel's murder in 1947, the mobsters didn't waste time. Within hours, Siegel's old pal Moe Sedway along with Gus Greenbaum, who had headed the mob's Phoenix operation, were at the Flamingo and in charge. Author Mario Puzo playfully juxtaposed the names a bit to create the fictional Las Vegas casino owner "Moe Greene" for the 1969 book, *The Godfather*.

Greenbaum and Sedway made a success of the Flamingo, turning a $4 million declared profit the first year. That success prompted organized crime families to get more and more involved in Las Vegas casinos. Keeping a low profile, they got men with little-or-no criminal records to front the resorts. Behind the scenes however, undeclared and untaxed money constantly vanished from the establishments' profits. Initially, as Syndicate head, Meyer Lansky was overall responsible for collecting, and then dividing, the skim. With Las Vegas "open," all of the crime families participated and benefitted. The Syndicate needed someone on the scene to oversee the action and ensure that all the families operated in harmony and benefited accordingly.

There was bit of toe-stepping, intimidating, posturing, individual retaliations, and bruised egos, but by and large the families got along. Tony "Joe Batters" Accardo had became Chicago crime boss in 1945 after the guy challenging him for leadership, Dago Lawrence Mangano, was mowed down in a drive-by hail of bullets. Accardo followed Al Capone and then Frank Nitti as Don (leader) of Chicago.

Gus Greenbaum

Meanwhile Gus Greenbaum, a tall, slender, dapper gangster who had controlled Arizona with an iron fist, was a front man who exuded an air of respectability. In fact, in 1950 he was proclaimed the first Mayor of Paradise, the unincorporated area that included the Las Vegas Strip. He not only brought the struggling Flamingo out of debt, but controlled other casinos as well. However, he wanted out. He had succumbed to the omnipresent vices of Las Vegas and was gambling, womanizing, drinking to excess, and using drugs. He went back to Arizona.

When the Riviera Hotel & Casino was about to open in 1955, Tony Accardo and the Chicago mob reached out to Greenbaum to return and run the casino. They didn't own the hotel but wanted their own man inside running things. Greenbaum rejected the offer and learned you don't say no to the mob. After his sister-in-law was brutally murdered in Phoenix, Greenbaum hastened back to Las Vegas to manage the Riviera. As one of the Syndicate's main men in town, he even had to order the executions of two connected mobsters for the effrontery of robbing a Syndicate hotel. In fact, pulling the trigger on those two was Jimmy "The Weasel" Fratianno, a mobster who later turned informer. The pressure and easy vices of Las Vegas got to Greenbaum and his gambling and drug habits got worse, causing him to eventually personally skim from the hotel. That embezzlement was noticed by Chicago and on December 3, 1958, both he and his wife were found in their Phoenix home with their throats slit.

Marshall (Johnny Marshall) Caifano

In 1955, once Greenbaum was busy with the Riviera, the Chicago family under Tony Accardo and Sam Giancana decided to send 5'5" Marcello (Marshall) Caifano to Las Vegas as chief enforcer. Caifano was mean and credited with at least 10 murders by that time and was proud of that fact. Another reason underboss Giancana sent his longtime friend Caifano was so he could spend more time with Caifano's wife. FBI agents who surveilled the Chicago gangsters learned that every Friday night Giancana and the beautiful blonde Darlene Caifano spent time together at a motel. It was even reported that Caifano knowingly traded her off to Giancana for the "Don" chair of Las Vegas.

Caifano was a violent enforcer who demanded his way and got it as casino people cowed to him out of fear. Some called him a psychopath. He was vain, loud, and incredibly intimidating. He legally changed his name to Johnny Marshall, but he still stood out like a common hood. Sheriff Ralph Lamb ordered him to "keep a low profile or get out of town," but that was hard for him to do. His name kept popping up with unsolved murders and he was also suspected of starting the 1960 fire that destroyed one of the original Strip casinos, the El Rancho Vegas. It seems he was kicked out of the place just a few hours before the fire. He was suspected of mutilating and murdering a former mistress, killing a former Chicago cop, strangling gangster Louis Strauss, and assassinating Chicago racketeer Teddy Roe. Caifano was also in Beverly Hills the night Siegel was murdered and knew Al Smiley, the man Siegel was with.

Caifano's public profile was his downfall. When the List of Excluded Persons (Black Book) came out in 1960 with 11 names including Caifano's, it meant he was banned from Nevada casinos. He fought it for a while and hid out in the Desert Inn, but was caught and kicked out. In 1964 he went to prison for extortion. He was released six years later; sometime thereafter the man who testified against him lost his life.

One of the mob's most violent enforcers escaped receiving the same likely "mob pension plan" that was awarded Siegel and Greenbaum by being in prison. He went to Florida, where he died of natural causes at age 91.

Johnny Roselli

Johnny Roselli (sometimes spelled Rosselli, real name Filippo Sacco) had earlier been sent by Al Capone to Los Angeles where he worked with Jack Dragna. He was assigned to control operations in Hollywood and Las Vegas, but spent most of his time in Hollywood. The dapper and slick Roselli became close friends with movie producers and eventually produced several early gangster movies. As a Hollywood insider, Roselli was also part of the mob's multi-million dollar extortion effort against the motion picture industry.

For his role, Roselli was fingered by informer Willie Bioff, convicted, and served six years in prison. After release in 1954, he became an important link for the mob in several "open" venues around the country. As for Bioff, he never knew what hit him. In Phoenix in 1955, his pickup blew up when he turned the ignition.

In 1957 with the opening of the mob-controlled Tropicana Las Vegas, Chicago wanted Roselli to become the main enforcer in Las Vegas. His reputation precluded him from getting a Nevada casino operating license, but he still helped Meyer Lansky and Frank Costello insure the families received their fair shares of the illegally skimmed casino revenues.

Within a month, the law received its first proof of mob skimming when Costello was shot down in New York in April 1957 by a member of the competing Genovese family. Costello wasn't killed, but the police found a handwritten piece of paper in his pocket that outlined the Tropicana's profits, wins, markers, payoffs and other incriminating evidence. Asked about the note by a Senate Subcommittee on Organized Crime, Costello took the Fifth Amendment 22 times.

Roselli meanwhile went on to make the Tropicana a success and serve as an important link between Las Vegas and the crime families. He was responsible for shaking down the other hotels and skimming where he could. He was everywhere. Roselli was even involved with the CIA plot to kill Cuban Prime Minister Fidel Castro.

That broad reach created a high profile that cost him. Upset that Roselli was bothering the legally licensed places, Clark County Sheriff Ralph Lamb publicly embarrassed him and prevented him from entering casinos.

That destroyed his effectiveness in Las Vegas. He went to Los Angeles where he was given a five year sentence for rigging a Friar's Club card game. After release, he was investigated for his role in the Castro plot. While he divulged nothing of importance, the mob was still upset he even testified without their permission. In 1976 a Florida fisherman found a 55-gallon drum floating in a bay off Miami. Stuffed inside were the remains of the mob's former go-to guy Johnny Roselli.

There was no question as to who controlled Las Vegas.

Off the Top
The Art of Skimming

As long as there's been gambling, there have been people attempting to get the edge, to cheat, to figure out how to "stack the deck" in their favor. Instead of complex cheating systems, in Las Vegas the mob just stole the profits in the form of "skimming."

The crime families earned millions by hiring and having their own people inside the casinos to "skim," or remove, untraceable cash from gaming tables and slot machines, then use couriers to distribute the cash back to the Syndicate.

The mob had the casinos involved underreport the actual gambling income for several reasons. There was less income for the owners of record; in some cases the legitimate casino owners went broke while the mob secreted off with their profits. Even if the mob had at least some ownership percentages, which they usually did, by taking it first they avoided paying taxes to local, state, and federal governments. And of course, it was a great way to get huge influxes of cash for the mob families to share.

It was easy and lucrative, a hands-off, mostly non-violent, white-collar conspiracy. And it was pervasive. Each of the major casinos had a "manager of skimming," regardless of his official title.

In the early days before controls were set up, owners or managers could just go in a counting room, stuff a few packets of bills in their coat, or suitcase, and walk away. Later the state began mandating electronic surveillance and controlling and carefully monitored the keys for the boxes. Each counting room soon had five people, all authorized by the Nevada Control Board and independent in authority from the casino itself. The jobs were all specific and sign-ins became mandatory.

The "soft count" room is for counting bills and currency, and the "hard count" room handles the voluminous amount of coins.

The creativity involved in "skimming" knew no bounds and went on blatantly throughout the 1960s and 1970s. When Howard Hughes started buying Las Vegas casinos, he immediately started losing money on previous "cash cows." Johnny Roselli and his pals delighted in fleecing the eccentric billionaire.

At one hotel, three crap tables were in operation on the graveyard shift, yet only two were reported open. At the third table dealers made their drop (money and markers) into the black metal box below the table. With a duplicate key, shift bosses would get the unreported income.

An interesting scam utilizing an auxiliary "phantom" change booth not even listed anywhere on the casino's record was uncovered at the Stardust. The brazenness and creativity of that elaborate skim even impressed the control board. The phantom booth was filled with coins skimmed from the hard count room. They got those coins by rigging the scale so it would report the wrong amount for the weight of the coins.

Then they put all those extra coins in the undeclared change booth. All day long the change girls would put bills into the booth to get change for the gambling customers, thus unwittingly converting the skimmed coins into paper currency. The paper bills were then converted into larger bills at the casino cage, and at the end of each shift, the manager walked into the "phantom" booth and pocketed all the large bills. By the mid-1970s, four Midwest organized-crime families (Chicago, Kansas City, Milwaukee, and Cleveland) were involved in the hidden ownership and widespread skimming of the Argent-controlled casinos and the Tropicana. They each had ownership and control of, and/or participated in the illegal removal of cash from, the involved gaming establishments.

One wealthy woman, Mitzi Briggs, the heiress to Stauffer Chemical, lost her entire fortune by investing in the Tropicana in 1975 after hearing about casinos making 20% profit. The Kansas City mob used the charming Joseph Agosto to keep stringing her along while they depleted her fortune. Frank "Lefty" Rosenthal ran the skim operation during his tenure in Las Vegas for the mobs. It was reported that Bill Presser (a Teamster official and father of future Teamster president Jackie Presser) and Teamster Roy Williams received about $1,500 a month for their roles in the skim. In 1979, Nevada gaming control authorities found evidence that $7 million had been skimmed from the Stardust alone. In 1983, a federal grand jury in Kansas City indicted 15 organized crime figures on charges related to skimming at the Argent casinos in Las Vegas, and the next year 11 of them received long prison terms.

During the mobster-controlled years in Las Vegas, casino skimming was a way of life.

Tony Spilotro and Frank Rosenthal
Real Mobsters from "Casino"

The 1995 Martin Scorsese movie "Casino" was based on the real lives of Tony "The Ant" Spilotro and Frank "Lefty" Rosenthal. In the movie they were Nicky Santoro (played by Joe Pesci) and Sam Rothstein (played by Robert DeNiro). The non-fiction exposé book *Casino* by Nicholas Pileggi that inspired the movie, however, took no such precautions and used their real names, documenting their lives and atrocities. Tony Spilotro, born in 1938, became known to local Chicago law enforcement at an early age and was arrested many times. In the mob he got on the good side of emerging leaders such as Joseph "Joey Doves" Aiuppa, James Torello and Joseph "Joey the Clown" Lombardo. Spilotro became a "made man" in 1963 after squeezing a man's head in an industrial vice to get a confession. His star was rising within the ranks and for a while he was assigned to a large bookmaking operation.

He had known the bookmaker Frank "Lefty" Rosenthal since childhood, and in 1962 both were implicated in trying to fix games by bribing college athletes. Spilotro pled guilty and Rosenthal pled no contest to the charges.

The previous year Attorney General Robert Kennedy was clamping down on illegal gambling activities and Rosenthal was called to testify before Senator McClellan's committee. It is reported the mob was impressed with Rosenthal after he invoked the Fifth Amendment 37 times.

After living in Miami, Rosenthal then moved to Las Vegas in 1966 where bookmakers were more than welcome. Rosenthal is credited with creating the first Race & Sports Book Parlor in Las Vegas. The sports book he set up theater-style at the Stardust was virtually copied by every other casino on the Strip. As a handicapper he literally set the line for bookmakers across the country.

Rosenthal created his own public persona, hosting his own weekly Stardust-sponsored TV show, "The Frank Rosenthal Show," and he was able to snare Frank Sinatra as his first guest.

Lefty met Geraldine (Geri) McGee, a Vegas stripper and hustler (played by Sharon Stone in the movie). He immediately flipped over her and they got married on May 1, 1969. They had two children, Steven and Stephanie, and Rosenthal kept his wife in luxury.

By 1971 Lefty Rosenthal was manager at the Stardust and his star was in ascendancy. He was shocked to see his old pal, the Chicago hoodlum responsible for so much mayhem, Tony "The Ant" Spilotro, swagger into town, and more shocked to realize the clout he carried. In Chicago Joey "Doves" Aiuppa assumed leadership of the mob and sent Spilotro to Las Vegas to succeed Marshall Caifano as the organization's main representative and enforcer. Enforce he did too, as it was noted that there was a 70% spike in the Las Vegas murder rate after Spilotro's arrival. Rosenthal, whose background precluded him from getting his own casino license, nevertheless ended up running the Stardust, Hacienda, Fremont and Marina casinos for Argent, on behalf of Allen Glick.

While Glick was the owner, Rosenthal the manager, and Spilotro the enforcer, the real chain of command was reversed. Glick had to relinquish all decisions to the mob in the form of Rosenthal. And Rosenthal learned he had to take orders from the 5'5" "Ant," who was one real mean individual.

Spilotro and Rosenthal worked together to embezzle profits from the casinos, which were then sent back to Chicago and other Midwest "families." Rosenthal was responsible for the actual management of the casinos; Spilotro's primary task was to control casino employees and other personnel involved in the skimming, and follow the dictates of Chicago.

On his own, Spilotro (under the alias Tony Stuart) took over the gift shop at the Circus Circus Hotel & Casino from which he conducted business. That hotel was owned by Jay Sarno, who had developed the property with a $43 million Teamster Pension Fund loan. As strings for the loan, the Circus Circus became controlled by the Midwest mobs. Spilotro himself invested $70,000 in the Anthony Stuart Ltd. gift shop at Circus Circus and when it was sold in 1974, he reaped $700,000.

Always looking to expand his income, Spilotro for many years had led a group of about eight burglars called the Hole in the Wall Gang. In 1976, Spilotro, along with his brother Michael Spilotro, and Herb "Fat Herbie"

Blitzstein opened The Gold Rush, Ltd., a Las Vegas combination jewelry store and electronics factory which became a headquarters for fenced goods. The three were joined by other gang members including Frank Cullotta, Ernest "Ernie" Davino, Lawrence "Crazy Larry" Neumann, Wayne Malecki, Leo Guardino, and former Las Vegas detective Joseph Blasko.

Cops who had worked with Blasko were disappointed with their old pal's crossing the line, and later revealed he did enjoy the drama of undercover work in which he often pretended to be a hit man.

Following a botched burglary on July 4, 1981, Cullotta, Blasko, Guardino, Davino, Neumann, and Malecki were arrested and each charged with burglary, conspiracy to commit burglary, attempted grand larceny and possession of burglary tools. Cullotta turned state's witness, testifying against Spilotro, but "The Ant" was acquitted.

Spilotro's legal counsel in Vegas was provided by mob defense lawyer Oscar Goodman, who later entered politics and became mayor of Las Vegas in 1999. In 2007 he won a third and final term by a landslide of 84%.

It was a woman that caused a serious rift between Rosenthal and Spilotro. Unlike the movie version, Geri McGee Rosenthal had known Spilotro before Frank met her and they resumed their old affair after

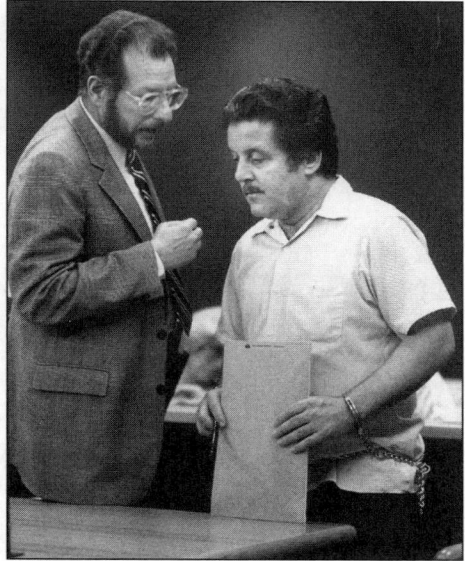

Tony (The Ant) Spilotro (r.) in court with Attorney Oscar Goodman
(Las Vegas Sun photo)

she became Mrs. Rosenthal. The Rosenthals eventually divorced in January 1981. After stealing a significant portion of Rosenthal's savings, Geri died in a Los Angeles motel on November 9, 1982 of an apparent drug overdose. Rosenthal himself survived an assassination attempt in 1982 after his car was rigged with explosives. His life was spared only because his car, a 1981 Cadillac Eldorado, had a metal plate under the driver's seat which saved his life. The explosion in the Tony Roma's parking lot almost knocked police officer Clarence "Rich" Richwalski off his motorcycle as he was out front idling at a signal on E. Sahara Road.

In 1988 Rosenthal was placed in the Black Book and had to leave Las Vegas. He returned to Florida where he remained a bookmaker, passing away in 2008 at age 79.

Meanwhile Spilotro's star was waning. He was placed in the Black Book that legally prevented him from being physically present in any casino in December 1979. That blacklisting was thanks to the testimony of Jimmy "The Weasel" Fratianno. Then in the aftermath of the Hole in the Wall Gang arrests, Frank Cullotta became convinced Spilotro had a contract out on him and turned informer, putting a lot of heat on Las Vegas and organized crime. He went into a witness protection plan.

In January 1986, a meeting was held with top Chicago mobsters including Joe Accardo and Joey Aiuppa. Everyone at the meeting was in agreement that Spilotro had to go and his execution was ordered. Lured to a non-existent meeting, Spilotro and his brother Michael were savagely beaten and buried in an Indiana cornfield.

At the time of Spilotro's death in 1986, the FBI suspected him to be responsible for at least 22 murders, including the 1963 murder of Leo Foreman, a real estate agent/loan shark. Foreman was tortured by repeatedly being stabbed with an ice pick and had pieces of his flesh cut out, before being shot and killed.

Spilotro was implicated in the 1962 Chicago murders of Bill McCarthy and James Miraglia, who were in debt to Spilotro's old boss Sam DeStefano. Popularized in the media as the "M&M Murders," the bodies of Miraglia and McCarthy were discovered in the trunk of a car in Chicago. Both had been badly beaten and had their throats slit. Additionally, McCarthy's head had been placed in a vise, popping out his eye. The FBI believes Spilotro was also involved in the murder of his former mentor Sam DeStefano in 1973, and in the brutal torture murder of loan shark enforcer William "Action" Jackson.

Spilotro is further suspected of murdering Danny Siefert who was to be a principal witness in a fraud case, but was shot in front of his wife and four-year-old son in September 1974 before he could testify. Spilotro was also a suspect in the murder of Allen Dorfman, the Teamster executive who helped the mob get the loans, who was gunned down in 1983. Spilotro may have been involved in the attempted murder car bombing of his former partner Lefty Rosenthal. Rumors on the street even implicated Spilotro in the murder of former Chicago mob leader Sam Giancana.

In 1986 Spilotro's old godfather, Chicago mob boss Joey Aiuppa, was convicted of skimming profits from Las Vegas casinos and received 28 years in prison.

While it took a while for all of the mob's tentacles to unhinge and release their symbiotic grip, an extremely violent chapter in the history of Las Vegas was coming to an end.

Nevada's Unsocial Register
THE BLACK BOOK

n 1953 Nevada tightened its rules on who could receive a gaming license. That
year the Nevada Legislature decreed that an applicant for a gaming license
could be found unsuitable if convicted of a felony, larceny, narcotics or firearm
violation in the past five years, was under age 21, or wasn't a U.S. citizen.

That covered casino licensing, but didn't completely solve the problem as
wise guys skirted the rules with hard-to-tackle end runs, trick plays, and subter-
fuge. By the late 1950s, there were still enough unsavory guys running around
the casinos that Nevada worried about its image. Nevada Governor Grant
Sawyer decided some changes were needed to clean it up. The 1955 session of
the Legislature took gaming control away from the Nevada Tax Commission,
creating today's Gaming Control Board (they investigate and recommend) and
the Nevada Gaming Commission (which has the final say-so.)

Out of the Gaming Commission came Nevada's Black Book, a list of the
people Nevada didn't want anywhere near a blackjack table, a craps table, or
anywhere in a casino for that matter.

The first edition of Nevada's Black Book (List of Excluded Persons) came
out on June 16, 1960 and included only 11 names: John Louis Battaglia;
Marshall "Tony Marshall" Caifano (Chicago mob enforcer); Nick and Carl
"Cork" Civella (St. Louis mob); Mike Coppola (Miami); Louis Tom Dragna
(nephew of Jack), key member of the Los Angeles family for over 30 years;
Robert L. "Taco Bob" Garcia (various Southern California locations); Sam
Giancana (Chicago mob leader); Motel "Max Jaben" Grazebienacy (Kansas
City mob); Murray "The Camel" Humphries (Chicago); Joseph Sica (Los
Angeles).

Over the years there have been a total of 56 names entered in the book,
and as of April 2011, 34 remain, including Louis Tom Dragna, age 91, the only
survivor from the original 11.

One woman is listed, Sandra Kay Vaccaro, who along with her husband
John Vaccaro (also listed) were defendents in one of Nevada's largest slot cheating cases. The first cheaters to earn a Black Book nomination, they may have
rigged $20 million in jackpots. John got nine years in prison plus the listing.

Johnny Marshall (Caifano) decided to challenge the authority by refusing
to leave a casino, and the gaming board's first chairman, Raymond Abbatico,
told the casino involved to kick Caifano out. The owners refused. After immense pressure from gaming control agents from Carson City, management
sagely decided to kick Caifano off the premises. Caifano filed suit in federal
court in October 1960, complaining that Governor Sawyer, the gaming board,
and the hotel had violated his civil rights. The Nineth Circuit Court of Appeals

upheld the state's right to ban people from places with "privileged licenses," as they are called—like a business that reserves the right to refuse service to anyone. The only temporary Black Book listing was in 1967 when Ruby Kolod, part owner of the Desert Inn, was convicted of threatening a Denver lawyer. The board mainly wanted to keep him away from the Tournament of Champions golf match at his Desert Inn golf course. His name was removed three weeks later.

Rather than making it a huge list of hundreds of people like New Jersey did when they legalized gambling, Nevada's regulators wanted to keep their list exclusive. Even when Frank Rosenthal's name was added in 1988, 28 years after the first list, his was only the fourteenth person on it. One state official said they were mostly interested in the impact of the industry's product (gaming) on society. Keeping out the bad guys keeps gaming's image shiny and helps the tax men. If the casino is cheated, don't forget—the state loses money. Can't have that.

Showcasing the Ruthless
GLAMORIZING GANGSTERS

There's something deliciously attractive to a goodly number of people about peeking into the windows of law breakers. It seems the more horrendous the infraction, the more seductive the enticement. Somehow society has fed on this perverse attraction and has tried to sate this ghoulish curiosity.

Books have been written about gangsters, violent movies about them have been box office hits, and even a top television show "The Sopranos" brings these fringe people into America's living rooms, tending to normalize their violent behavior. As I write this, there are 455 mob-related items for sale on eBay.

Given the history of the Syndicate, the mob, organized crime, the mafia, or whatever you want to call them in Las Vegas, it should come as no surprise that some endeavor to capitalize on the city's history of mobsters. After all, they even gave the mob's famous defense attorney, Oscar Goodman, a third term as mayor.

Another example: in shining glory out in the garden of the Flamingo Las Vegas is a bronze memorial plaque of Benjamin "Bugsy" Siegel, the tough and vain hoodlum whose brutal assassination focused attention on the Las Vegas casino business and led to the growth of the modern city.

Vegas Mob Tour

For those seeking to be close to the criminal element, there is the Vegas Mob Tour which takes the curious to former crime scenes and locations where mobster movies were shot. Based at the Greek Isles Hotel & Casino, the Mob Tour features guys with black fedoras, black shirts and broad ties who talk out of the sides of their mouths, saying things like "yous, and "dose" as they take you around town regaling stories on the criminals who used to prowl there, making it sound as if they were on intimate terms with them.

Your morbid curiosity can be teased at the parking lot of Tony Roma's restaurant where Frank "Lefty" Rosenthal's Cadillac Eldorado car was wired and exploded.

Then you'll get to see the street, but not the actual house (present owners don't want to be bothered by the lookee-loo ghouls), where Sherwin "Jerry" Lisner was repeatedly shot, strangled with an electrical cord, and dumped in his swimming pool. It seems Lisner ticked off chief enforcer Tony "The Ant" Spilotro who ordered the hit, which was carried out by Frank "The Rat" Cullotta and Wayne Malecki. Cullotta, who turned informer, is still alive and has aided the Mob Tour people with "his side of the story," for example, admitting that after the Lisner hit, he calmly went out and got a pizza. Of course, if you want to learn more about "The Rat," you can buy "Cullotta" the book, or "Cullotta" the DVD—both available at the Vegas Mob Tour office at the Greek Isles. The 2½-hour tour runs six nights a week (6 p.m.) and costs more than $50.00.

Las Vegas Mob Experience

The Tropicana Las Vegas got into the act on March 29, 2011, when it opened its $24 million Las Vegas Mob Experience. The 27,000-square-foot theme park is full of high-tech bells and whistles, including holograms and interactive computer chips.

Guests even get to display latent gangster mentality by voting whether a "cheater" is released with a warning or gets "beaten up." The Mob Experience offers 1,000 artifacts including items donated by Tony Spilotro's son and mother, Bugsy Siegel's daughter (who is still alive), Meyer Lansky's grandson, and others. Instead of Tony Roma's parking lot, the Tropicana has the ignition key to the car that exploded there.

Mayor Oscar Goodman, Mouthpiece for the Mob

There are numerous Las Vegas stories of gangsters like Moe Dalitz reaching for respectability. In many cases there has been, and still is, a hazy reality between the mob and the city. An interesting story is that of 12-year Las Vegas Mayor Oscar Goodman (1999-2011).

Goodman came to Las Vegas in 1964, was admitted to the Nevada State Bar and served as Clark County deputy public defender in 1966 and 1967

Las Vegas Mayor Oscar Goodman
(City of Las Vegas file photo)

before he opened his own practice. As a high-profile defense attorney once considered one of the nation's top trial lawyers, Goodman represented numerous mobsters. His clients included Syndicate boss Meyer Lansky, Stardust manager Frank "Lefty" Rosenthal, and Chicago mob enforcer Tony "The Ant" Spilotro. In 1999 Goodman ran for mayor of Las Vegas and won with 64% of the vote. In 2003 he was reelected with 86%, and in 2007 he won a third and legally final term with 84% of the vote. His mayoral tenure as well as his background has been provoking and controversial. His bizarre comments have offended many, but he didn't care, enjoying the shock value his boozing and colorful image has projected.

He once publicly received a $100,000 Bombay Gin endorsement fee saying it would be donated to charity. However, half of it was earmarked for a private school run by his wife. He was also accused of using his political influence to further the career of his attorney son.

He calls himself "The Happiest Mayor in America," and has never publicly apologized about zealously defending the mobsters, saying they had a constitutional right to a defense.

He really ticked off law enforcement when he once said he'd rather his daughter date Spilotro than an FBI agent. In fact, the mob enforcer had attended her bat mitzvah party, which was even held at a lodge rather than a casino so Spilotro could attend.

To extend Goodman power, Oscar's devoted wife Carolyn Goodman became a late entrant in the 2010 mayoral race, winning 37% of the primary vote out of 18 candidates. In June 2011 she clobbered the remaining challenger to succeed her husband as mayor. Oscar has said he wished he could be mayor for life. It seems that in Vegas I wouldn't bet against him.

Mob Museum

In 2002, Las Vegans were stunned but not surprised that their mayor would be the catalyst and main supporter of the non-profit Mob Museum. Officially called the Las Vegas Museum of Organized Crime and Law Enforcement, it is finally set to open in December 2011 in a former post office and courthouse where Oscar Goodman tried his first case.

In the initial uproar, community activists were concerned about the possible glorification of organized crime. Italian-Americans were upset about possible profiling.

A poll conducted at that time indicated that while tourists thought it might be a neat idea, the majority of Las Vegans were against the entire concept.

Undaunted, Mayor Goodman rallied forces to make his vision a reality. He enlisted the aid of former Nevada Governor and U.S. Senator Richard H. Bryan to serve on the board of directors. He also enlisted, and this is a paradox, retired FBI Special Agent in charge of Las Vegas Ellen Knowlton for the non-profit board.

She got FBI brass support by creating exhibits and displays to help tell "their side of the story." One FBI spokesman said "We support it because we want to make sure the mob isn't glorified in any way." Knowlton added that they didn't want younger and more impressionable guests to be enticed into a life of crime.

Three key exhibits within the museum include "Mob Mayhem," "The Skim," and "Bringing Down The Mob." This museum will even display the actual wall from Chicago's St. Valentine's Day Massacre.

In a public information statement, Mayor Goodman said, "Las Vegas has a wonderful, colorful history, and the Mob Museum will educate visitors about the impact organized crime had on this great city. This isn't done to glorify organized crime, on the contrary it is to show how law enforcement successfully managed to gain the upper hand."

This current Las Vegas spotlight on crime is not unprecedented as Americans have long been drawn to these scofflaws who have committed murder and mayhem for personal advancement. Entrepreneurs have also bused tourists to mob haunts in Newark, Kansas City and Chicago.

And by the way, the Sopranos are also represented in Vegas. See "The Sopranos' Last Supper," a fun, dinner and dancing parody of the Emmy award-winning show. Aren't those mobsters a hoot?

CHAPTER 5

The Mississippi of the West

Racism was blatant in the early years of Las Vegas. Black entertainers could not even dine in the hotel/casinos where they performed. Bucking the trend, the first integrated casino, the Moulin Rouge, opened in 1955.

It took yet more time and some defiant posturing and bluffing to relieve the racial tensions of early Las Vegas.

A Color Barrier
RESTRICTED AND SEGREGATED

In a March 1960 meeting of civic leaders, casino operators, media members, and NAACP officials, an agreement was signed to end segregation on the Las Vegas Strip. While at least something was on paper, it was by no means the end of racial discrimination in Las Vegas.

Among other negative images, Las Vegas long endured a history of racism, so much so it had been called the "The Mississippi of the West." Las Vegas has always had a black population, with early settlers being primarily railroad workers: porters, crewmen, janitors, or maids. Approximately 50 black people lived in Las Vegas by the early 1920s, and some locals went out of their way to make them feel unwelcome.

A very conservative Ku Klux Klan group formed in Las Vegas. It took Clark County's first clerk, and later district attorney, Harley A. Harmon to squelch KKK activity in 1922 by letting the locals know he had a list of all who had participated in a recent Las Vegas Klan cross burning. The list was not made public, but the fear of disclosure pretty much caused the cravens to disband. Even so, the hooded group did later march down Fremont Street in 1924.

In the 1930s, most black Las Vegans lived on Block 17 (same block as the Lady Luck Hotel & Casino), between Second and Third streets, that was designated for "non-white" residents. They spilled into an eight-block area between First and Fifth streets and from Stewart to Ogden. Bars, brothels and restaurants had encroached on what was mainly a residential area.

As residents began moving away, most of the black population gravitated to the more inexpensive West Las Vegas area. Restrictive covenants in Las Vegas at the time, which prohibited sales or even rentals to blacks, kept them in West Las Vegas even if they could afford other areas.

Another restriction in those days for minorities was in some public gathering places like movie theaters. In 1928, businessman Ernie Cragin opened the El Portal Theater, the city's first. There, blacks and other minorities, primarily Hispanic, were steered to the left; whites could sit on the right or in the middle. Other theaters later offered the balcony for blacks. Las Vegas businesswoman and civil rights leader Lubertha Johnson recalled that the police really enforced segregation at the El Portal. "If you insisted on NOT sitting against the wall, the police were called. All the theaters were segregated, but it seems that others didn't make the effort to see that this policy was carried out like Mr. Cragin did."

After Cragin was elected mayor of Las Vegas in 1943, the racial situation got worse. Police actively enforced segregation and even closed the Star Bar in West Las Vegas because, according to the *Las Vegas Review-Journal,* the "bar has been playing to a mixed trade, with Negroes and whites encouraged to congregate in the establishment promiscuously."

World War II saw a huge influx of people into the Las Vegas area, many blacks included, to work in the war-time magnesium plant at nearby Henderson. Blacks from the South were stunned to encounter living conditions worse than what they had left. Many were forced to live in segregated facilities provided by employers, or in the poorer West Las Vegas, which had become a minority enclave. Black soldiers stationed in the area were in for a surprise when they tried to take a little R&R in Las Vegas. Those raised in the North were especially offended at being denied access to casinos and popular night life venues. The friction was palpable and fights and riots broke out. In August 1943 a West Las Vegas clash with police left two wounded. The next year one soldier was killed, and four (including one policeman) wounded in further rioting. This just resulted in more restrictions. One base even declared Las Vegas off-limits to its black soldiers.

Just as J.T. McWilliams' western town site was a poor step-child to the "railroad" city, West Las Vegas continued to be a poor step-child to the rest of Las Vegas. It was mostly a slum with inadequate or nonexistent infrastructure lacking good, or even paved, roads and a properly functioning sewage system. Perpetuating an intractable circle, Mayor Cragin responded to requests for public works improvement projects by insisting that property values there did not justify expenditures to make improvements.

Needless to say, black Las Vegans were not fans of Mayor Cragin, and even non-blacks agree that his inaction made West Las Vegas one of the worst slums in the western U.S. Racism in Las Vegas became worse. It was no longer just at the El Portal Theater; in the 1940s the city also nudged black businesses aside by refusing to renew their business licenses unless they agreed to move to West Las Vegas. Businesses, particularly the casinos and nightclubs, refused to serve blacks at all. By then, even in the Southern states, blacks were generally served, albeit they were segregated and had to use back doors.

Slow to Change

There were a few bright spots, if one can call an absence of discrimination a bright spot. On October 10, 1944, the Huntridge Theater, owned by Hollywood stars Loretta Young and Irene Dunne, opened and became the first non-segregated theater in Downtown Las Vegas. Out on the Strip, one of the biggest ironies was that black singers and entertainers who were responsible for attracting tourists to the casino shows could not even stay or dine in the places they worked. According to Ed Reid and Ovid Demaris in their 1963 exposé *The Green Felt Jungle*, "Negroes like Louis Armstrong and Eartha Kitt are acceptable to the hoodlums as long as they stay out of the way and don't invite their relatives and friends to the shows." Even Sammy Davis Jr., a headliner at the Frontier, rather than live with his peers in the hotels, had to live in a rooming house in West Las Vegas for many years. Black performers were even denied stage dressing rooms, so they had to sit around outside by the swimming pool between acts.

Dancer Harold Nicholas noted, "If you were black, you experienced prejudice. It wasn't a real horrible thing for us; we went through it. We noticed it mostly in the South and in Las Vegas, where we couldn't stay in the hotels where we entertained. But that began to change." One of the biggest changes for black performers in the 1950s was the opening of Moulin Rouge on Bonanza Road on the west side, the first non-segregated casino/hotel in Las Vegas. The story of the Moulin Rouge is the shining light in the struggle of Black Americans in Las Vegas.

The Moulin Rouge
FIRST INTEGRATEd CASINO

It was actually several white guys who foresaw a need for an integrated casino in Las Vegas—one that would be open to all, to sleep, to dine, to gamble, to play. By 1955 virtually all the casinos on the fabled Strip were totally off-limits to blacks, unless they were entertainers or part of the work force. Even then, most sections of the establishments were still unavailable to the entertainers.

Will Max Schwartz and a few other white investors, (New York restaurateur Louis Rubin, real estate developer Al Bismo, and others) built and opened the Moulin Rouge at 900 West Bonanza Road, between Downtown Las Vegas and the heart of West Las Vegas, between the predominantly white Strip and the largely black west side. The upstart Moulin Rouge opened on May 24, 1955, at a cost of $3.5 million. Two stucco buildings housed the 105-room hotel, the casino, and a theater. When it opened, the Moulin Rouge was fully integrated and black entertainers and guests had the run of the entire place. The original Moulin Rouge dealers were white because blacks had previously been denied that position, so there were no qualified black dealers. The Moulin Rouge concept was so unique at the time it made the cover of *Life* magazine on June 20, 1955.

World heavyweight boxing champion Joe Louis (who was given a few ownership points) was the welcoming host. While the integrated establishment was unique, it was the entertainment that made the Moulin Rouge a legend. The greatest names in black entertainment, such as Louis Armstrong, Pearl Bailey, Nat King Cole, and Sammy Davis Jr. performed there.

The upstart casino became so popular that white performers, including Jack Benny, George Burns, Bob Hope, Dean Martin, and Frank Sinatra would drop in after their own shows on the Strip to gamble and render impromptu performances. Eventually a 2:30 a.m. "Third Show" was added to accommodate the crowds. White casino employees from the Strip flocked to catch the late show and see the biggest names in entertainment. Jazzman Benny Carter was the first musical director, and Pearl Bailey's cousin Bob Bailey, who sang with Count Basie, was brought in as entertainment director to book the best talent available.

Moulin Rouge *(photo courtesy City of Las Vegas)*

Unfortunately that bright and shining star that was the Moulin Rouge turned out to have a short life. It fizzled and sputtered and in November 1955, after a stellar six months, the Moulin Rouge closed its doors. By December 1955, the owners declared bankruptcy. Some concluded that the Moulin Rouge was a victim of the overall racism in Las Vegas. According to the authors of the 1963 book *The Green Felt Jungle*, "...it did not appeal to the country's wealthiest Negroes, who resented being restricted to the Moulin Rouge."

All of the reasons behind the closing may never be fully understood, but Bob Bailey, who went on to become the first black TV personality in Las Vegas, felt that its very success precipitated its demise. He offered his opinion that the gamblers followed all of the showgirls over to the Moulin Rouge which really ticked off the Strip hotels. The mob-run resorts retaliated by forcing a boycott of that "Nigrah joint." He said they even put up notices in the dressing rooms that cast members who went to the Moulin Rouge would be fired.

However, this appears to be an exaggeration as, while a few casinos forbade their employees from gambling at the Moulin Rouge, there was no boycott.

It appears the resort failed because of numerous things: management skimming profits and failure to pay some construction bills and other debts. Mechanics' liens closed the Moulin Rouge.

Over the years, the Moulin Rouge closed and re-opened many times. For a while the hotel was owned by Sarann Knight-Preddy, the first black woman to hold a Nevada Gaming License.

The Moulin Rouge has been shuttered for decades and was declared a National Register of Historic Places site in 1992, and is also listed on the Las Vegas Historic Property Register. Ownership changed hands several times and there have been a series of fires. In foreclosure at the time, a 2009 fire destroyed the landmark hotel, leaving just the familiar cursive "Moulin Rouge" sign, which was saved for the Neon Museum. Even though city leaders have decided to tear down what remains, the burned-out building and tall shell of a tower still sit in a fenced lot and can be seen from the nearby freeway junction.

The short but vibrant life of the Moulin Rouge was gone, but it became a catalyst for the civil-rights movement in Las Vegas. The hotel became the spark needed to bring an end to segregation on the Strip

Achieving Equality
TENSIONS IN THE DESERT

It was a black dentist named James McMillan who forced a stand-off between the black community and the mob-run Strip casinos. McMillan, who was born in Mississippi and reared in Detroit, came to Las Vegas in 1955 to tie in with his old dental partner Dr. Charles West. McMillan said, "There was disrespect everywhere," referring to everything from his difficulty in getting a dental license and getting into the dental association to the forced living accommodations in West Las Vegas. He noted there were a few people in the desert city working to end the discrimination, "David Hoggard, Woodrow Wilson, Lubertha Johnson, and a couple of preachers were here before I got here and were working tremendously hard." Hoggard was a police officer, Johnson ran a grocery store, and Wilson worked out at Basic Magnesium in Henderson.

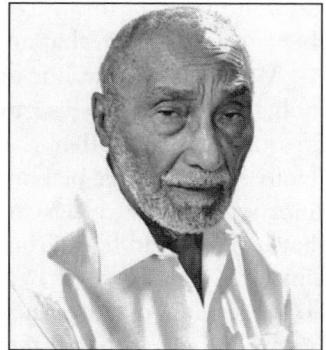
James McMillan *(photo courtesy Nevada Oral History Program)*

Lubertha Johnson *(photo courtesy Nevada Oral History Program)*

McMillan joined them in the local chapter of the National Association for the Advancement of Colored People (NAACP), soon becoming president. His tactics were to write letters to businesses that refused to hire blacks, and to picket and boycott those who continued the practice. It was obvious that the most in-your-face offenders were the major casinos, hotels and restaurants. So, in 1960 McMillan fired off a letter to new Mayor Oran Gragson, giving him 30 days to come up with a plan to eliminate discrimination or blacks would march on the casinos. Las Vegas Mayor Gragson and City Commissioner Reed Whipple came up with a counteroffer. They promised more city jobs for blacks and more business and home loans for blacks (Whipple was an officer of First National Bank) if the demonstration was called off. They declared they did not have jurisdiction to force the Strip resorts into accepting blacks. McMillan turned down the offer even though he had been bluffing. He then had 10 days to organize a major protest, something he had never done before. While he got busy trying to rally the black community, he began receiving death threats. The Strip hotel owners sent him a message through an intermediary, Oscar Crozier, owner of a small West Las Vegas gambling club. The mob on the Strip didn't mince words. "Cut it out or we'll drop you in Lake Mead" was their terse memo.

Scared but undaunted, McMillan had Crozier reply to them, "All I'm trying to do is make this a cosmopolitan city, and that will make more money for them. You tell them that and let me know what they say."

With the bottom line of more gambling dollars dancing in their vision, the mob and other Strip resort owners answered "Okay," and a nervous McMillan breathed easier. Rather than face possible riots and civic disturbances, they finally agreed to let black people into the restaurants, the hotels and the casinos where they could eat, gamble, and everything else. The tense situation that likely would have erupted was diffused. The NAACP group was relieved. Until the resort owners backed down, they knew that to save face they had to do something, create some sort of major disturbance. The surprise agreement certainly shelved that urgency.

Moulin Rouge Agreement

A meeting was hurriedly arranged by then-Governor Grant Sawyer between hotel owners, city and state officials, and local black leaders. The agreement to end discrimination on the Las Vegas Strip was signed on March 26, 1960 in a conference room of the vacant Moulin Rouge. Those attending what became known as the Moulin Rouge Agreement included McMillan, Dr. Charles West of the NAACP, Mayor Gragson, and Las Vegas Police Chief Ray Shaeffer. The meeting was mediated by *Las Vegas Sun* publisher Hank Greenspun.

It was a defining moment, but actual and complete desegregation took years. Over the objections of some, in 1961 Nevada state legislators created the Nevada Commission on Equal Rights of Citizens. It still was an uphill battle. In their first two cases of discrimination, four subpoenaed witnesses were too scared to testify.

During the 1960s, civil rights battles were supplemented by protests over the Vietnam War. A group of community leaders were able to suppress and thwart a couple of early demonstrations on the Strip. In October 1969 a race-related riot erupted in West Las Vegas and more than 20 people were sent to the hospital. No one was killed, but it took hundreds of police officers to restore order.

Howard Hughes

While changes were slowly being made, it did not stop older holdouts from their ingrained attitudes. The Howard Hughes years in Las Vegas began in 1967 when he took up domicile in the Desert Inn, which he later purchased. An avowed bigot, Hughes was even more racist than the integration mindset of the times. He wrote his right-hand man Robert Maheau, "Now I have never made my views known on this subject. And I certainly would not say these things in public. However, I can summarize my attitude about employing more Negroes very simply—I think it is a wonderful idea for somebody else, somewhere else."

Maheau, who loved tennis, initiated the Howard Hughes Open, with a payout second only to the U.S. Open, to be played at the Desert Inn. However, the night before the tournament Hughes learned that black tennis star Arthur Ashe was scheduled to play and wanted the entire tournament cancelled. He feared that the Desert Inn would be invaded by "hordes of Negroes."

Ruby Duncan

Civil Rights activist Ruby Duncan came to Nevada from Louisiana in the early 1950s and also learned why they called Las Vegas the "Mississippi of the West," discovering the entrenched racism first-hand. For more than 25 years she addressed a lot of underlying issues, such as hunger, literacy, health care, and voting rights for minorities.

Her work for women and children resulted in the first medical facility for the West Las Vegas area. She pioneered and helped bring about the Work Incentive Program, Women and Infant Children Nutrition Program, CETA dollars, food stamps, and early diagnostic testing for children. The tireless Ruby Duncan also led efforts to bring West Las Vegas its first school lunch program, public library, and public swimming pool. She also led the creation of daycare centers, crime prevention programs, job training resources and job placement programs. Duncan served as a delegate for Nevada at the 1980 Democratic National Convention and was a major contributor in the betterment of race relations in the previously embattled Las Vegas community.

For her efforts she was the 2009 recipient of the Margaret Chase Smith American Democracy Award. Past recipients of the prestigious award included the history-making Rosa Parks and Watergate Judge John Sirica. She was nominated by Nevada Secretary of State Ross Miller.

Don Barden

Sheer numbers of gambling visitors to Las Vegas helped tip the scales toward a more permissive attitude. In 1970, 6.7 million people visited the handful of Strip and downtown casinos. That number exploded to just under 40 million visitors by the year 2000. And they were spending money, dropping over $30 billion into the Vegas coffers, eating, sleeping, seeing shows, and of course, gambling.

Studies had indicated that black Americans from California took 2.35 trips to Las Vegas versus 1.6 for non-blacks. They also tended to budget more for gambling and were loyal to the casino/hotels where they stayed.

These, and other similar statistics, were encouraging to a black entrepreneur named Don Barden of Barden Companies.

Barden had created the country's largest cable television franchise and was well known in real estate development and radio broadcasting. Recipient of numerous honors, including some from the NAACP, former President Jimmy Carter, and the United Negro College Fund, Barden became the first black American to own a casino chain, Majestic Star Casinos.

In 2002, Barden made Las Vegas history by purchasing the 638-room Fitzgeralds Casino & Hotel downtown. With other properties in Chicago, Denver and Memphis, Barden had a base from which to promote his new Las Vegas acquisition.

While previous politicians might have attempted to impede the deal, Las Vegas Mayor Oscar Goodman and Nevada state assemblyman Morse Arberry Jr. worked hard in the background to make the Fitzgerald's deal fly.

It was a real sign that times had changed in Las Vegas.

CHAPTER 6

THE CHANGING FACE of GAMBLING

Once billionaire Howard Hughes began to buy up casinos, new financial laws came into being which virtually rang a death knell to the days of mob rule.

The state, emboldened with the new Nevada Gaming Commission, imposed and enforced strict gaming controls.

The casinos of the future would be run by corporations who fine-tuned marketing concepts to appeal to an ever-widening audience.

Redefining Itself

Polishing the Strip's Image

By the 1960s, Las Vegas had survived a lot of bad press from around the world, revealing the proliferation of organized crime figures behind the casinos. The image was one of total corruption on top of its wide-open attitude, offering non-stop gambling and adult entertainment.

One of the ways casinos could counter this image was to make the town more family-friendly. The decision was not favored by all; indeed, numerous old-timers and dealers questioned kids in casinos, but an initial change started tentatively in the 1960s.

The reason to become family-friendly at that time was primarily to counter that negative image. As you can see, not all of the new casinos that opened on the Strip during the 1960s created family destinations.

Westward Ho — 1963

A smaller Western-themed casino/motor hotel called the Westward Ho opened next door to the Stardust in 1963. Calling itself "the friendliest casino" in Las Vegas, its three swimming pools gave kids something to do while their parents gambled. They also offered an inexpensive "jumbo hot dog." The friendly Westward Ho was closed in 2005 after a 42-year run.

Castaways — 1963

In 1963 the Castaways Casino opened on land where one of the original Strip roadhouses, the Red Rooster, perched. Thumbing their collective noses at the emerging family trend, the Castaways owners featured shows with topless women swimming around a large aquarium.

The Castaways property was sold to Howard Hughes in 1970, and it was purchased by Steve Wynn in 1987, where he erected the Mirage.

Aladdin — 1966

The Aladdin Hotel & Casino too bucked the half-hearted family trend when it debuted in 1966. Originally opened in 1963 as the Tally Ho, the Arabian-themed Aladdin was long a popular entertainment venue and was the site of the Elvis-Priscilla Presley wedding. And it was adult in tone. Before it was imploded in 1998 to make way for Planet Hollywood, I roamed the silent hallways where the sounds of drilling for demolitions had replaced the familiar din of a vibrant casino. Fixtures, furnishings and souvenirs went for almost give-away prices as the Aladdin was being prepped for its doom. The image of the Aladdin's veiled employees wearing sexy gossamer gowns wafted through the darkened rooms.

Caesars Palace — 1966

Jay Sarno, who would later build Circus Circus, opened Caesars Palace, the most expensive ($19 million) and opulent casino to date in 1966. He bought the land from Kirk Kerkorian and borrowed the money from the Teamsters Central Trust Fund.

In naming it, Sarno felt that Julius Caesar evoked a sense of royalty and wanted the guests to feel the same. It now has 3,348 rooms and 166,000 square feet of casino space. Toga-clad employees and the vast Forum Shops continue to attract visitors. Free shows at the Forum Shops, which include animatronic statues coming to life, have been delighting and attracting children and adults since 1993.

1960s Las Vegas Strip *(photo courtesy Classic Las Vegas)*

Circus Circus — 1968

The opening of Jay Sarno's Circus Circus in 1968 officially signified that kids were not only allowed in Las Vegas, they were encouraged, at least in some places. Outside of the Hacienda, which had small kiddy pools and a go-cart track, the Circus Circus became the first major Las Vegas casino-hotel to specifically target youngsters. It featured a second-floor midway of county fair-style games and almost round-the-clock trapeze acts and strolling clowns.

There was non-stop action and could have been distracting to a blackjack player pondering a "hit" with aerialists soaring overhead. Owners later added the 16-ride Adventuredome theme park "Grand Slam Canyon" behind the hotel.

The Circus Circus casino originally opened in the familiar tent structure without a hotel and a later high-rise now offers 3,774 budget rooms, further attracting families looking for a bargain. It is the only Strip hotel that also has an RV park. Initially, Sarno even charged admission and hoped to keep gamblers in, but it soon became apparent that gamblers were uncomfortable playing below jugglers, clowns and high-wire acts.

Las Vegas Hilton — 1969

There were fewer hotel openings during the next 20 years, and most were back to being adult-oriented. For example, just off the Strip on the site of the Las Vegas Downs horse racing track, Kirk Kerkorian built the Las Vegas Hilton. It opened in 1969 as the International Hotel, at the time the largest hotel in the world. It is still the largest Hilton property. It has an illustrious history of entertainment and sporting events, beginning with opening-night performer Barbra Streisand.

Kids on Hold

The next two decades (1970s, 1980s) saw fewer casino/hotel openings, sort of a leveling-off period with money tighter amid a recession. But the Strip still welcomed the following new casinos: Barbary Coast (1978), Imperial Palace (1979), Bally's (1985, emerged from original MGM Grand, which suffered a disastrous fire in 1980), Gold Coast (1986), and the carnival-themed all-suite The Rio, across the I-15 Freeway (1990).

Not all reached out to families. For the most part, casino operators just "bit the bullet" and continued to offer their various forms of gaming to a willing public. The negative image never really went away and many capitalized on it. They were proud to be a part of "Sin City." The casinos had invested time, money and creativity in their businesses, which existed for the sole purpose of taking money from their guests—business as usual, just leave your money!

It wasn't until the 1990s, when competition from various venues around the country ate into the bottom line, that Las Vegas decided to become America's family destination. But by that decade's end it became obvious that "attracting families" was not the soundest decision. However, reversing the trend became as formidable a task as putting the Genie back in the lamp at the Aladdin.

First Female Dealers
Changing With The Times

I t probably comes as no surprise that the first female blackjack dealers in Las Vegas were hired not for ability, but for appearance—and flashing skin was the major job requisite! Of course, there were female Keno runners and cocktail waitresses, but no dealers.

It was April 1966 and the small Silver Nugget Casino in North Las Vegas hired two female blackjack dealers, Dianne McMillin and Jaye Boack, for the 1 to 8 a.m. shift. It was a gimmick to attract male gamblers. Management was afraid to hire topless dealers because the Attorney General earlier said he would go to court to get an injunction against them. To counter the topless claim, the pair was provided with chiffon transparent tops and pasties.

From that inauspicious start, it would be several years before female dealers were in the mainstream in Las Vegas. The Harolds Club in Reno was the first Nevada casino to utilize female dealers. Founded in 1935, Harolds Club shortly began to hire female dealers when they rightfully decided that the women might attract more female customers, thereby broadening their customer base. It proved to be a wise decision and by World War II and the scarcity of men in much of American industry, about 90% of Harolds' dealers were female.

In Las Vegas by 1971 there were several casinos willing to use female dealers. The first two were the Silver Slipper on the Strip and the Union Plaza downtown. The Golden Nugget downtown was another casino that had been experimenting with female dealers in the early 1970s. Executive Murray Erhenberg had left the Golden Nugget and joined the Argent (Stardust, Fremont, Hacienda, Marina) team when Frank "Lefty" Rosenthal was the head man.

Erhenberg and Rosenthal discussed the possibilities of hiring female dealers and went down to Fremont Street to observe. Rosenthal was impressed, "The better ones were able to effectively cut and stack chips, shuffle, scoop, place the winning bets exactly where they belonged in a smooth friendly manner. They had winning smiles and were not aware that we were privately auditioning them."

Although he ran into resistance from the "old guard" casino managers, he initially hired 12 "most qualified and attractive" women, four for each shift, to start at the Stardust. The move was copied by the others and there would always thereafter be female dealers on the Strip.

Today there are women in all levels of casino management, but it took a long jump from those first few entry jobs as dealers. One woman director of casino operations who worked into the position the hard way admitted that back then it was tough getting into management. "There were plenty of women

116

dealers. We were the eye candy behind the table. But I don't know if it ever occurred to the guys (in charge) that we might one day want to do more than deal." She added, "Smart women are all over the industry now."

It took a little more time, but appearance finally became less of an issue than skill, initiative, and intelligence.

Howard Hughes
A Billionaire's Impact

Probably no one made a greater impact on Las Vegas than Howard Robard Hughes, billionaire heir of a tool company that revolutionized oil drilling, record-setting pilot, Hollywood movie producer, and eccentric tycoon. In the four years between 1966-1970, he almost bought the whole town.

Hughes was no stranger to Las Vegas when he began his buying spree in 1966. He had visited the desert town during World War II, previously staying at the Desert Inn, El Rancho Vegas and the Flamingo Las Vegas. In 1953 he leased a small, five-room cottage near the Desert Inn, calling it the "Green House." A year earlier he had purchased about 40 square miles of federal land just west of Las Vegas from the Bureau of Land Management (BLM). Originally known as "Husite," it is now the master-planned community called Summerlin.

Before his move to Nevada in 1966, Hughes had sold his interest in Trans World Airlines (TWA) for $546.5 million netting him a tremendous profit over his $80 million purchase price.

On Thanksgiving eve that year Hughes quietly came into Las Vegas aboard a private train. His entourage moved the by-then frail tycoon by van, dolly, and service elevator to the rented penthouse suite at the Desert Inn. He never budged from that suite for four years, having to buy the hotel to remain.

He not only leased the penthouse, but the entire top floor of suites and all the rooms in the floor below that. When Hughes remained past his 10-day reservation, owner Moe Dalitz was getting antsy. With New Year's upcoming, a lot of high rollers were due and their suites were occupied by people who didn't even gamble. Dalitz pleaded and tried to kick the group out. But Howard Hughes had major clout too and got his right hand man Robert A. Maheau to notify Teamster leader Jimmy Hoffa to call on their behalf.

The impasse finally ended when Hughes decided to buy the resort rather than move. He bought his first Las Vegas hotel for personal reasons, and it cost him $13.25 million. What made a Las Vegas investor out of Hughes was when he realized incredible relief from the heavy taxes he owed for his TWA profits. The government recognized casino gross as "active income," thereby sheltering plenty of Hughes' tax burden. According to Maheau, "Hughes called me and said the purchase of the hotel 'solved my tax problems.' He said we need to buy more of them. All of the elements were in place and Hughes had the money to do it—and no board of directors to answer to."

Maheau said he started looking for resorts and Hughes soon bought the Sands ($14.6 million, including 183 acres), Frontier ($14 million), Castaways ($3 million), and the Silver Slipper ($5.3 million). All of the casinos came with huge parcels of land. He also made a $30.5 million bid on the Stardust, but the U.S. Securities and Exchange Commission, fearing a monopoly, halted the sale. The government did allow him to buy the bankrupt 31-story Landmark patterned after Seattle's Space Needle for $17.3 million. Hughes quite simply wanted to be the biggest player in town. The presence of Howard Hughes in Las Vegas alone was important. His incredible wealth and power, plus the fact that he was one of the country's large defense contractors, tended to lend legitimacy to the entire gaming industry.

State and local officials went out of their way to accommodate Hughes, even after running into his myriad eccentricities. For example, he refused to leave the Desert Inn, and in applying for a casino license, refused to be photographed, fingerprinted, or even fill out financial disclosure papers. In 1967, the Nevada Gaming Commission still awarded Hughes a license to run the Desert Inn.

Hughes may have been a clean owner, but the mobsters were still active in many casinos, skimming away wherever they could. No way could they leave a man with pockets that deep untouched. It is reported that the mob skimmed over $50 million from the Hughes-owned casinos. Five of his seven "money-makers" lost money and he reported Nevada operations losses all four years (-$700,000: 1967; -$3.2 million: 1968; -$8.4 million: 1969; and -$13 million: 1970).

Hughes later blamed Maheau for stealing from him, and Maheau said that Hughes was buying properties "to boost his ego, rather than as sound business investments." Hughes' benign business neglect, impulsive, poor and late decisions, waffling and changing his mind, combined with his blatant racism and perverse paranoia actually made it a wonder he was able to hang on to any of his properties.

As an example of how paranoia dictated decisions, Hughes is said to have purchased the Silver Slipper casino across the street from the Desert Inn because the bright lights from the rotating slipper bothered him. Also, as

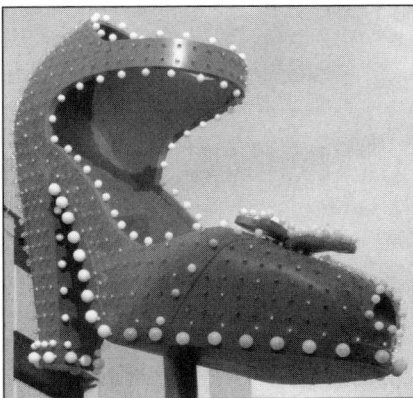

Neon Silver Slipper

the toe of the slipper would stop between rotations and face his penthouse window, he feared a camera could be planted in the toe by someone, maybe even the government. After several attempts at requesting that the slipper be turned off, Hughes purchased the casino, had the slipper filled with concrete, and dismantled the rotating mechanism.

Another "only Howard Hughes" move was when he paid $3.6 million to acquire the local CBS affiliate, KLAS-TV, from former *Las Vegas Sun* publisher Hank Greenspun. A night owl, Hughes wanted to control which late-night movies it ran. He then set up his own schedule of three "westerns" or "airplane" movies played back to back each night. Hughes often waffled in making the selections, hampering the station's scheduling and advance notices.

Hughes' eccentricities might have gotten a destitute person locked up. He had phobias, manias, delusions, and a morbid fear of germs. During his entire four years in the Desert Inn penthouse, it was never cleaned, Hughes himself rarely bathed, and he grossly kept his bodily waste in sealed jars in a closet. He had a team of male Mormon nurses who looked after him and he never saw anyone else. He even ran his empire through memos to Maheau, who never met the man face to face.

Hughes left Las Vegas as stealthily as he arrived and it was a week before anyone knew he was gone. On Thanksgiving, 1970, he was wheeled out of the hotel and placed on a plane to the Bahamas. By the time Hughes had left Las Vegas on November 25, 1970, he had become Nevada's largest private employer, largest casino owner, largest property owner, and largest mining claims owner. His Nevada holdings were worth an estimated $300 million. His empire included Harolds Club in Reno, nearly every vacant lot on the Las Vegas Strip, an airline, several Nevada ranches and about 2,000 mining claims.

It has been said that Hughes "chased the mobsters out of town." That by itself is not true. But the presence of Hughes in Nevada brought the image of legitimacy to Las Vegas and paved the way for the era of corporate rule. Thanks to Hughes, the Nevada Legislature revised state laws to allow corporations to be licensed to operate casinos without having to conduct background checks on each and every shareholder. That law transformed respectability and a clean corporate image to Las Vegas in stark contrast to the city's undesirable mob image. Las Vegas changed to a corporate-run town.

Even longtime entertainer Wayne Newton, when asked what he felt was the single most influential change in Las Vegas, quickly said, "When the state of Nevada allowed public companies to own casinos. That was the turning point in this town. By the government blocking Hughes from additional purchases, it paved the way for corporations. Unfortunately, with corporations the 'personal touch' has been lost along the way."

Paul Laxalt, Nevada Governor at the time, even said that Hughes' investment in Las Vegas had given the city the "Good Housekeeping seal of approval."

After leaving Las Vegas, Hughes went to the Bahamas, Canada, London, Nicaragua, and Mexico before he died in 1976 of kidney failure. His holdings went into his Summa Corporation which, as he left no will, made a lot of very distant relatives wealthy.

Gaming Controls
HoldiNq THE LiNE

Nevada today has one of the most effective gambling control systems in the world. It didn't come by accident. It's only fitting that the state in the vanguard of legalized gambling was first to try to "keep the wolf out of the hen house," minimize cheating and theft, keep the industry as honest as possible, and of course, collect taxes.

Nevada's gambling history is older than the state itself. There actually was a basis for those old Western movies. Cowboys did sit around saloons with swinging doors drinking and playing cards. In 1861 while still a territory, Nevada actually prohibited all gambling; that was the law when Nevada became a state in 1864. That didn't work for the cowboys and miners who wanted to gamble, so in 1869 against the governor's veto, the legislature legalized numerous games and imposed the first license fee.

In 1907, two years after Las Vegas came into being, state legislature redistributed gambling tax income, with slot machine fees going to the state, and the rest retained by the county.

In 1910 gambling was again prohibited by a righteous legislature. Violators were considered felons and officers were authorized to "seize and destroy" gambling apparatus. That was a tough law, so in 1915 upon Governor Tasker Oddie's recommendation certain games were allowed as long as they were for prizes not exceeding $2.00.

With the 1931 state-wide legalization of gambling, the state established a schedule of license fees and empowered the counties with major responsibilities. The state got 25% of the total revenue and the counties got the rest. If the establishment was in a city or town, the county had to share.

That worked pretty well until the mid-1940s when Clark County was about to surpass its northern cities in population, clout, and gambling income. But the state was still rife with cheaters and con men who fleeced tourists from roadside attractions, and Nevada could no longer afford to allow local sheriffs to investigate licenses. The state also wanted more of the lucrative gambling tax revenue.

The Nevada Tax Commission, whose members met part time, was overall responsible for licensing and tax collection. In 1946 the commission levied the first taxes on gambling. Robbins Cahill assumed responsibility of the commission and had the onerous duty in 1947 of trying to get new Flamingo owner "Bugsy" Siegel to pay his $5,000 tax due. After a stand-off, Siegel paid, and his later murder prompted the state to take another look at its regulations.

In 1949 Nevada's legislature gave the commission authority to make background checks, deny licensing if warranted, and allow fingerprinting of employees.

One of the biggest changes occurred in 1955 with the creation of the Nevada Gaming Control Board (The word "Gaming" is much more socially acceptable than "gambling.") to act as the enforcement and investigative arm of the Nevada Tax Commission.

The Gaming Control Board is empowered to investigate qualifications of license applicants and has the authority to inspect and examine the gaming premises as well as all equipment and supplies; and demand access to and inspect, examine and audit all papers, books and records of applicants and licensees. The board is composed of three full-time members who serve four-year terms, appointed by the governor.

In 1959, at the request of new Governor Grant Sawyer (dubbed by the media as the "hang tough" governor), legislators completely overhauled the state's gaming control machinery. Sawyer was concerned that many casinos were still run by mobsters and that even if he couldn't kick everyone out, maybe he could keep worse ones from coming in. Legislature thus created the Nevada Gaming Commission, with the Gaming Control Board its investigative arm.

The five members of the commission are appointed by the governor and serve four year terms in a part-time capacity. It was the commission that created the "List of Excluded Persons" called the "Black Book" in 1960, with the encouragement of Governor Sawyer, who was anxious to maintain a clean image for Nevada gaming. In 1961 Governor Sawyer stood up to fellow Democrat, the zealous new U.S. Attorney General Bobby Kennedy who wanted to deputize 65 federal agents and conduct raids on the main Nevada casinos. The "hang tough" governor convinced Kennedy that Nevada was taking steps to sanitize gambling and that any "federal raids" would be merely witch hunts that would give his state a "black eye." The raids never occurred.

The arrival of Howard Hughes in late 1966 prompted the next important gambling legislation. In 1967, at the urging of Governor Paul Laxalt, the state required casinos to file audited financial statements, and more importantly, passed a law allowing publicly traded corporations to obtain casino licenses. This law was refined in 1969.

The corporation law began to rapidly change the face of Las Vegas casino ownership. In 1975 Nevada gambling revenue exceeded $1 billion for the first time, and only two years later Clark County by itself attained that milestone. Also in 1977, Nevada passed a bill that allowed Nevada-based casino licensees to operate casinos outside Nevada's borders. The state also moved to shut down the Aladdin Hotel & Casino for having hidden owners. Show director James Tamer got listed in the Black Book for that and also went to prison.

Under Corporate Rule
BROADER VISIONS

The lone wolf days of individual or limited partnership ownership of Las Vegas hotel casinos went the way of the wide open spaces on the Strip. After the state set up laws to spur corporate ownership, it's a rare casino today not managed by a boardroom of executives beholden to Wall Street. Most of the Las Vegas Strip casinos today are owned by two corporations, MGM Resorts International and Caesars (former Harrah's) Entertainment. Other major players in Las Vegas are Barrick Gaming, Boyd Gaming, and Las Vegas Sands Corporation.

MGM Resorts

In addition to 12 Las Vegas area casinos, MGM Resorts International (formerly MGM Mirage) has six casino resorts outside of Las Vegas and one in Macau, China. After the MGM & Mandalay companies merged in 2005, MGM was the world's largest gaming company. MGM Resorts International now has 28 properties in five states, annual revenues of $6 billion, and control of 40% of the slots, 44% of the table games, and 36,000 hotel rooms on the Las Vegas Strip.

Caesars Entertainment Corporation (Harrah's)

When Harrah's and Caesars merged in 2005, Harrah's surpassed MGM Resorts International as the world's largest gaming company. In 2008, Harrah's was acquired by Apollo Management and TPG Capital in a leveraged buyout.

Renamed Caesars Entertainment Corporation in December 2010, in September 2009 the company bought $140 million in debt of the Planet Hollywood Casino, giving them nine Las Vegas properties (Paris, Bally's, Flamingo, Imperial Palace, O'Shea's, Rio, Bill's Gambling Hall, and Caesars Palace). Caesars Entertainment also owns three casinos at Lake Tahoe, one in Reno, one in Laughlin, 24 throughout the other states, and four internationally.

Operating the 42 properties (with more under construction), Caesars Entertainment has yearly revenues of around $8.8 billion, and more than 70,000 employees. In November 2010 Caesars/Harrah's Entertainment scrapped a planned $575 million IPO (initial public offering).

Wynn Resorts

Wynn Resorts owns Wynn Las Vegas, Encore Las Vegas, Wynn Macau, and Encore at Wynn Macau. (See chapter on Steve Wynn).

Boyd Gaming

Boyd Gaming owns several downtown casinos, the Station casinos, and other off-strip casinos. Boyd's big new project is Echelon Place, a $4 billion, 63-acre complex on the Strip at the former site of the historic Stardust, and the Westward Ho. In 2009, construction was placed on hold at Echelon Place which has plans for four hotels, a casino, theaters, convention space, spas and shopping. Boyd Gaming and Coast Casinos merged in February 2004 in a deal reportedly worth $1.3 billion. Coast had the Barbary Coast, Gold Coast, Orleans, and Suncoast hotel/casinos.

Las Vegas Sands Corporation

Las Vegas Sands Corporation operates three resorts that have over 7,000 rooms. The Venetian complex is on the site of the original Sands Hotel & Casino. In addition, the corporation is a big player abroad, with three major hotels in Macau, one in Bethlehem, and one in Singapore.

Barrick Gaming Corporation

Barrick Gaming Corporation is a private company founded by D.W. Barrick and Stephen Crystal which operates several hotels and casinos in Las Vegas. In 2004 Barrick Gaming purchased several properties from Jackie Gaughan, a longtime Downtown Las Vegas casino owner, for $82 million. The casinos included The Gold Spike, The Plaza, The Vegas Club, and The Western. Gaughan retained the El Cortez Hotel & Casino. In October, 2004, Barrick also acquired the Queen of Hearts Hotel & Casino and the Nevada Hotel & Casino from Ann Meyers, rendering Barrick one of the largest landholders in Downtown Las Vegas.

Modern Las Vegas is not the same old Las Vegas. No longer are mobsters with a handful of bent-nose associates running the show. After the corporations got a hold, and the cost of a big new casino reached the billions, it became very difficult for not only the mobsters, but any lone wolf to operate. There are still privately held casinos and some do quite well, generally catering to specific markets. But the Las Vegas of today is mostly under corporate rule.

Harrah's Market Analysis
They Got Your Number

When Mr. and Mrs. Average Joe go out gambling, they might be unaware that their every movement is not only monitored, but was most likely carefully planned, plotted, and even orchestrated—to the degree that the casino probably nudged them that it was time for them to go. The casinos have really learned what makes 'em tick.

Casinos have long understood that creating the proper environment for gambling has generated more gambling dollars. That's why the casinos have few doors, no windows, and no clocks. They want the player to lose track of time, not know whether it's day or night, to have a hard time finding the exit, and be engrossed in the action. Even the cacophony of coins tumbling, slots being pulled and general noise creates a sense of excitement. Then there's "Scent Science," which recognizes the powerful sense of smell and how it can release inhibitions to play havoc with one's emotional conditioning and create pleasant sensations. The casinos know. Almost every Strip casino resort has attached metal devices about the size of a microwave oven to their ventilation systems. The boxes vaporize highly aromatic oils into the ducts, where the airflow dilutes and distributes them. It's another edge, a lingering sense of euphoria.

However these days more and more casinos are learning that the physical marketing draws are not enough—they prefer to get inside the minds of the gamblers, discover what makes them tick, and lure them in. The pioneers in studying gamblers' habits and acting accordingly were the college-educated mathematicians and marketing experts at Caesars (formerly Harrah's) Entertainment.

There's a reason Harrah's has been so successful. The company, founded by William F. (Bill) Harrah who opened a small Reno bingo parlor in 1937, not only had a different genesis from the Las Vegas operations, but a longtime history of bucking the trend. He opened Reno's Harrah's Club in 1946 and was far away enough from Las Vegas to have been left alone by mobsters. Plus, Bill Harrah himself had a unique approach to the business: unquestioned honesty, fair play, and a squeaky clean image. The casino itself was spotless, and featured carpet when his competitors still had sawdust on the floors. He hired mostly clean-cut young people, set up company rules and regulations, and parlayed efficiency into profits.

Harrah's went public in 1971, and became the first casino listed on the New York Stock Exchange in 1973. Bill Harrah died in 1978, but the corporation he founded not only didn't miss a beat, it got stronger—and mostly as a result of taking a business approach to entertainment. In 1980 Harrah's Inc, which then had two hotel casinos in Reno and one in Lake Tahoe, was acquired by Holiday

Inns, Inc. Holiday Inns at the time had 1,600 hotels and interests in two casinos, a casino under construction in New Jersey, and 40% ownership of the Riverboat Casino, adjacent to the Holiday Inn on the Las Vegas Strip. The Holiday Inn/ Harrah's marriage allowed for growth, but

Harrah's Las Vegas

some of the properties remained in a time warp with low ceilings and bad floor plans.

In 1990 the company spun off the marginal casinos and Phil Satre became president. A lawyer, Satre wanted to bring the company out of doldrums and set about hiring talent. In 1995 Harrah's Entertainment was formed and another spin-off retained the profitable casinos. Before Satre, most casino executives rose from the gambling pits, long on job experience, short on formal education.

One of Satre's hires was John Boushy, who came with a master's degree in applied mathematics. The son of two college professors, Boushy was named VP of strategic marketing and performed a longitudinal tracking study. His data convinced Satre to start up a customer rewards program like the airlines and hotels. People signed up for the "Total Rewards" cards in droves with all sorts of benefits and perks as incentives. Giveaway driven, the more often the card is used the more comps and neat offers are sent. The more money wagered, the better the freebies.

Other casinos followed, but Harrah's was always a step ahead of its competition, and more important—the gambling public. The magnetic swipe cards fed everything into the casino's database, every bet, how fast (velocity of play), how often, what odds, and pattern of play. Harrah's spent more time, man hours and effort compiling the results than other casinos. More MBAs and marketing experts joined the "Harrah's team," as former Stanford football star Satre referred to them. They diligently studied gamblers, learning all they could about them, their likes, dislikes, interests, and patterns.

They learned that the group producing most of Harrah's profits were not the high rollers that all casinos pampered, but low rollers, "average Joes" spending between $100 and $500 each trip. Their "low rollers" made up only 30% of the gambling base, yet they gambled so frequently they brought in 80% of Harrah's revenue, and nearly 100% of its profits! Harrah's discovered these people visited other Harrah's casinos. In 1992, before the proliferation of Indian and Riverboat casinos, Harrah's learned these "low rollers" made three trips a year to a casino. By 1997, with more casinos in strategic locations across the country, they were making five trips. By cross-marketing, they were able to lure these people into Harrah's casinos.

Harrah's had to tweak its approach in Las Vegas however, because customers reported that while back home they were recognized as important Harrah's customers, in Las Vegas they were just one of many. More professors joined Harrah's management team, all dedicated to improving the bottom line by luring the gambling dollar into their establishments.

One was Harvard Business School professor Gary Loveman, who took over the leadership when Phil Satre retired. He further segmented customers once telling Satre, "Some customers are worth very little to you, while other customers are very valuable…" The Harrah's executives were not as concerned with the operations of a competing casino as they were with other successful company models in retail and other businesses.

Using collected data they began to test theories, to offer the appropriate goodies to the "average Joes" so they would come more often and gamble longer. Focused on the bottom line, Loveman once noted that Harrah's gamblers only spent 36 cents of every wagering dollar at Harrah's. He told shareholders that if they could just encourage one penny more, their annual earnings would rise more than $1 per share. In one test in Mississippi they offered two groups of slot players different "goodies." One group was offered a "room, food, beverage, and $30 of free chips" package worth a total $125. The other group was offered $60 in chips for gambling. A long-held assumption went by the wayside when they learned that the more modest "chips only" offer generated far more gambling.

Harrah's learned not only what, but when and how to mail coupons to different segments of players—anything to encourage them to gamble more—to raise each group's average number of trips, say from 1.1 to 1.4 times a month.

Loveman noticed that many casino gamblers are often miserable, especially when losing. He trained casino employees to try to perk them up. By the player identity cards, the employees can instantly spot wins and losses. Noting someone losing, a "luck ambassador" is dispatched immediately to present them with a token gift and cheer them up.

Massaging the customers is one quotient. The product has to also be displayed in as seductive manner as possible, anything that will make people pass more machines. Taking lessons from Walgreens and Rite Aid, they placed high-demand products like Wheel of Fortune slots in hard to reach places forcing players past numerous other attractions.

A lot of casino companies began to do what Harrah's pioneered. And the results continue to enlighten. Consultant Bill Friedman, author of the 2000 book *Designing Casinos to Dominate the Competition*, discovered information in his 20-year study that invalidated some of the previously held mantras that bigger is better. He learned that after "location," the next most important entity for a successful casino was its "design."

The megacasinos that would sprout in the 1990s created their own problems with their size. Their all-inclusive attractions and broad spaces would draw hordes of people—but fewer than 10% would gamble! Gamblers felt uncomfortable in those environs. Conversely, the smaller, well-designed, more comfortable casinos did the best in terms of gambling revenue, with up to 87% of the people gambling. The bottom line is that the bottom line is all-important.

Folks who go to the casinos to play slot machines account for 60% of most casinos revenues. They are no longer ignored in favor of the high rollers, instead they are led, like tethered animals to the trough where they will deposit their money.

A Family Destination
SOMETHING FOR EVERYONE

Reaching out in the 1990s

By the 1990s, the venues and opportunities for gambling across America had been changing. No longer did Nevada have an iron grip on the dollars being offered to the gods of luck. New Jersey legalized gambling in 1978 and large casinos began springing up along the boardwalk of Atlantic City.

There was a nation-wide economic slump in the early 1980s, and money became tight everywhere. As states loosened their anti-gambling grip in anticipation of more tax revenues, Indian casinos and riverboat gambling began to proliferate. By 1993 gambling was the country's fastest growing industry. Americans gambled a whopping $394.3 billion that year with 75% of it spent in casinos.

According to *Gaming and Wagering Business*, Nevada got 46% of that, New Jersey, 19%, and the rest went to riverboats and Indian casinos. Las Vegas was no longer the only game in town.

Some casino operators concluded that one of the ways to attract more people is to draw in the families, create more places like Circus Circus. While this concept was vilified by some, several casino operators decided the time had come.

Mirage — 1989

The upscale Mirage Resort & Casino ushered in the megacasino age. The 3,000 room, $630 million hotel was opened by Steve Wynn in 1989 and drew families just to watch its outdoor 64-foot volcano in front of the casino erupt into action at regular intervals. Crowds would gather on the sidewalk to "ooh" and "aah" as the volcano came to life, hissing and spewing brightly-lit lava into a huge pond.

Wynn had said that providing tourists with a crap table and a few slot machines was no longer enough. He added that the industry had to provide special attractions in the form of more entertainment, more excitement, more thrills, fantasy even. "The Mirage will be perceived as changing Las Vegas," he predicted.

Excalibur — June 1990

Most of the new casino operators along the Strip were trying to outdo each other with opulence and luxury: the bigger, the fancier, the more expensive, the better. Not Bill Bennett. Bennett had taken over control of the Circus Circus from Jay Sarno and made it a real profit-maker by offering all sorts of bargains to attract an undiscerning market: inexpensive buffets, budget rooms, cheap t-shirt shops, and liberal low-price slot machines. Bennett built the King Arthur-themed, castle-like Excalibur Hotel & Casino, which opened in June 1990 and featured children's attractions, such as a large family swimming pool, an arcade, and a motion simulator called Merlin's Magic Motion Machine. A large arena with shows featuring jousting matches delighted young and old alike. When it opened with 4,032 rooms, it was the largest hotel in the world.

Luxor — October 15, 1993

The doors of the realm that is Las Vegas were thrown wide open to families during the last two and a half months of 1993 when three major casino-hotels (Luxor, Treasure Island, MGM Grand) opened, all of which offered family entertainment.

The Luxor Las Vegas, a huge pyramid befitting the hotel's Egyptian theme, was the tallest structure when it opened and has the world's strongest light beam atop it. There are 4,408 rooms, a 120,000-square-foot casino, and for the younger set, the Luxor featured indoor Nile River rides.

Treasure Island — October 27, 1993

Mirage Resorts, under Steve Wynn, opened the pirate-themed Treasure Island Hotel & Casino next door to the Mirage. It's swashbuckling features, such as the skull-and-crossbones marquee and a kid-friendly video arcade, drew in families, but the biggest attraction was out in front of the casino where live staged pirates battled on Buccaneer Bay right on the Strip. Treasure Island features 2,885 rooms, a 76,000-square-foot casino, and has been the home for the long-running Cirqúe du Soleil Mystère show.

MGM Grand — December 18, 1993

The MGM Grand was designed to be the first true "family destination" hotel in the Las Vegas area. Thus when it opened in 1993, it featured the Grand Adventures Theme Park behind the casino to provide activities for younger children.

As the third of the major hotels opening that fall, and the "new" largest hotel in the world, the MGM Grand was rampant with superlatives. Its 5,034 rooms today attract over 22 million annual visitors, and its 156,000-square-foot casino and 380,000-square-foot convention center make up just part of the hotel's overall humongous 5 million square feet.

New York New York — 1997

Just as some of the "family" casinos were beginning to scale back, in January 1997, New York New York Hotel & Casino opened. The new casino featured a New York City skyline complete with a one-half-size Statue of Liberty. For kids, though, the draw was the fun zone and 67-mile-per-hour roller coaster that wound through the place.

The Height of Family-Friendly

Reveling in their metamorphosis, several casino operators defended their changes. Robert Maxey, then President of MGM Grand Inc., waxed, "These new places will take Las Vegas to the next level. This will deliver on the promise that we've become a destination resort, not just a gambling curiosity." The major media lapped it up.

Not just buildings to house attractions, the themed hotel-casinos had become attractions, each offering something different and unique. They wanted tourists wandering around the sidewalk in front of the Strip to stop in and be entertained.

Did it work? Yes and no. Tourist numbers to Las Vegas skyrocketed. By early 1995, monthly visitors were already a whopping 24% ahead of projections and had surpassed those of Orlando, Florida. By the end of the year, Las Vegas doubled the tourist traffic of Orlando by attracting 29 million visitors. By the end of 1995 Las Vegas was in the catbird seat.

But it was a new breed of visitor, not the hard core gamblers of previous times, nor even those couples who dressed up for a night on the Strip. Shorts, tank tops, t-shirts, flip flops, fanny packs, and baby strollers had become the new and accepted "costumes" on the Strip, replacing the more sedate attire of an earlier era.

More People, Less Money

Casino operators like Steve Wynn noted with chagrin that while there were more people, there was less money! It turned out that the middle-class folks lured to Las Vegas by the newer "family-oriented" mega-resorts were not big spenders. With less disposable income, they were even considered "cheap." They came for the free entertainment, the budget-priced rooms, the value-packed family buffets, and any freebie they could get their hands on. In short, they did not leave much money on the tables. That's a mortal sin in a place like Las Vegas.

The conundrum was that while hotel occupancy rates hovered over 90%, incredible in any economy, many visitors never entered the casinos. The spending numbers on a per person basis dropped drastically, cutting into projected profits.

Something had to be done, and raising prices was the first knee-jerk reaction, so of course they did that. No longer content with just casino revenue, they decided to squeeze profits out of everything. Loss-leading restaurants, bars, and hotel rooms were now required to make money. Free drinks, inexpensive rooms, giveaways, and inexpensive food for the most part vanished like slacks and evening dresses on the Strip.

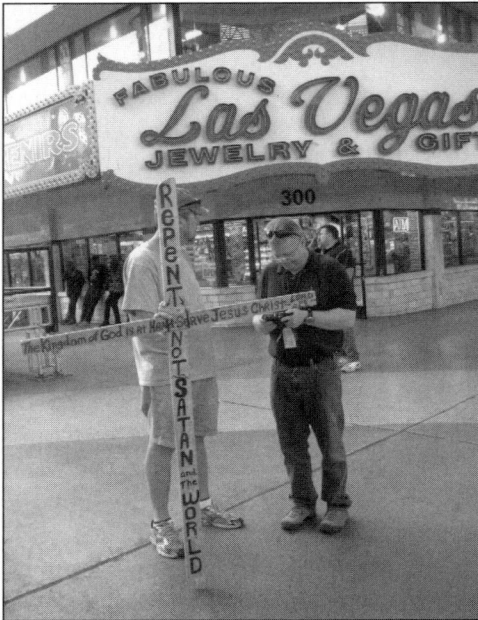

There are varying opinions on the perceived vices of Las Vegas

Casino owners bickered, many blaming the "family" joints for even wasting airline seats on non-gamblers.

Resisting the changes, a lot of old-timers echoed the same sentiments, "This place was better when the mobs ran the joints." In time, the casino operators, realizing that their primary goal is to compete for that gambling dollar, started phasing out of the kiddy, babysitting business. Family scale-back had begun.

In a private interview, entertainer Wayne Newton even mentioned that the "kiddy" experiment was fortunately short-lived. "Gamblers did not want to be stepping over baby carriages," he said.

Retired Las Vegas Metropolitan Police Lieutenant Dennis Larsen added, "This is an adult playground. There have always been half-naked women around."

There was also concern about image. "This is an oil and water situation," stated William R. Eadington, director of the Institute for Gambling and Commercial Gaming at the University of Nevada, Reno about casinos with attractions for children. "The two are just absolutely inconsistent with each other. It may create a backlash of public opinion against the industry."

Scaling back

At the Excalibur, the former open stage foyer was first to go and is now occupied by The Shoppes. The adult Octane lounge now occupies the stage where a cover band performs nightly. They've renovated the former family pool area to make it more adult-friendly: doubling its size, adding cabanas, fire pits, sun decks and a secluded relaxation pool.

The Luxor got rid of the Nile Ride and added a hip, two-floor, 26,000-square-foot nightclub that is one of the city's largest.

The Treasure Island in 2003 largely abandoned its pirate theme for a more contemporary resort in efforts to focus more on adults. The original arcade and kid-friendly pool areas were replaced with an adult-friendly hot tub, contemporary nightclub, and party bar. The famous skull-and-crossbones sign at the Strip entrance was replaced by one reading simply "ti" that is also a large LCD video screen.

At the MGM Grand, in an attempt to reverse its family appeal, in 2000 the hotel underwent a major renovation, removing a kiddy-based "Oz" theme to emerge more art-deco. The ill-conceived Grand Adventures Theme Park performed poorly, and did not reopen for the 2001 season. It was replaced by a conference center and condominiums. Now billing itself as The City of Entertainment, the resort still has numerous activities—they're just not geared for kids.

Now mostly run by large corporations, the Las Vegas casino business will never be the same. The bottom line has always been the most important thing, and gamblers provided most of that. The baby carriages would be better tolerated if Papa dropped a bundle.

CHAPTER 7

ENTERTAINMENT CAPITAL of the World

There's a reason Las Vegas has earned the sobriquet "Entertainment Capital of the World."

Performers like Liberace, Frank Sinatra and the Rat Pack, Elvis Presley, and Wayne Newton have set the pace for dazzling and exciting shows that today feature extravaganzas, magicians, and more.

There's truly something for everyone at a Las Vegas show or nightclub.

Entertainment Capital of the World
"I Go For The Shows"

Gambling may have defined Las Vegas, but world-class entertainment has nurtured and glamorized it. Shows rarely seen elsewhere—the biggest names in entertainment, gala extravaganzas, and cutting edge acts—have rightfully given Las Vegas the title of Entertainment Capital of the World. Some people, when asked about their frequent visits to Las Vegas, blithely respond, "I go for the shows." The shows take the spotlight off the green felt tables and one-armed bandits. The shows are designed to fill the casinos, and lure the people to where they can be parted from their money, and enjoy doing it. "Didn't win, but we had a good time."

Casino entertainment goes back to the old saloon days of yesteryear, when a sultry singer with too much makeup and a honky-tonk piano player would try to drown out the cacophony of unruly and raucous crowds.

The early Las Vegas casinos created entertainment that set the tone for all that would follow. It has been a case of one-upmanship ever since. Back in the 1930s, Judy Garland appeared on stage with her sisters at the Meadows. During the 1940s major performers began appearing even in downtown shows.

The El Rancho Vegas, the first and only resort on the Strip back in 1941 initiated a small intimate showroom and booked a wide variety of performers: singers, comedians, instrumentalists, and dancers to entertain hotel guests, including star-quality headliners such as: Pearl Bailey, Lita Baron, Milton Berle, Ben Blue, stripper Lili St. Cyr, Billy Daniels, singer Lena Horne, Gy Landis, Joe E. Lewis, Ann Southern, Sophie Tucker, and crooner/actor Rudy Vallee.

Not to be outdone, the Strip's second casino, the Last Frontier, immediately started booking big name entertainment, something it became known for throughout its long history. Some of the celebrities to perform at that resort during the 1940s and '50s included the biggest names of the time: Sophie Tucker, Mandrake the Magician, Marx Brothers, Judy Garland, Ronald Reagan, Frank Sinatra, Sammy Davis, Jr., Eddie Albert, Jack Carter, Henny Youngman, Tommy Dorsey's band, and Josephine Baker.

The Thunderbird, which opened in 1948, was another early leader in attracting big name entertainment, including Rosemary Clooney, Donald O'Connor, Mills Brothers, Tony Martin, and Mel Torme to Las Vegas. Most Las Vegas casino resorts soon had a main showroom for the big names, and a smaller lounge show. The lounges normally had a small cover and maybe a two-drink minimum.

The person most responsible for the concept of quality lounge entertainment was Bill Miller, who became 10% owner and entertainment director of the Sahara Hotel & Casino in 1953. A former nightclub owner from New Jersey, he felt the lounges would produce income on their own. In that vein, for the Sahara's Casbah Lounge he hired vocalist Louis Prima, his partner and wife Keely Smith, and their backup band Sam Butera and the Witnesses for a seven year gig at a total $10,500 a week. It was a big, radical new idea that worked. They were so popular singing the likes of "That Old Black Magic" that they were promoted to the big showroom.

Lounge entertainment had become such big business entertainers wanted to work them for the widespread recognition they afforded. During the '50s and '60s, casino lounges often provided continuous entertainment from dusk to dawn at no charge to the customer except the cost of drinks. Many entertainers got their starts in them, including Sonny and Cher. Other top lounge entertainment attractions included performers like Don Rickles, Buddy Hackett, Shecky Greene, and Alan King.

Choreographer Donn Arden first broke with that successful star formula in 1950 with a dance troupe that opened the Desert Inn. Then in 1957, Jack Entratter brought fame to the Sands Hotel with the chorus line of Copa Girls. Resorts then tried to out-spectacular each other with their shows.

The Dunes *(photo courtesy Larry D. Moore, cc 1983 under Creative Commons ShareAlike License)*

Bare Breasts on Stage

At the Dunes in early 1957, Harold Minsky introduced shock value with the debut of "Minsky's Follies," the first time that topless showgirls were seen on a Las Vegas Strip stage. The show borrowed from vaudeville, Broadway, burlesque, and Paris, but what made it a real knockout success were the bare-breasted dancers. Things would never be the same in Vegas.

Donn Arden followed with the "Lido de Paris" at the Stardust in 1958. He offered a large stage production with topless showgirls. Imported from France, "Lido de Paris" was acclaimed as even more spectacular than the Paris original. It was so popular it enjoyed a 31-year Las Vegas run. The success of the "Lido" extravaganza encouraged other resorts to try big production shows. Arden himself developed the show "Jubilee" at Bally's which has been featuring showgirls for over 25 years. The Tropicana countered in 1959 with the spectacular Folies Bergére, a showroom favorite. A half century later, it remained the longest-running show in Las Vegas history, finally closing in 2009.

There are currently 11 Las Vegas shows that feature topless performers.

Originally the Las Vegas showgirls were dancers who accompanied and supported the headliners with a little glitter. Their successful image morphed them into headliners themselves.

Today productions like "Jubilee," the "Blue Man Group," "The Producers," Disney's "Lion King," "Le Rêve," "Phantom," or the six Cirqúe du Soleil shows in town: "Mystère," "O," "Zumanity," "Ka," "LOVE, The Beatles," and "Criss Angel Believe" are packed and prosperous. Other big Las Vegas shows included illusionists Siegfried and Roy and their white tigers. They first played Las Vegas in 1967 at the Tropicana. Later they performed at the MGM Grand and the Stardust, and were named the Las Vegas Show of the Year in 1972. In 1990 they inked a lifetime contract for an annual guarantee of $57.5 million with owner Steve Wynn to appear at The Mirage. In total, they performed in 15,000 Las Vegas shows. Their act closed in 2003 after Roy was severely mauled by a tiger during a show.

Strip developer Steve Wynn introduced another new type of show for the Treasure Island Hotel & Casino. "Mystère," a unique circus production from Canada which opened on Christmas 1993, was such a hit other permanent Cirqúe du Soleil shows like "O" and "Zumanity" have followed. "Mystère" is still going strong 17 years later.

The shows and stage productions have been the defining entertainment in Las Vegas. There are literally scores of shows going on all the time. Some are intimate, some are grand, some are sexy, few are bland. There is a show for everyone—every taste and interest. No other city offers such choices.

There are big productions, singers and headliners, impressionists and magicians, oldie revivals, sexy shows for men and women, jousting, acrobat and circus shows, animal shows, and free shows. The big productions fill huge stages in theaters with upwards of 1,500-2,000 seats.

There have been a host of magicians, illusionists, and impersonators: Danny Gans, David Copperfield, Wayne Brady, Nathan Burton, Rich Natole, Terry Fator, Steve Wyrick, Dirk Arthur, Dixie Dooley, and others.

Lately, a number of nostalgia shows have been exploiting the past talents and fame of others.

Sex sells and there are more sexy shows in Las Vegas than in Paris, New York, San Francisco and Rio de Janeiro combined.

Wayne Newton noted that Las Vegas entertainment has been cyclical though the years with different types of shows gaining favor before taking a backseat to a current and new trend. He cited the original singers and stars; the various and numerous magic shows; the impressionists; and the big circus productions.

In addition to the big shows, many of the longtime Las Vegas performers have become legends if not institutions, and their shows are the embodiment of Las Vegas.

It seems there truly is something for everyone in Las Vegas these days. There's a reason to go for the shows.

Liberace

PERFORMER iN PURPLE

O ne of the most flamboyant performers to headline Las Vegas was also one of the most durable, delighting crowds of mostly women for over 42 years. Walter "Lee" Liberace, an admitted fan of composer Frederic Chopin, graced his piano with his trademark candelabra because in a movie Chopin had one.

The pianist was working in Montreal for $350 a week when invited to Las Vegas by Last Frontier entertainment director Maxine Lewis. He told her he was making $750 a week, so she agreed to match it. After he arrived in December 1944, she was impressed and made the contract for $1,500. To attract an audience Liberace personally passed out flyers for his show along Fremont Street.

In 1947, Bugsy Siegel tried to get the popular performer for his new Flamingo, offering to double Liberace's then weekly salary of $2,000 a week. The loyalty/money dilemma facing Liberace was solved when Siegel was murdered.

Through the years Liberace, with his talent and his unique flamboyant, over-the-top persona, continued to draw big crowds. His outrageous outfits were the talk of the town, appearing in gold lamé in one show, purple velvet the next.

Each contract brought him greater success. His weekly take was bumped to $50,000 in 1955 for performing at the newly opened Riviera. When he opened the Las Vegas Hilton in 1972, he signed a contract for $300,000 a week.

Liberace's last performance was a two week engagement at Caesars Palace in 1986. He died the following year at his Palm Springs home at age 67. To say he was a pioneer in Las Vegas entertainment is an understatement. He *was* Las Vegas entertainment, often called Mr. Showmanship. He paved the way for so many other unique shows to follow.

In tribute to the Vegas icon, there was a Liberace Museum in Las Vegas at 1775 E. Tropicana Ave. in Liberace Plaza, which opened in 1979. Along with the world's largest collection of rhinestone and other memorabilia, the museum housed rare pianos (one played by Frederic Chopin and one owned by George Gershwin), antiques, jewelry, custom autos, and elaborate costumes from the entertainer's million-dollar wardrobe.

Liberace Plaza artwork

The Liberace Museum closed its doors in October 2010 and the vast collection has been put in storage.

Frank Sinatra
"THE WORLD ON A STRING"

I f there was ever an entertainer who defined an entire town, it was Frank Sinatra. Sinatra owned Las Vegas, where his 43-year presence created the image of hip, cool, carefree, and fun. From his first Strip performance at the Desert Inn in September 1951, until his last at the opening of the MGM Grand on New Year's Day, 1994, old "Blue Eyes," from Hoboken, N. J., "The Chairman of the Board," held sway as top headliner in a city of headliners.

Celebrities and other stars even came to see Sinatra, whose presence elevated the Western-feeling town to one of sophistication. "He brought unmatched excitement to the Strip…," eulogized actor Gregory Peck following Sinatra's 1998 death, adding, "With his little gang of merry men, he established forever a sense of free-floating fun and frolic that captured the imagination of the world."

Sinatra would forever be identified with the Sands Hotel & Casino, which opened in December 1952. Manager Jack Entratter had sold his famous Copacabana Club in New York to open up the Sands and, continuing his New York success which featured the likes of Danny Thomas and Lena Horne, signed Frank Sinatra to perform in the Sands' Copa Room in 1953. Sinatra received two points at that time and his ownership was bumped up to 9% in 1961, by which time he memorialized the Copa Room.

The Rat Pack

By the late 1950s, Sinatra started inviting a few of his pals to share the stage with him and a major chapter in the history of Las Vegas entertainment was born. The impromptu antics of what would be called the Rat Pack delighted the crowds for two shows each night. The Rat Pack (Sinatra, Dean Martin, Sammy Davis Jr., Joey Bishop, and Peter Lawford) were cool and fun with their shoot-from-the-hip craziness on stage.

Together in 1960 they made the classic Las Vegas casino-heist movie, *Oceans Eleven*, produced by Sinatra's Dorchester Productions, also starring Angie Dickenson, Buddy Lester, Cesar Romero, Richard Conte, and other popular actors.

While Sinatra was the king of Nevada entertainment, his personal life involving his known association with mobsters and his virulent temper created numerous problems for him. In 1963 he was forced to relinquish his gaming license and sell his majority interest in the Cal Nevada Lodge at Lake Tahoe because he welcomed the blacklisted gangster Sam Giancana there.

Then in 1967 he got into a fist fight and drove a golf cart through a plate glass window at the Sands after Howard Hughes bought the place and had his credit cut off. Following that episode, Sinatra began performing at Caesars Palace.

In 1970 Sheriff Ralph Lamb threatened to throw Sinatra in jail after another argument over casino credit resulted in a gun being drawn by the crooner's combatant.

Despite his eccentricities, Sinatra continued to entertain, even wooing a newer, younger audience to his upbeat shows. In 1981, the Gaming Commission even approved re-licensing Sinatra when he applied for his consulting interest in Caesars Palace.

Like most of the major players behind Las Vegas and the Strip, Frank Sinatra too was a paradox. It appears he often felt things should have gone, like his song, "My Way." But his talent, his charisma, his energy is still missed. Following his death, the lights on the Las Vegas Strip were dimmed, in tribute to the entertainer who lit up the Strip by himself.

Elvis Presley
The King in Sequins

Elvis Presley may be dead, but don't tell anyone. He lives on in Las Vegas. You can get married with "Elvis" officiating, go skydiving with "Elvis" and his clones, buy "Elvis" art, clothing, caps, t-shirts, ashtrays, and get your photo taken with the "King" himself on Las Vegas Boulevard. The "Las Vegas

Elvis" himself was a reincarnation of the earlier singer, the one who hit stardom with "Blue Suede Shoes" and "Jailhouse Rock." It was a different, more flamboyant star who dazzled almost half of all Las Vegas visitors between 1969 and 1977. The earlier, younger Elvis was no more. At the height of his fame, he even served in the U.S. Army, as did a lot of us. I saw him as I followed him through Fort Hood and over to Germany, where in olive drab he blended in with the rest of us. But even by then his popularity was astronomical. In 1956, before the army and only 21 years old, Elvis first performed in Las Vegas at the New Frontier. The swivel-hipped entertainer with sideburns was extremely popular with teens around the country, but failed to "wow 'em" in Vegas at that time.

In 1963 he returned to Las Vegas to film the movie "Viva Las Vegas," which co-starred Ann Margret. He was back again on May 1, 1967 when he married Priscilla Anne Beaulieu at the Aladdin Hotel.

By 1969, Elvis's film career, which spanned 33 mostly so-so movies, was waning and he rarely performed publicly. So when Kirk Kerkorian completed his International Hotel and asked Presley to be the exclusive act in the International's showroom, Presley, through his manager Col. Tom Parker, readily agreed. While Barbra Streisand opened the huge 2,000 seat showroom, it was Elvis who later brought the crowds.

On July 26, 1969, a different Elvis Presley introduced his new act

Elvis Presley and Ann Margret in "Viva Las Vegas" *(photo courtesy MGM)*

on the International stage. Inspired by singer Tom Jones, who enjoyed a sexy rapport with his audiences, and the ever-flamboyant Liberace, Elvis, now in a sequined white jumpsuit, strutted, kissed the women, tossed out sweaty handkerchiefs, and emitted unrestrained energy all to a new noise level accompanied by more than 50 musicians and two soul and gospel choirs. Elvis truly had created a new Elvis and re-achieved mega-star status with yet a different audience.

Elvis played exclusively at the International Hotel (which became Hilton Las Vegas in 1971), for a total of 837 consecutive sold-out performances in front of 2.5 million people. At the end of Elvis' first month, the International's showroom had earned more than $2 million, becoming not an inducement to attract gamblers, but the main attraction. His contract called for two four-

week appearances, two shows a night. At only $125,000 a week, it was puny by any standards. However his manager Col. Parker, an inveterate gambler, was "comped" to the max, including unlimited casino credit. Needless to say, he lost and lost big, about $50,000 to $75,000 each night!

Meanwhile, after the shows, Elvis and entourage would head for the penthouse, which was well stocked with food, booze, pills, and women. The pills eventually got the best of Elvis Presley and a plethora of them contributed to his heart attack in 1977 at his Memphis home. Of all the Las Vegas entertainers, Elvis Presley is the individual people are most loath to part with. His legacy includes memorabilia at the Hard Rock Cafe, a statue in front of the Hilton Las Vegas, imitators and impersonators not only in Las Vegas but around the world, and websites and chat rooms everywhere where people who refuse to believe he's actually dead can commiserate with each other. The King lives on.

Wayne Newton
"Danke Schoen, Mr. Las Vegas"

Often called "Mr. Las Vegas," if it seems Wayne Newton's name has graced casino marquees all your life, you're probably right. Wayne Newton has performed over 30,000 solo shows in Las Vegas for half a century and is still at it. While his biggest hit was the 1972 song "Daddy Don't You Walk So Fast," he is best known for crooning "Red Roses for a Blue Lady," and his signature song, 1963's "Danke Schoen."

Born Carson Wayne Newton in Virginia in 1942, he learned the piano, guitar, and steel guitar at the age of six. As part of a USO show, he performed in front of President Harry Truman while still in the first grade. His asthma forced the family to move to Arizona, where he attended high school. Wayne and his brother Jerry formed a duo and appeared in Grand Ole Opry roadshows and on the television show *Ozark Jubilee*. While still in high school, they inked a deal with the Fremont Hotel in Las Vegas to begin performing in 1959. That was extended to a five-year gig for The Newton Brothers.

In 1962 the Newton Brothers performed on the immensely popular Jackie Gleason Show, who invited them back 11 more times. Almost a half century later, Newton admitted that he learned a great work ethic from Gleason, who was a perfectionist who would even sit in the audience during rehearsals.

Later going solo, Wayne was noticed by numerous celebrities and comedian Jack Benny hired him to open his show. After that engagement was over, the Flamingo Las Vegas offered Newton another opening act, for Jack Carter this time, but the singer requested his own headline act, even offering to do it at the original salary. He was granted the headline show and the rest is history.

Supported at first by locals, soon the tourists came and he has since performed live to over 40 million people.

Newton became part owner of the Aladdin Hotel in 1980-1982, but was unsuccessful in acquiring majority ownership in 1983.

By 1994, Newton had performed his 25,000th solo show in Las Vegas. In 1999, he signed a 10-year deal with the Stardust, performing 40 weeks out of the year, six shows a week in a showroom named after him. In 2005, with the eventual implosion of the Stardust, Newton went to the Las Vegas Hilton to do 30 shows.

Wayne Newton was a major Las Vegas star and even appeared in numerous television shows and 13 movies, a couple in which he even played himself, like *National Lampoon's Las Vegas Vacation.* In 2001, Newton succeeded Bob Hope as chairman of the USO Celebrity Circle. He says his USO shows have been the highlight of his career, and in support of the military still has veterans in his show stand to be recognized.

In 2005, he inaugurated a re-ality television show called *The Entertainer.*

A limber Newton was even featured on the *Dancing With The Stars* television show in 2007, paired with Cheryl Burke. "I really loved the experience," said Newton, "But it's hard. The steps are so precise and disciplined. I guess I always thought dancing should be more fun." To celebrate his fiftieth year of crooning to appreciative audiences on the Las Vegas Strip, in October 2009 he began performing his newest show, a limited engagement production "Once Before I Go" at the Tropicana. Backed by three singers and an orchestra, it was a real fun nostalgic romp through

Author Greg Niemann and Wayne Newton

five decades of Newton with most of the biggest names in show business. He also played a few of the 15 instruments he's mastered over the years.

It will seem strange being in Las Vegas and not seeing Wayne Newton's name in neon, not that he plans to quit. "I'm an entertainer," he said with a smile. "As long as I can bring happiness to people, that's what I want to do."

Continuing to entertain people, in November 2010 Newton announced plans to offer tours of his 10,000-square-foot home Casa de Shenandoah beginning in late 2011.

As a reminder to visitors of his impact on Las Vegas, the address of Las Vegas McCarran International Airport is 5757 Wayne Newton Blvd. Wayne Newton and Las Vegas have been a very good fit. According to media guru Merv Griffin, "Las Vegas without Wayne Newton is like Disneyland without Mickey Mouse."

Scene at the Nightclubs
Making it Rain

For a lot of Las Vegas visitors, the nightlife is the big draw. The Las Vegas nightclubs are some of the biggest, most innovative, most state-of-the-art, and most seductive around. It's a see-and-be-seen world, and there are enough hot bodies, including celebrities, around to melt the polar ice cap.

In fact, some celebrities have been providing the most fun throwing money away to a crowd as delighted to see the currency as they are the celebrity. Called "making it rain," athletes, musicians, rock stars, television and movie personalities, and others who feel they have enough to ostentatiously share a little bit have been in the habit of carrying wads of bills into a nightclub and throwing handfuls of bills in the air to "rain down" among the merrymakers.

One of the most prolific and generous "rainers" is Floyd Mayweather, Jr., the flamboyant boxer nicknamed "Pretty Boy." The successful pugilist chalked up 38 straight wins and six world championships in five different weight rankings. He lives in Vegas and when he celebrates, others benefit. One club owner said he's seen Mayweather "make it rain" at least 20 times. And with Mayweather, they're not singles either. He'll stuff his pockets with about $20,000 cash and "let 'er rip," showering club goers with $100 bills. He once told a reporter, "With me it's entertainment. We're in the Entertainment Capital of the World." Mayweather restrained himself from "showering" the ABC stage, however, when he was a *Dancing With the Stars* contestant.

NFL cornerback Adam "Pacman" Jones is another athlete known to part with his cash in Las Vegas nightclubs. The controversial party-goer has been spotted "making it rain" at Minxx Gentlemen's Club, among others. Mindfreak illusionist Criss Angel and then-girlfriend "Peep" star Holly Madison showered the crowd at the LAX club in the Luxor with $100 bills when they celebrated their December birthdays in 2008.

NHL star goaltender Ray Emery visited the The Bank, Bellagio's swank nightclub, in May 2009 and let $1,000 in singles fly in the air. The eccentric and colorful basketball star Dennis Rodman was the all-time "rain" champ. For over 10 years he'd enter nightclubs with plastic garbage bags full of various denomination bills to dispense on the crowds. UFC fighter Rampage Jackson made it rain in June 2009 when he climbed on stage at Body English and threw $1,000 of his MMA winnings into the air.

Once an unknown guy just showed up at a club on New Year's Eve 2007 with a backpack stuffed with bricks of bills. He threw out about $5,000 at midnight and continued the spree through the night. There are numerous others who have become "rainmakers" in Las Vegas, and nightclub habitués really never know who's going to show up next. Might not be a bad idea to keep tabs on that Mayweather though.

Sightings

A lot of people go to the clubs hoping to spot a celebrity or two. That's called "sightings" by those who make a practice of it. There's probably no better place on earth, even Hollywood, than Las Vegas to discover a sighting or two, especially in the clubs.

After all, the big names are paid to show up. Most people wait in line to shell out an expensive cover charge, "grease" the maître d' for a table, much less a decent one, and buy exorbitantly priced drinks. Yet many top personalities are paid $50,000 or $100,000 just to show up and be seen.

Of course, the clubs make sure the media is alerted, photos are taken, and "their" club will be the next "hot spot." After all, today's "in" place will someday be replaced by another.

The Clubs

Most of the nightclubs are in the major Strip casinos, and most of the casinos have nightclubs. The dress code varies from funky to sexy to very provocative to crank-up-the-heat. They run the gamut from poolside to high rise, from intimate to multi-storied. A night out hitting the clubs will definitely enhance one's Vegas experience, and they are much more crowded in the wee hours than before midnight.

There's a gang of pulsating hot spots, in a myriad of decors and themes to choose from, even one called appropriately Rain Nightclub at the hip Palms Casino Resort. The Palms was opened in 2001 by entrepreneur George Maloof and, teamed with Playboy, has been one of the hottest "in" places ever since. At the grand opening socialite Paris Hilton wore a $1 million dress fashioned from poker chips.

Rain Nightclub at the Palms, puts the "sin" back in Sin City, with private cabanas, water booths, and skyboxes overlooking the massive dance floor. Special effects include rain and fire.

Moon/Playboy Club, also in the Palms Resort, has glass tile floors, a retractable roof and two patios overlooking the lights of Vegas. A lot of celebrities have been seen at the several Palms venues.

XS is a luxurious poolside club at the Encore Hotel. The height of hedonism, you can even buy a $10,000 cocktail there. It comes with men's silver cufflinks and an 18K gold woman's necklace replete with black pearl.

Pure Nightclub at Caesars Palace is huge, featuring 36,000 square feet in four rooms with different types of music, including the seductive Pussycat Dolls Lounge. Pure attracts celebrities like Lindsey Lohan and football star Jerry Rice among its 5,000 party goers each weekend.

LAX at the Luxor welcomed the year 2010 as one of the city's hottest, attracting A-List celebrities. Its 26,000 square feet featured a state-of-the-art sound system over two floors of rich red leathers and oversized mirrors.

MIX Nightclub is on the 64th floor of the Mandalay Bay Resort. There are incredible views even from the bathroom stalls which feature floor-to-ceiling windows.

Body English at the Hard Rock Hotel is a rock star's kind of place and is frequented by locals and celebrities alike. NASCAR star Jeff Gordon was spotted entering a dance contest there.

The Bank at Bellagio is expensive and classy, featuring a mix of hip-hop and techno. Business casual for men, yet as often the case in Las Vegas, anything for women.

Coyote Ugly at New York New York is a funky saloon-type place that can get really wild with women dancing on the bar.

Tao is an Asian-inspired nightclub at the Venetian. Numerous bars and go-go dancers make this a fun place. There are models in rose-petal-filled bathtubs to greet visitors. Model Pamela Anderson once set tongues wagging when she stepped in one to join them.

Jet, the Mirage's nightclub, has three dance floors and smaller party rooms. The multi-level club features an upscale sound system.

For a supersensual experience, the **Tryst** nightclub at the Wynn Hotel is hard to beat. With a 90-foot waterfall lagoon surrounding the dance floor, it's romantic and intimate. There are even sexy pole dancers.

Studio 54 at the MGM Grand has four dance floors, exclusive areas and semi-private lounges.

Privé at Planet Hollywood is one of the better spots for "sightings" as A-List celebrities have often visited the club where chic imagery meets upscale decor. Originally opened by celebrity owners, it seems like there's always a "name" on the property.

The Las Vegas nightclubs have become legends unto themselves, extending that Sin City image that is Las Vegas. They attract mostly a younger crowd who opt not to sit for a stage production, and are the current "rage." There are a lot of them; they are generally very pricey; they are big and sexy, and even if nobody decides to throw money your way, you will still have a memorable time.

Chapter 8

Sin City Stories

What's Sin City without stories, both true ones as well as those myths and urban legends that tend to endure and flourish through the years?

There have been Las Vegas scandals that have even had the locals' tongues' wagging. And nothing gets them talking more than yarns about whales and big spenders.

Myths and Urban Legends
You'll Never Believe This, But...

M
yths and local legends are everywhere. Good eyebrow-raising stories have survived even though never documented or substantiated. Las Vegas is no exception; in fact Sin City has an abundance of them. Gamblers, by nature, are superstitious, and the stories passed off as absolutely true generally center around the slot machines, but other yarns that continue to circulate tend to be more bizarre in nature.

Dead Hooker Story

It seems a couple in Las Vegas complained about a horrible odor in their room. They called the manager who sprayed the room with strong chemicals. They returned to the room later and the strong odor was still there, but they were finally able to go to sleep. In the morning the smell was so powerful they called the manager, demanding a new room. He went to their room and as the stench seemed to be by the bed, he lifted back the mattress to discover a decomposing hooker crammed into the box springs.

When I first heard this one in the early '90s, my source named the couple. Dubious, I called the man in Salt Lake City and he said it happened to another couple at the hotel. He seemed excited and sincere and I'm sure he believed it, but I've heard the same story since. Some versions don't include the poor woman's occupation. But the people who tell this story seem to swear by it.

Bodies in the Dam

A story often heard in southern Nevada has it that several (some versions claim up to seven) bodies of construction workers on Hoover Dam were buried in the huge concrete structure. It is documented that there were 112 deaths, directly or indirectly associated with the five-year project, mostly heart attacks and heat strokes, although there were accidents too. None, however, were buried within the dam.

Even if someone had fallen into the concrete, it was poured in small slabs, each curing before the next slab was poured, and someone falling in would have been noticed and retrieved.

Fresh Kidneys For Sale

A persistent rumor that began in the early 1990s tells of a man having drinks with an attractive lady at a Las Vegas bar and then blacking out. He awakens in a hotel bathtub covered with ice. The phone is on the floor nearby with a note, "Call 911 or you will die."

The panicked man does and is rushed to the hospital, where doctors inform him that one of his kidneys has been removed, apparently by a gang specializing in selling "human organs" on the black market.

The story gained such momentum around the country that the National Kidney Foundation asked anyone who has had his or her kidneys removed unintentionally to please call. So far no one has.

Ready To Hit!

A persistent belief among slot players is that of "hot" machines, one that's ready to pay off big. Some players hog a machine that's been paying off smaller amounts "knowing it's ready to hit." Truth is, each pull of the handle or push of the button is totally random. The opposite is also true. Some players shun a machine that just paid off big. The next spin is just as likely for another jackpot as the one before.

I've Got Rhythm

Some players insist that you can't just put one coin in a machine and move on because it spoils the rhythm of the machine. Well, machines are inanimate and don't take dancing lessons. Ain't no rhythm.

Mega Bunk to Megabucks

The huge payoffs of Megabucks, the linked progressive network of slot machines, are enough to set tongues wagging, whether or not the waggers know what they're talking about. When the jackpots start at $10 million and go up until someone lines up the three Megabucks symbols, there are plenty of wishful stories.

Rumors especially fly following a big win, like the anonymous guy in 2003 who hit for almost $40 million. According to "those who know," the guy died right after, with at least three versions of his demise. Not true; he's alive and rich.

Another Megabucks death story is about an elderly woman in 2002 who lined the symbols up and died on the spot as her heart failed from the shock.

The woman was 74 at the time, survived the surprise just fine, and traveled to Europe with some of her winnings.

Every time a new casino in Las Vegas opens, there are dedicated Megabucks players swarming the place. It seems a persistent rumor has it that the next Megabucks payoff will be at the newest casino. Apparently the feeling is that "those in charge" made a payoff to ensure one of their machines hit. Bunk. It is pure chance.

Winning Big

Someone turned a $400 Social Security check into $1.6 million playing blackjack. It's listed on a web page as fact, but I've been unable to document it. Too good to be true?

Losers Usually Recover Pawned Goods

Contrary to a common perception, people who pawn their jewelry or other items in Las Vegas generally return to reclaim their belongings. From 75-90% of the time the items are reclaimed, according to pawn shop employees in several Las Vegas locations.

The mean estimate was 80%, offered by almost everyone in the business. And, according to a North Las Vegas EZ Pawn Shop employee, most of the people hocking merchandise are not gamblers but locals who run short of cash between paydays.

Even busy shops like the one on TV's *Pawn Shop* show (713 S. Las Vegas Blvd.) concur. Adam Harrison of the black-shirted Harrison family immediately said, "80%" when asked about retrievals. Of course, wheeling and dealing and buying and selling is something else.

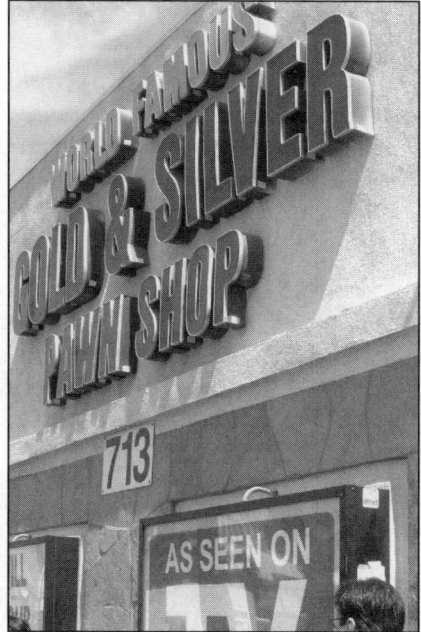

Gold and Silver Pawn Shop featured on the History Channel

True Stories

It Happened in Vegas

Frontier Justice

L as Vegas's first permanent Anglo settler, O. D. Gass, became a Lincoln County justice of the peace. He was called upon to preside over a case in which one Paiute Indian shot another. Gass, knowing that any judgment would bring trouble from one Paiute faction or the other, announced that everyone should adjourn to the ranch house for dinner.

He left one Indian to guard the prisoner. As they dined, a gunshot was heard. Everyone ran outside, to discover the defendant dead, and the guard standing with a smoking gun. He had tried to escape, the guard explained. Gass was surprisingly calm about the incident.

Lost Sexual Powers

Ed Kraus, a truck driver working on the Hoover Dam, sued the contractors, Six Companies, Inc., because he claimed he lost his sexual powers due to exposure to carbon monoxide fumes in the tunnels. The defendants used undercover agents and got prostitutes to belie his impotence. Kraus lost his case.

A Parade Ghoul

Indian outlaw Queho, who terrorized southern Nevada in the early twentieth century, was found dead in a cave in 1940. The Las Vegas Elks Club put his mummified remains on display, and on at least on one occasion propped his body up for a ride in the Helldorado Days parade down Fremont Street.

Best What?

Virginia Hill, Ben "Bugsy" Siegel's former girlfriend, had dated a number of mobsters before she was called before the 1951 Kefaufer Committee dealing with organized crime. Senator Estes Kefaufer did not expect her blunt response for the world to hear when he asked her the secret of her success. She coyly batted her eyelashes and said, "Senator, I'm the best damn cocksucker in the world."

Sorry, Mr. President

Singer Frank Sinatra was chastised by the Nevada Gaming Control Board for his underworld ties and forced to sell his casino interests. Nevada Governor Grant Sawyer admits in his book *Hang Tough* that President John F. Kennedy tried to intervene on Sinatra's behalf. Sawyer politely told the President to mind his own business. While the crooner still performed in Nevada casinos, he owned no part of them.

Benny Had a Heart

Benny Binion, a longtime casino operator who had earlier served a 42-month prison sentence for tax evasion, did have a heart. When a North Carolina preacher lost $1,000 of church money shooting craps at Binion's Horseshoe Club, Benny gave it back. He said, "God may forgive you, preacher, but your congregation won't."

Shut up, Sign

Actor Lee Marvin stayed at the Mint Hotel downtown back in 1966 and Vegas Vic, the huge 40-foot neon waving cowboy across the street at the Pioneer Club bothered him, especially when Vic would say "Howdy, Pardner" every 15 minutes. Marvin complained and the management forever turned off the recording to the future bliss of nearby guests. Vegas Vic finally stopped its waving in 1991, but is still there.

Whoa, Moe!

Moe Dalitz was a mobster whose decades of running Vegas casinos gave him a veneer of respectability. However the following encounter shows he was still connected. Boxer Sonny Liston had been drinking and had some words with the 64-year-old Moe. As Liston raised his fist, Dalitz is reported to have stared him in the eyes and said, "If you hit me, nigger, you'd better kill me. Because if you don't I'll make one telephone call and you'll be dead within 24 hours." Now Liston was no Rhodes scholar, but he was smart enough to lower his fist and slink away.

Let There Be Light

The tip of the Luxor pyramid contains a fixed-position spotlight that points directly upward and is the brightest beam in the world at over 42 billion candle power. It is visible from anywhere in the Las Vegas valley at night, and can be seen at flight level from above Los Angeles, over 275 miles away. Engineers claim the light can be observed from space.

All or Nothing

Many erroneous versions of this story abound, but they're usually based on this true one. Benny Binion created history by raising table stakes at his Horseshoe Club. In 1980 a gambler named William Lee Bergstrom asked if he could really bet $1 million. When assured he could, he said he'd be back.

A couple of months later he showed up with a suitcase stuffed with $777,000, even apologizing for not raising the entire million.

Binion let him bet it and he put the whole suitcase on the "Don't Pass" line in craps. The nervous woman rolling the dice "sevened out" in three rolls, and Ted Binion escorted the lucky guy out to his car. He returned several times over the next few years, betting, and winning, amounts from $90,000 to $590,000. Then in November 1984, he arrived with an even $1 million. Again betting it all on the "Don't Pass" line, this time the shooter made seven, winning on the first roll. Even though over the years Bergstrom was ahead, losing that million apparently got to him. He committed suicide three months later.

For the Want of A Dollar

It's true. In 2001, a 22-year-old Utah man was playing the Megabucks machine at the Stateline Hotel and Casino in Wendover, Nevada. He was distracted talking to a friend and played one spin for only two dollars instead of the requisite three. Yep, he hit that time and it cost him—losing the $7.96 million jackpot at the time. He did receive a $10,000 consolation prize. Ugh!

Nighttime Scenery

The only nighttime National Scenic Byway in America is Las Vegas Blvd., the glittering Strip from Sunset Road north to Sahara Blvd.

That's Tall

At 1,149 feet, the Stratosphere Tower is the tallest freestanding observation tower in the United States and the tallest building west of the Mississippi River.

The Golden Arm

On May 28, 1989, the late Hawaiian Stanley Fujitake was so hot at the California Club crap table he became the club's charter member of its "Golden Arm Hall of Fame." How hot was he? He held the dice for 3 hours, 6 minutes, making 118 straight rolls. The casino's hall of fame now lists about 200 hot shooters who held the dice for one hour or more—but nobody has yet made it close to Fujitake's feat.

The Fremont Hotel & Casino has similar recognition called the Sharpshooters Circle, about 25 people who have held the dice for 50 or more rolls. Again, nobody close to 118 rolls.

Benny's Offer

Benny Binion had a memory and took care of his friends, one of whom was California author Jack Holder's grandfather, D. M. Sampley, a Piper aircraft distributer. In 1979, after Jack ferried in a small plane for his granddad, he joined the older man with Binion at Benny's Horseshoe restaurant booth "office."

"Last time I saw you Jack, you were in diapers," chortled the casino man. "Your grandpa's family to me, so if there's anything you might need in my town, you just let me know. And I mean *anything*," he added with a wink.

Jack flew in a few more craft for his granddad over the next few months and always went to the Horseshoe. Once, while playing Blackjack, he noticed an attractive cocktail waitress named Irene giving him the eye. After a while, the pit boss approached Jack and whispered, "That Irene is a doll, eh? The boss sent word to remember what he said. Anything you want, Jack, just let me know."

Jack almost dropped his cards, but that was pure Benny Binion. No limits, no strings, and taking care of people.

"Welcome" to an Icon

In 1959 a small sign company named Western Neon won a $4,000 bid from Clark County to construct a welcome sign for the south end of the Strip. Western's Betty Willis got the assignment, drew the letters by hand and placed them in an eye-catching diamond shape outlined with neon and lights, added coins spelling out "Welcome" and a twinkling star. Her result has become one of the best known images in the world. The sign was listed in May 2009 on the National Register of Historic Places by the Department of the Interior.

Las Vegas Welcome

Whorehouse or School?

Sen. Harry Reid (D.-NV) admitted in his book *The Good Fight* that by the time he was born in Searchlight in 1939 prostitution had replaced mining as the leading industry there. There was a law that prohibited prostitution or selling alcohol within so many feet of a school. So when it was discovered that one club was in violation, they did what you might expect Nevadans to do—they moved the school!

Liberal Booze Laws
Tipplers Welcome

I t's noticeable to arriving visitors, booze is. People with open alcoholic beverages are everywhere. They are out on the sidewalks, in casinos, and in markets and shops, carrying open bottles, cans, plastic cups of beer, plastic hi-ball glasses, and fancy fluted glasses of colorful exotic drinks. Kinda makes the Skid Row tippler and his flask take a back seat to the real boozers—the tourists.

Folks who quickly get into the act with their own container know that back home they could never get away with such public flaunting of liquor. The laws in most states run the gamut from counties that are totally dry to all sorts of restrictive state and municipal laws. In most places the venues and times booze can be sold is tightly regulated, as is keeping the beverages within the walls of the drinking establishments. And so on.

Now Las Vegas is a 24-hour town and the laws support that. Nevada liquor laws are different and have evolved into the most liberal in the U.S. Even Tijuana has laws about open drinks in public places.

Most notably, there are no legally-mandated closure days, or even hours, for Nevada establishments serving alcoholic drinks. And there are no days or hours during which a store may *not* sell liquor. Alcohol can be purchased 24/7 from any licensed Nevada business whenever it is open and wants to be selling drinks and/or packaged liquor. The only Nevada alcohol restriction is the legal age minimum of 21 for drinking, purchasing, and possessing alcohol.

Nevada state law today even makes public intoxication legal and *prohibits* any county or city law from making it a public offense. Public intoxication is at least a misdemeanor in most states. The Nevada exceptions are if intoxication is an element in a civil or criminal offense, such as DUI. Laws do prohibit providing alcohol to minors, fake IDs, and/or other crimes, but boozing, or even drunkenness by itself is fine, and welcomed. The laws haven't always been that liberal, nor the interpretation or punishment meted out that consistent.

Boulder City was set up as a dry town and booze was not legal there until 1969 when the state laws prohibiting counties and municipalities from making booze illegal were enacted.

For trivia buffs, there is still one dry Nevada municipality, Panaca, a town settled by Mormons in 1864. Originally part of Utah, Panaca was redrawn by Congress into Nevada in 1866. Panaca remains dry only because it was grandfathered into the state law.

suffices.

Six Months in Jail

Before booze laws became more liberal in the late 1960s and 1970s, public drunkenness in Las Vegas was definitely not tolerated. And Municipal Court Judge Richards was the one to enforce the rule. Longtime police officers all have their favorite Judge Richards stories, from way back before 1973 when the City of Las Vegas Police Department merged with the county officers to become the Las Vegas Metropolitan Police Department.

It seems the Skid Row tipplers liked to get off the hot streets during the dog days of a desert summer. And Judge Richards was quick to oblige. A young officer named Dennis Larsen who would eventually retire as a Lieutenant recalls his first arrest in 1971, "His name was Clarence Creel and Judge Richards wanted to give him six months in jail for public drunkenness. I started to advise Creel on how to get the sentence reduced and he looked me incredulously and said, 'You must be new here, boy!' Old Clarence was looking forward to the food and a bed." Six months was the standard sentence in those days and those who shifted between the streets and the jail mostly welcomed it. After the Metropolitan Police Department was formed, Judge Richards retired and the state began enforcing (or non-enforcing) the relaxed drinking laws from hard-nosed to soft-liberal. Maybe those skid row boozers of the 1960s and early 1970s did not mind sitting in jail for six months, but that's hardly any way to treat a tourist. Let 'em walk around anywhere they want. Booze is just another Las Vegas attraction in the city that never sleeps.

Scandals Erupt Everywhere
When Reality Fails to Shock

Nevadans are hard to shock anymore. Just when they think nothing can "top this one," something does. The scandals that constantly erupt across the entire Silver State emerge from every corner of society, and like windblown sand from a desert dust storm, they infiltrate everything to settle as part of the state's unique personality. The scandals are not limited to boorish celebrities and threatening mobsters. Politicians and businessmen have often led the scandal list from the early days of statehood to the present. The huge amounts of money in Nevada have proved too tempting for many. And the law has sometimes been bent.

Unsolved murders have long been a part of Nevadan lore, and still are. So are sullied politicians, from back in 1901 when Senator Clark (Clark County namesake) was caught trying to bribe four legislators with $34,000 to get elected, to the present. There's no shortage of tongue-wagging shockers. Here are a few.

Governor Gibbons

Republican Governor Jim Gibbons (2007—2011) had been accused of plagiarism, favoring donors, sexual assault, and corruption—while a congressman. After elected governor in 2006, he'd been accused of land deals, influence peddling, undeclared donations, and hiring an undocumented nanny. He endured a difficult and titillating divorce and also saw his approval rating drop to as low as 10%. One female blackjack dealer summed up public sentiment by saying, "Jim Gibbons is an embarrassment."

The conservative was defeated in the 2010 Republican primary by Attorney General Brian Sandoval (2011—) , who won the seat over Senator Harry Reid's son Rory Reid (D.).

Then There is Ensign

In a bizarre situation, Republican Senator John Ensign (2001—) admitted that during 2008, he had an affair with a campaign staffer, who was also a longtime family friend. But that's not all. The Christian conservative then fired her and her husband in 2008, giving her a $25,000 severance package. Then it turns out that Ensign's parents made a $96,000 "gift" to the woman and her husband.

Senator Ensign is facing an investigation from the Senate Select Committee on Ethics concerning potential felony violations of lobbying laws, and in March 2011 withdrew from the 2012 Senate race.

Federal Judge Impeached

The only sitting U.S. federal judge ever impeached was Nevadan Harry Claiborne, a former Las Vegas city cop and later law partner of Las Vegas Mayor Oscar Goodman. He was impeached by the U.S. House of Representatives and convicted by the U.S. Senate for tax evasion in 1986. He was charged with accepting a $30,000 bribe from Mustang Ranch brothel owner Joe Conforte to get the FBI off his back.

He was convicted for failing to pay taxes on more than $100,000 and went to prison in 1986, serving 16 months. Back practicing law in 1987, he began suffering from health problems and eventually shot himself to death in 2004.

G-Sting

Las Vegas strip club owner (Jaguars and Cheetahs) Michael Galardi admitted that he paid between $200,000 and $400,000 to "certain public officials" to sway political matters his way. The operation called "G-Sting" netted three Clark County Commissioners—Dario Herrera, Lance Malone, and Mary Kincaid-Chauncey—who were busted, convicted, and jailed, while a fourth, former commissioner Erin Kenny cut a plea deal.

U.S. District Judge Larry Hacks called the 2007 G-Sting political corruption case "some of the rankest corruption of local government that has ever occurred in Nevada." Well, that's saying a lot.

Sting — Operation Yobo

An earlier (1983) big corruption case saw the downfall of five popular political leaders, Nevada State Senators Floyd Lamb and Gene Echols, Clark County Commissioners Woodrow Wilson and Jack Petitti, and Reno City Councilman Joe McClelland in an FBI sting. Lamb, brother of popular former Clark County sheriff Ralph Lamb, was the FBI sting's initial target, but greed snared the others as well. FBI agent Steve Rybar discussed a $15 million loan deal and Lamb allegedly wanted a 1% "finder's fee."

The others indicted in the scandal, called Operation Yobo by the FBI, were convicted of accepting lesser bribes. All five served time.

Financing the Final Four

The NCAA charged University of Nevada, Las Vegas (UNLV) basketball coach Jerry Tarkanian in 1976 with 10 violations of its rules, including recruiting players with criminal backgrounds and weak academic credentials. One of the charges alleged that a player received a B grade in a class he never attended. UNLV was found guilty and fired Tarkanian. The coach sued, and in October 1977 was granted a permanent injunction prohibiting the suspension. Say what?

Tarkanian continued to field winning teams, four times making it to the final four and wining all the marbles in 1990. The scandal that got his resignation in 1992 was when the *Review-Journal* published photos of his star players in a hot tub with a convicted sports fixer.

Merchandise With Legs

Scandals continued to plague UNLV. In 2007, eight students (five football players, two track team members, and one cheerleader) were arrested for stealing merchandise from an upscale department store in the Forum Shops.

One member worked there and rang up piddling amounts for the others and they walked out with their arms full. The clerk, a freshman football player, admitted to doing it at least 10 times and offered to return about $1,600 of it. Wonder what grades they were getting.

Tailhook — One Rowdy Convention

The Tailhook Association –a private organization for active, reserve, and retired naval aviators—has held its annual convention in Las Vegas every year since 1963. They may have been obnoxious before, but in 1991, they set new highs, or lows, for ugly behavior. Held at the Las Vegas Hilton that year, the group's vulgar and unlawful behavior that included groping women resulted in 90 instances of indecent assault, $23,000 in property damage, and some major forced retirements and reassignments in the naval hierarchy. What happens in Vegas doesn't always stay in Vegas.

Fate of a Union Man

Al Bramlet, who rose from dishwasher to head the powerful, 22,000-employee Culinary Workers Union, made a lot of enemies on both sides of the table. He was hated by other union leaders, his own rank and file members, and establishments that tried to resist his encroaching union. Seems they had firebomb problems. Oops! He apparently made one enemy too many—the mob.

On February 24, 1977 Bramlet flew back to Vegas from a short trip to Reno. Seen waiting for him at the airport were three men. Bramlet vanished and his body was found in the desert by hikers three weeks later. The reason for his untimely demise was presumably over a portion of the culinary local's $42 million pension fund. Some $16 million of the fund had already been loaned out and backed by Las Vegas gambling bosses.

Feisty Frank

Frank Sinatra got his way in Las Vegas, until Howard Hughes intervened, that is. After learning that his casino credit line had been suspended by Hughes, an angry and drunk Sinatra drove a golf cart through a plate-glass window. Sinatra reportedly threw chips in the face of a casino employee and defied hotel security officers who tried to quiet him. He staggered into the Garden Room, the Sands' 24-hour restaurant, where he found casino manager Carl Cohen and overturned his table. Shortly after that, "blue eyes" moved his show to Caesars Palace.

Who Killed Rapper Superstar?

Tupac Shakur, a rap music superstar, was in a car heading to a nightclub with Death Row Records owner Marion "Suge" Knight after a Mike Tyson fight on September 7, 1996. A gunman from the back seat of a passing white Cadillac opened fire and four bullets struck Shakur, who died six days later from the wounds.

His murder was never solved, though it is thought to be connected to an East Coast-West Coast gangsta-rap rivalry. What stunned Las Vegans was the brazenness of the act in a crowded location.

Minxx Shootings

In February 2007 NFL "bad boy" Adam "Pacman" Jones was involved in an altercation with a Minxx strip club dancer, allegedly slamming her head on the stage. He left, but according to the club owner a member of Jones' entourage returned with a gun and opened fire, damaging equipment and hitting three people, including the security guard who was shot twice.

Former professional wrestler Tommy Urbanski was also shot rendering him paralyzed from the waist down. Jones insisted he did not know the shooter and ended up cutting a plea deal admitting to conspiracy to commit disorderly conduct, a misdemeanor.

Jones was later sued by Urbanski and his wife in civil court, also contending that Jones had "bitten his left ankle" in the earlier scuffle.

The cornerback apparently paid $15,000 to various people involved in the episode. A Tennessee Titan at the time, Jones was suspended for the season, and later went to the Dallas Cowboys, who cut him at the end of the 2009 season because of his continuing off-field antics.

O.J. Busted

While Los Angeles defense attorneys got O. J. Simpson a "not guilty" verdict in the murder of his wife and another man, he wasn't so lucky in Las Vegas. O.J. Simpson, the man civil courts held responsible for those wrongful deaths, went to jail for a lesser crime. In September 2007, Simpson and a few others entered a memorabilia collector's office at the Palace Station Hotel & Casino where weapons were brandished and threats were made. The former football-playing criminal was found guilty of 12 counts in October 2008 and sentenced to prison for nine years.

He's Too Young

Paris and Nicky Hilton created a big ugly scene at Pure nightclub on New Year's Eve 2005 after Paris' 20-year-old boyfriend Stavros Niarchos, grandson of a Greek shipping magnate, was denied admission. They returned the next night to apologize.

Trashing the Place

Around the same time, Niarchos and his buddies made such a mess of their Hard Rock Hotel room with a pillow fight that he had to put $25,000 on a credit card. Apparently a broken sprinkler head caused a lot of water damage. While Daddy okayed the bill, young and clueless Niarchos couldn't understand the fuss, saying, "It's all going to be paid for."

Paris — Continued

Paris Hilton was busted for possession of cocaine while a car passenger in front of the Wynn Hotel and Casino. Shunning the adverse publicity, Wynn promptly barred the self-indulgent socialite from entering their properties. This prompted TV personality Jay Leno to remark, "I'm not sure what Paris is banned for, but I think we can rule out card counting."

The "Sin" in Sin City

Privé nightclub at Planet Hollywood, a top "in" place was a favorite "sin place" it seems. The Gaming Control Board busted Privé for numerous violations, including prevalent drug use inside the club, prostitution, and accusations that Privé employees have assaulted customers, both physically and sexually.

During the initial 12 months after opening in November 2006, emergency crews responded to 61 calls that included reports of overdose, rape, and traumatic injuries. In 2007 police also responded to 52 reports of assault or battery, along with reports of fighting, guns, and prostitution. The club was also cited in March 2008 for allowing topless or lewd activity among customers.

Best not pass out there either. The management was also accused of tossing out drunken customers and leaving them unattended in the casino or parking lot, sometimes in "various states of consciousness." Planet Hollywood owners agreed to pay a $750,000 fine.

"Beautiful" Murderers

Craig Titus and his wife Kelly Ryan were "in" people, both beautiful, respected health celebrities, gurus who seemingly had it all: money, prestige, and a loyal following. They were famed bodybuilders who conversely were destroying their bodies through heavy drug use and a wild party mentality.

They went too far in December 2005, when their 28-year old personal assistant, Melissa James, was found dead in the couple's torched-out Jaguar. There were allegations of a love triangle and even of Titus earlier trying to arrange a murder-for-hire scenario. The couple fled to Massachusetts where they were later arrested. They pled guilty to the murder and both received long prison sentences. The titillating true story is told in Glen Puit's *Fire In The Desert*.

Busted by Blow Flies
THε WiTcH oF LAS VεqAS

A nother desert disappearance had tongues wagging far beyond Las Vegas. The alcoholic mother of Brookey Lee West vanished from her Las Vegas apartment in 1998. When asked, West said her mother went to stay with her brother in California.

However, in February 2001 Las Vegas police responded to employees complaining about an odor coming from a self-storage unit. There, they found the decayed body of West's mother, Christine Smith, stuffed in a garbage can. There were also books on witchcraft and the occult in the storage locker.

The authorities suspected West of killing her mother, with whom she had frequently fought. However, so much time (3 years) had passed that a medical examiner testified that he was unable to determine how Mrs. Smith died. West said her mother had died peacefully of natural causes, and that she had panicked and crammed the decaying remains into the garbage can. The case was solved with forensic evidence as a prominent entomologist determined that blow flies, insects that usually appear on corpses right after death, were nowhere to be seen on the body. Instead, most of the larvae found came from scuttle flies, or "coffin flies," insects that cannibalize dead bodies after they have undergone initial decomposition. The significance of the blow flies' absence meant that Smith had to have been put into the garbage can either directly after she died or while she was still alive, barring the blow flies' access to the corpse. (Coffin flies, on the other hand, could have gotten to the body because they often tunnel through tiny nooks and crannies.)

That indicated that West lied about what she did with her mother, and after only two hours of deliberation, a jury found Brookey Lee West guilty of her mother's murder. West is currently serving a life sentence at a prison in southern Nevada, but the strange bizarre story goes beyond the single act of matricide.

Journalist Glenn Puit pursued the strange case and uncovered a pattern of abuse and as he called it, "...a 40-year saga of crazy criminal behavior. When you put it all together, it's truly frightening." Back in 1961, West's mother Smith tried to kill a married man by blasting him with a shotgun after he broke off their affair. The man survived, and Smith spent five years in a prison for attempted murder. Seven-year-old West and her brother were then sent to live in an orphanage. In later years Smith bragged about the shooting.

West's father, Leroy Smith, was just as strange, a gun-toting white supremacist who worshipped Satan and practiced witchcraft.

Then Brookey West was herself embroiled in a custody battle in the mid-1980s with the father of her 8-year-old daughter. West wanted to give the girl up for adoption, but the child's father Ronald Viramontes refused to sign away his parental rights. So West's father Leroy sent Viramontes a threatening letter that included pentagrams and satanic curses. Four days after the letter, a masked man knocked on Viramontes' door and shot his 86-year-old grandmother in the chest. She survived, and the case remains unsolved.

The violence continued. Leroy Smith's new wife Diane believed West turned her husband against her in an attempt to take over his finances as he was dying of cancer. She claimed West, with Smith's encouragement, zapped her with a stun gun that would have killed her if a blanket hadn't partially blocked the electric jolt. No charges were filed in the incident. "She had a history, along with her father, of trying to eliminate people when they got in their way," Clark County prosecutor Scott Mitchell said of Brookey Lee West. "Once you showed yourself to be in opposition to anything Brookey Lee West wanted to do, your life was in danger."

Take the case of Howard Simon St. John, a down-and-out alcoholic and drug addict who was in a detox center in California. West, at the time a successful technical writer who drove a Jaguar, went to the detox center where her mother attended Alcoholics Anonymous meetings, but she seemed to be trolling for a new husband. She met St. John and within a month they were married. Shortly thereafter St. John told friends that West wanted him to burn her Jaguar so she could collect on the insurance. Days later, the car was torched.

About a week later, West shot St. John in the neck during a domestic dispute. When he was released from the hospital, St. John admitted to an insurance investigator about the Jaguar scam. St. John foolishly reunited with West, and two weeks later his body was found in Sequoia National Forest—shot in the back. Police recommended murder charges against West, but for some reason prosecutors decided not to file a case. When Clark County prosecutors heard of the St. John murder, they were more determined than ever to convict West in her mother's death. During the three years her mother's body was rotting in the storage unit, West collected her mother's Social Security checks and continued to study witchcraft.

Prosecutor Mitchell said West, then 52, was a victim of her success. "She just got overconfident," he said. "She got away with so much for so long, she just became a little too casual." (See Glenn Puit's book: *Witch: The True Story of Las Vegas' Most Notorious Female Killer*).

Murder in the Desert
The Black Widow

S oap opera writers could well hone their trade by observing the titillating goings on in Las Vegas.

Take the story of Margaret Rudin, dubbed "The Black Widow" by the press, in which public opinion shifted with each new revelation. Convicted in 2001 of murdering her fifth husband, real estate magnate Ronald Rudin, for $11 million, the Nevada Supreme Court ruled against her final appeal in May 2010.

This riveting story has it all: money, an adulterous affair, multiple marriages, insecurities, jealousies, a brutal murder, and a wife on the lam. Rudin's body was driven to a remote area and stuffed in a trunk where it was set ablaze, and her subsequent flight made her an FBI Top 10 fugitive. Add a pathetically laughable attorney, mix it with three appeals, the first denied, the second approved, and you have all the ingredients for an award-winning soap.

Margaret Rudin (née Frost) was born in 1943 and was shuttled around 15 states in her first 15 years. She divorced her first husband, with whom she had two children, citing emotional abuse. Her second marriage lasted from 1974 to 1976, and few people, including her third husband Philip Brown, even knew about him. Then Brown himself paid her $10,000 in lieu of alimony when they divorced in 1979 after a short marriage. This time the husband filed against Margaret citing emotional cruelty.

Margaret relocated to Las Vegas in 1980 sharing a mobile home with others before she met and married Richard Krafve, a struggling businessman, but one with a large inheritance from his father. Krafve was astute enough to make Margaret sign a prenuptial agreement but still paid her $32,000 when they divorced in 1987. This time she claimed that he was abusive toward her.

With her children grown and gone, she told friends she wanted to meet a real cowboy. At a Las Vegas church, she met Ronald Rudin, who enjoyed affecting the Western look complete with cowboy hats and boots. After they married in 1987, Margaret Rudin became so jealous of her new husband she began to follow him, including placing a surveillance telephone recording machine in his office. Rudin himself got antsy about his bride and made beneficiary changes during their first year together. In 1988, he filed for divorce, but they reconciled.

While still uneasy in his relationship, Rudin secretly signed a document stating that if he should die violently, the suspect or suspects in his death would be denied any inheritance he left them. Yet, for some reason Mr. Rudin still increased his wife's share of his business to $11 million. Their marriage suffered all sorts of outrageous ups and downs until December 1994, when the real estate man disappeared. Mrs. Rudin, then 51, did not report him missing for four days.

After a month-long search, his skeletal remains were discovered in remote Eldorado Canyon about 45 miles from Las Vegas. His body had been crammed in an antique trunk purchased by Margaret just months before his disappearance, driven there and set ablaze. An autopsy revealed that he had been shot.

Margaret Rudin quickly became a suspect but fled to Arizona, where following an airing of *America's Most Wanted* television show, she was recognized by a neighbor. Before they could arrest her, she fled again, to Massachusetts, and lived with a firefighter for two years before her eventual capture in 1999. Her boyfriend in the East didn't even know she was wanted.

But the plot thickened as in Las Vegas, police uncovered that she was having an adulterous affair with an Israeli man and theorized that he might have helped her with her husband's murder and/or disposal of the body. It was determined Rudin was shot in the head while he slept. Her alleged accomplice Yehuda Sharon had rented a van the night of Rudin's disappearance and was given "transactional immunity," but continued to deny any knowledge of the crime.

She was brought to trial in 2001 and it quickly became a media circus. It came out that both Margaret and Ronald had affairs. Also among those testifying were Rudin's three former wives, one of whom called him an abusive alcoholic.

Margaret had had the alleged crime-scene bedroom remodeled and repainted after her husband's disappearance. Still, matching blood samples led to a murder conviction and in May 2001 Margaret Rudin was sentenced to life in prison with the opportunity for parole in 20 years. She was definitely not helped by her pro-bono attorney, one Michael J. Amador, who was as valuable as his free counsel. Trying to make a name for himself he accepted the case, bragged about how great he was during his opening statement, and his overall performance was so bad and bizarre at least one potential juror complained to the judge. Another called him "The laughingstock of the jury room."

Rather than have a mistrial declared, Amador got two attorneys to assist at the eleventh hour. After the trial ended, Rudin got new lawyers who made Amador the focus of their appeal. Faced with a long list of incompetence, Amador surprisingly responded with what would be construed as a threat. Nevertheless, the 2002 appeal was denied by the Nevada Supreme Court.

Later attorneys in their motion for a new trial argued that Amador was unprepared and spent his off hours during the major trial at strip clubs. He was frequently unprepared for witnesses, the lawyers alleged, and secretly pursued book and movie deals on the case. He was even accused of leaking information to the *National Enquirer*. That convinced District Judge Sally Loehrer in December 2008 to rule that attorneys for Margaret Rudin weren't prepared to defend her at her 2001 trial. She also ruled that Rudin's main attorney at the time, Michael Amador, wasn't effective.

For his part, Amador remained unfazed and unrepentant about his performance on the sensational trial. His behavior still seems as bizarre as ever. In November 2009 he was arrested in a pub parking lot fight in which he pulled a semi-automatic from his waistband and shattered a car window. As for the Black Widow, Margaret Rudin? Well, her 10-week trial was one of the longest criminal trials in Las Vegas' history and was telecast on *Court TV*, covered by CBS *48 Hours*, and spawned a book titled *If I Die…*(by Michael Fleeman) in reference to Ron Rudin's changed will if he died violently.

Margaret Rudin has spent most of a decade behind bars and after her final appeal was denied it looks like she will remain there.

The Binion Family Saga
Money, Drugs, and Murder

I f you haven't yet found all the elements for a good soap opera in the other scandals, consider the suspicious death of Lonnie "Ted" Binion. It had a little of everything: inherited casino wealth, scion of a prominent family, murder, a secreted treasure, drug addiction, infidelity, a topless dancer, the dancer's "other" boyfriend, mob associates, burglary, sibling rivalry, and much more. In fact, Hollywood screenwriters would really be hard pressed to top this scandalous true Las Vegas story. Then again, the story of Ted's dad is pretty interesting too. We'll start there.

Benny Binion

Las Vegas casino legend Lester "Benny" Binion was a street-smart Texas bootlegger who created Binion's Horseshoe Casino in downtown Las Vegas.

In Texas during the 1930s, Benny was twice convicted for bootlegging. He graduated to numbers, running an illegal lottery and organizing crap games. With so much money around, Benny began carrying three pistols with him at all times. He apparently needed them, too. He killed a fellow bootlegger in 1931 in an argument. His defense was he thought the guy was going to stab him. He was convicted of first degree murder and was given only a two-year suspended sentence because the dead man was a known "bad guy" and violent killer himself. Such was justice, Texas-style.

Binion used his guns again in 1936 when it was reported that he and a henchman had stalked a rival numbers operator and emptied their 45s into the unarmed man. Benny then shot himself in the armpit and turned himself in. He said the guy pulled a gun on him and shot him as he was raising his hands. Binion then allegedly grabbed the man's gun, turned it away, pulled his own gun and shot the rival dead. He was acquitted on this one—his self defense argument held up.

By the early '40s, Binion was politically connected and the reigning mob boss in Dallas. The Texas violence got worse, and several of Binion's rivals died, including the Fort Worth mob boss who was murdered. The Chicago Mob then entered the Dallas market; additionally, Binion lost some contacts in the 1946 elections, and so he headed for greener pastures, Las Vegas.

One of Binion's Dallas enemies, Herb Noble, followed him to Nevada and their feud made the Hatfields and McCoys look like a roadrunner cartoon. Noble had a lot of enemies and before he was eventually killed in 1951 by a homemade bomb placed near his mailbox, he had survived over 11 attempts on his life. He was shot in the back; his car was riddled with bullets, and he found dynamite wired to his car starter, for example. After his wife was killed in a car bomb attempt, Noble forever blamed Binion and tried to even the score. In fact, he was caught loading his private plane with bombs and a map of Binion's Las Vegas house.

Benny, schooling-shy but street savvy, found lots of opportunity, legal opportunity, in Las Vegas. In 1947 Binion bought into the Las Vegas Club on Fremont Street with J. Kell Houssels Sr. Later in 1951 he opened his own casino, the Horseshoe Casino, down the street. Binion became famous for creating the biggest action in town by raising crap table limits tenfold over the competition to $5,000. He knew how to bring in gamblers and later started the World Series of Poker, creating an important casino game out of what had been a backroom operation.

The law caught up with Binion. He lost his gambling license and went to Fort Leavenworth federal penitentiary in 1953 for tax evasion. He was forced to sell controlling interests of the casino to pay the legal fees. He served 3½ years and the family later regained control of the Horseshoe but Benny had to serve as a "consultant" as he was denied a gaming license. Son Jack became president; son Ted was casino manager, and wife Teddy Jane ran the casino cage. In 1970, son Jack began hosting the World Series of Poker (WSOP) at the Horseshoe, eventually becoming the largest poker tournament in the world. The $10,000 WSOP event has grown from the eight people who originally played to many hundreds today. Poker was not a big profit maker for casinos, but the increasing popularity brought in the people. Benny Binion knew people and their habits. Realizing that everyone was "comping" the big players, he decided to pay attention to the smaller players. He advised, "If you want to get rich, make little people feel like big people."

In addition to offering the highest limits and the poker tournaments, Binion's offered $1 million on display so folks could get their picture taken standing next to a million dollars.

In 1988, the Horseshoe expanded by acquiring the Mint Las Vegas, a high-rise hotel next door, a move that his children had to talk the unwilling Benny into. He saw no need for a hotel for his casino, but he did like the added casino space. That expansion provided room for Binion's first poker room.

Benny Binion, a true Wild West character, with big 10-gallon hat, cowboy shirt, and a gun handy all his life, died of heart failure on Christmas Day, 1989. He was a tough guy but an innovative businessman who changed the way casinos operated in Las Vegas. Among the 1,000 people at his funeral, casino developer Steve Wynn said, "He was either the toughest gentleman I ever knew, or the gentlest tough person I ever met." U.S. Senator Harry Reid, in reflecting on Binion's contributions, said: "He's my hero. Nevada is a better place because of him!"

The Controversial Death of Ted Binion

Lonnie "Ted" Binion, born in Texas in 1943, had an older brother, Jack, and three sisters: Becky, Brenda, and Barbara. Ted was involved early on in his father's casino. As casino manager, Ted was the public face and became well known. He loved living the high life, partying with high-profile guests, and flirting with attractive women.

Ted was intelligent, an avid reader, and mathematically gifted where he could easily mentally calculate odds in gambling transactions. However, he developed a severe marijuana and heroin problem. He was arrested in 1986 on drug trafficking charges and began drawing attention from the Nevada Gaming Commission also for his association with mobster "Fat Herbie" Blitzstein, a former pal of Tony "The Ant" Spilotro. Ted was stripped of his gaming license for his continued association with Blitzstein. Their friendship ended in 1997, however, when Herbie caught three bullets in the back of his head, gangland-style. In 1998, Ted was also banned from even entering the family's casino and was forced to sell his 20% interest to his younger sister, Becky Binion Behnen.

On top of his drug and mob problems, Ted became enamored with Sandy Murphy, a topless dancer at Cheetah's, a club he frequented. His wife decided she'd had enough of Ted's infidelities and left, taking their daughter with her to Texas. Ted and Sandy began living together and the Gaming Control Board also began surveilling his girlfriend.

After his banishment from the family casino, Ted had a dilemma. Inside a big vault in the basement of the Horseshoe Club was Ted's huge silver collection. It totaled six tons of silver bullion, casino chips, paper currency, and over 100,000 rare coins—worth at least $7 million total. Ted either had to sell the cache or relocate it to a secure spot. So Ted hired Rick Tabish, a guy he met in a restaurant urinal, to help him build a place for it and move it. Rick was a contractor who owned a small trucking company, MRT Transport. Ted owned a vacant lot in downtown Pahrump, Nevada, about 60 miles from Las Vegas and wanted a concrete bunker built there.

So Rick constructed a 12-foot-deep concrete bunker on the desert floor and MRT trucks were used to transport the silver to the vault. The only two people who had the combination to the vault were Binion and Tabish. Ted trusted Tabish; in fact, sometimes the three of them, Ted, Sandy, and Rick, socialized publicly together.

Most likely Ted never knew the facts about Tabish, the son of a wealthy man who himself had a hard time making a go of anything. He was involved in several thefts and burglaries and was convicted of shipping cocaine via FedEx. Knowledge about Rick Tabish's past might have changed things for Ted. Or maybe not.

The city was then stunned to learn that on September 17, 1998, Ted Binion was found dead in his Las Vegas home by his girlfriend, former stripper Sandy Murphy. Empty pill bottles were found near the body, and an autopsy revealed that he died of a lethal combination of the prescription sedative Xanax and heroin, with traces of Valium. While the initial cause of death appeared to be a drug overdose, Las Vegas homicide detectives suspected that the scene had been staged, as his body didn't show the typical signs of a drug overdose.

The scandalous and salacious story was uncovered bit by bit, and a public thirsty for more lapped it up. It turned out that for some time Murphy and Tabish had been romantically involved, and Binion was beginning to suspect that Murphy was cheating on him, thus creating the proverbial triangle.

Then the Pahrump vault was discovered two days after Binion died, as sheriff's deputies caught and arrested Tabish on the site unearthing the silver. Oops.

In June 1999, Sandy Murphy and her lover Rick Tabish were arrested for Binion's murder, as well as for conspiracy, robbery, grand larceny and burglary. They were each charged with murder and burglary charges connected to the removal of his fortune from the vault on the desert floor in Pahrump.

In 2000, in a widely publicized trial Murphy and Tabish were convicted of murdering Ted Binion and both received life sentences. The prosecution convinced the jury that Murphy and Tabish had conspired to kill Binion and steal his riches, drugging him into unconsciousness and suffocating him.

But the show is not over. The Nevada Supreme Court overturned the convictions in 2003 because of improper jury instructions, and after a second trial was held in 2004, the pair was found not guilty of Binion's murder, though they were convicted for conspiring to commit burglary and/or larceny, burglary and grand larceny. It seems the Nevada dramas are never over when they're over.

Becky Binion Behnen and the Horseshoe

Becky Behnen already had Ted's 20%, and she acquired controlling interest of the family casino after an ugly legal battle with her older brother Jack. It ended with Jack being bought out, only retaining a token 1% interest, necessary for him to keep a Nevada gaming license. Jack moved on to other gambling interests. In July 2006, he became chairman of Wynn International, responsible for opening the Wynn Macau. He continues working with Wynn Resorts in a consulting role. Their other sister Barbara also developed a drug problem and had committed suicide in 1977. In fact, the defense for Tabish and Murphy tried to indicate that suicide ran in the family. Becky went on to have numerous problems with the Horseshoe. She became president while her husband, Nick, took over as manager. Among several unpopular measures, she removed the iconic $1 million backdrop display. She changed how poker fees were handled, and closed a restaurant which her dad had used as an office. The longtime profitable casino became debt-ridden.

She made enemies with other casino owners and several of the unions. In 2002 the Culinary Workers Union filed a complaint that she hadn't signed the collective insurance and pension payments. They reached a settlement in 2003; she signed the collective bargaining agreement and agreed to pay the owed money. However, the Horseshoe still fell behind and judgments were made allowing seizure by the union.

In 2004, regulators closed the casino to ensure owner Becky Binion Behnen could pay the property's mounting debts. The casino was sold to Harrah's Entertainment in early 2004. Harrah's then sold it to MTR Gaming Group who reopened in April 2004 renaming it Binion's Gambling Hall and Hotel.

The current owner is Terry Caudill, whose TLC Casino Enterprises acquired Binion's in January 2008 for $32 million. He too has been unable to make it profitable and the property's 365 hotel rooms closed in December 2009.

The saga of the Horseshoe is the saga of the Benny Binion family itself. There was bold daring, innovation, scandal, and then mismanagement, sort of a microcosm of Las Vegas itself.

Whales and Big Tippers
MONEY TO BURN

I n Las Vegas they call them "whales," for the largesse that dominates their actions. By some definitions just to be in that cetacean category, you must be willing to gamble about a half million ($500,000)—that's *each hour* you're playing!

Casinos do everything they can to harpoon a whale to play at their establishment, rolling out all possible luxurious perks. However, getting a whale aboard can be just as dangerous as the whale hunts of the nineteenth century. Even a mid-size casino can end up in financial jeopardy if a whale hits a hot streak.

Las Vegas hotel/casino managers figure only about 500 individuals worldwide make the elite list, and the comps are rolled out for them. Along with the best accommodations and dining, casinos do more, lavishing expensive gifts, providing private jet transportation, and even securing U.S. Visas for foreign whales (In fact, about 80% of the whale population is Asian).

Whales generally travel with a big entourage (Bodyguards, hangers-on, beautiful women), and usually tip big, win or lose.

Kerry Packer

By all accounts the biggest whale to have landed in Las Vegas was Australian media tycoon Kerry Packer (1937-2005). Packer gambled around the world and became a true legend due to his incredible betting, with both wins and losses.

He once set a record for the biggest single British gambling loss in 1999 when he dropped almost $28 million in London casinos during a three-week period. However, there were years he would win about $7 million during his annual UK gambling excursions.

In Las Vegas he liked to play seven blackjack hands at a time, making bets up to $375,000 per hand. On one occasion, he was said to have won $33 million at the MGM Grand Casino in Las Vegas. His big win actually caused the value of MGM Grand shares on the New York Stock Exchange to drop a few points the next day!

Then it was reported that he lost about $20 million at the Bellagio when he was stranded there in the aftermath of the 9-11-01 tragedies. The Bellagio dealers liked to see him coming. He regularly would leave a big tip—like $1 million to the dealers there (all 700 dealers shared it, but that's still almost $1,500 each). Previous to the early 1980s when casino rules changed, dealers kept their tips, rarely reporting them. That made dealing at the upscale casinos a lot more attractive.

Packer could be abrasive and unpredictable, but he was not cheap. One true story from the Stratosphere Casino revolves around a Texan who wanted to join his table. Packer turned him down and the Texan said, "Hey, I'm a big player too. I'm worth $100 million." (Some versions of the story say $60 million, but Packer's response actually happened). The Aussie, who was worth about $5 billion at the time, looked at the man, pulled out a coin, and said, "If you really want to gamble, I'll flip you for it."

Not willing to risk his life's fortune on a coin flip, the Texan retreated.

Terrance Watanabe

Terrance Watanabe became a trivia answer by earning a dubious record in 2007. In that one year he lost more than anyone in Las Vegas—almost $127 million, which nearly broke the Nebraska novelty manufacturer. Watanabe inherited the family business and was a philanthropist before the dual addictions of alcohol and gambling got the best of him. Initially losing at the Wynn Resort, his erratic behavior reached the attention of CEO Steve Wynn, who threw him out because of his compulsive drinking and gambling.

Watanabe found a home at Caesars Palace and the Rio, both owned by Harrah's Entertainment. They plied him with a suite and all the freebies he could ever want, including his favorite vodka. Watanabe was not a savvy gambler, choosing games that gave the house the biggest odds, like slots and roulette.

When he did play blackjack, dealers remarked that he ignored the basic game and made poor decisions which increased the house edge. Squirreled out of the city by his sister before he was totally broke, he left unpaid markers for $14.7 million, so Harrah's sued. Watanabe countered claiming that they kept him drunk to stay and play. The casino, supported by state law that says unpaid markers are like checks and a felony, claimed that he made adult decisions and alcohol is no excuse. However the legal issue is not so important in Las Vegas as moral or ethical ones. No pit boss or floor manager was willing to cut the guy off—not while he was so valuable to the casino, drunk and playing poorly or not. He alone accounted for 5.6% of Harrah's gambling revenue that year. That's a few million reasons to "look the other way" when a drunk is playing.

Watanabe, who faces 28 years in prison, has entered a residential treatment facility and moved out of state.

Harrah's Entertainment VP Jan Jones said, "We're in the gambling business. We had no reason to believe that Terry Watanabe was anything other than a big player with huge resources who made an adult decision to bet the money he did. Are we going to provide an environment that keeps him very happy? Of course we are."

Ausaf Umar Siddiqui

Ausaf Umar Siddiqui, like Watanabe, got into the casinos big time. "Omar" as he was called, was a purchasing VP at Frye's Electronics with a major gambling problem. It turns out he set up a shell company to fleece the company of more than $162 million in "kickbacks, $65 million from five vendors alone.

At the casinos, he would get behind and then pay what he owed. According to the IRS he sent more than $120 million to the Las Vegas Sands and MGM Grand companies alone between 2005 and 2008. He considered himself a major whale and loved to play high stakes baccarat. Of course, where there's the appearance of a whale, there are sharks circling. After Omar lost millions in Las Vegas, Donald Trump sent a private jet to fetch him to New Jersey, and gave him a $6 million credit line. He lost the $6 million in a few hours and was subsequently sued by Trump Taj Majal Associates. Of course, he's being sued by a lot of people, and if he ever plays baccarat again, it might be for matches and cigarettes in a grey-bar hotel.

Zhenli Ye Gon

Zhenli Ye Gon is a Mexican businessman of Chinese origin who made his money in the meth business. When he was busted in 2007 with over 500 grams, police also found $205 million hidden in his Mexico City mansion. He left a lot in Las Vegas too, having lost over $120 million at the tables there. A reputable East Coast newspaper reported that the Venetian Resort Hotel Casino appreciated Ye Gon so much it gave him a Rolls Royce.

Other Whales

Another "whale among whales" is Kamel Nacif Borge, a Mexican-born businessman of Lebanese descent. One of Mexico's richest men, he is also one of the world's biggest gamblers. It is reported that with all the money he lost at the Caesars Palace baccarat tables in Las Vegas, he could have bought the place.

Tokyo real estate investor Akio Kashiwagi liked high stakes baccarat and in 1990, dropped $10 million in an Atlantic City casino. He was stabbed to death with over 150 wounds two years later, rumored as revenge by the Japanese organized crime group Yakuza over some business deal.

Other whales who have frequented Las Vegas include Adnan Khashoggi, a Turkish-Saudi Arabian arms dealer, the Sultan of Brunei Hassanal Bolkiah, American sportsman (Lakers owner) Jerry Buss, and *Hustler* publisher Larry Flynt.

Memorable Tips

Mega-whale Kerry Packer and his tips are the dreams Las Vegas is made of. Appreciating the service from an MGM Grand cocktail waitress, he asked her if she had a mortgage. She said yes, so he asked her to bring it in the next day. She did and he paid it off for her—all $150,000! The free-spending "rain-makers" (Those who shower nightclubs with piles of currency) are obviously big tippers. Boxer Floyd Mayweather Jr. routinely tips $100, and once tipped $50,000 at one of his favorite strip bars. Actor Jamie Foxx and basketball player Dennis Rodman are also big tippers. Rodman is a big player too, admitting, "I lost $35,000 in less than a week at the Mirage in Las Vegas." Another basketball personality, Charles Barkley, was known for tipping a $500 chip every time he hit his roulette number, whether he was winning or not.

Comedian Drew Carey often tipped $5,000 for the Hard Rock Hotel dealers—and even more than that at the Vegas strip clubs. When the Hard Rock opened, it was reported that tennis star Andre Agassi bought in with $10,000, ran it up to $15,000 and then gave the whole pile to the dealers. Radio personality Howard Stern could not find a casino to allow him to bet $1 million on a single blackjack hand. However, the Hard Rock Casino let him bet $100,000 on one hand. Stern did, won, and gave the proceeds to charity.

Is a BMW Memorable?

It's hard to top Las Vegas stories—it's the one place in the world where anything can happen, and often does. A member of the Las Vegas Pussycat Dolls discovered an admirer really had a crush on her. She wouldn't go out with him but he asked her to meet him at the casino entrance for a gift. There on a flatbed truck was a brand new BMW! Don't know if she reconsidered or not.

The upscale nightclubs and strip clubs often attract free spenders. The VIP section at Tao nightclub in the Venetian has been frequented by outrageous tippers. One guy tipped a total of over $150,000 the first two years the place was open. There have been stories of other $20,000 plus tips being made there, including a $25,000 diamond-studded watch. Pure Nightclub's VIP section gets high rollers too, including the guy who wanted to give a cocktail server $50,000. At first, she refused but her co-servers talked her into accepting it. She "settled" to accept only $20,000.

There are a number of celebrities who frequent Las Vegas and play some serious money. Actor Ben Affleck was seen in 2001 betting three hands of $20,000 each to win up to $660,000. He tipped $100,000 back. Hockey great Wayne Gretzky enjoyed a credit line that allowed him to play up to $25,000 a hand, although he didn't usually play that high.

Casinos generally section off their areas for high rollers, to keep out the curious and smaller players. For example, gamblers at the MGM Grand Mansion are expected to play with $250,000 over two or three days to qualify for their high roller suites.

In addition to the athletes, actors, rappers, musicians and other entertainers, there are entrepreneurs and foreign guests who spend incredible amounts of money in Las Vegas. Oriental visitors sometimes bring the whole family and order exotic foods at special restaurants, not batting an eyelash at dropping $20,000 to $50,000 for one dinner.

The average American family that visits Las Vegas is hard pressed to earn in a year what many others throw away on a weekend. They see a different Las Vegas: inexpensive lodging, bargain buffets, freebies, dollar slots, and $10 blackjack. Then they'll go home and root for a guy who makes more for each three-point basket than the family man earns in a year. They are really two different worlds.

There are those who apparently have money to burn, and Las Vegas casinos do not discourage them. Casino owner Jack Binion once remarked, "I've often thought, if I got really hungry for a good milk shake, how much would I pay for one? People will pay a hundred dollars for a bottle of wine; to me that's not worth it. But I'm not going to say it is foolish or wrong to spend that kind of money, if that's what you want. So if a guy wants to bet twenty or thirty thousand dollars in a poker game that is his privilege."

Famous Sin City Quotes
My Take on Vegas

"What happens in Vegas stays in Vegas."

–Jeff Candido and Jason Hoff, advertising slogan written for the
Las Vegas Convention and Visitors Authority, 2002

"The night before I left Las Vegas I walked out in the desert to look at the moon. There was a jeweled city on the horizon, spires rising in the night, but the jewels were diadems of electric and the spires were the neon of signs ten stories high."

–Norman Mailer

"Presidents and presidential assassins are like Las Vegas and Salt Lake City. Even though one city is all about sin and the other is all about salvation, they are identical, one-dimensional company towns built up by the sheer will of true believers."

–Sarah Vowell

"When we first came here, the city had about 10,000 residents. Nowadays we have more employees than that in our organization."

— Bill Boyd, Boyd Gaming

"For a loser, Vegas is the meanest town on earth."

—Hunter S. Thompson

"It's a corny old gag about Las Vegas, the temporal city if there ever was one, trying to camouflage the hours and retard the dawn, when everybody knows that if you're feeling lucky you're really feeling time in its rawest form, and if you're not feeling lucky, they've got a clock at the bus station."

—Michael Herr

"In Vegas, I got into a long argument with the man at the roulette wheel over what I considered to be an odd number."

—Steven Wright

"In the case of an earthquake hitting Las Vegas, be sure to go straight to the Keno Lounge. Nothing ever gets hit there."

— Author Unknown

"Retirement is like a long vacation in Las Vegas. The goal is to enjoy it the fullest, but not so fully that you run out of money."

—Jonathan Clements

"As for poker, I've stayed away from that, even though when I was in Vegas for Ocean's Eleven, I would get accosted by these guys begging me to play. They just want to take my money. They see me, think "actor" and see some easy money."

— Matt Damon

"I love the live performances and Las Vegas. I also like making films that are being discovered by another generation. Having been a teen idol of the '60s is great because you realize you left your generation with a smile and good memories."

—Connie Stevens

"I shouldn't be near Vegas and have money in my pocket."

—Adam Sandler

"I've been in Vegas. That's where you get into the money thing. Boy, you get greedy in Vegas, you know. That's the only place that you can bet $25, get it up to $500 and refuse to quit."

—Louie Anderson

"Nevada's one of the most conservative states in the Union, but you can do what you want in Vegas and nobody judges you."

—Drew Carey

"No presidential candidate should visit Las Vegas without condemning organized gambling."

—Ralph Nader

"There's just no quiet in Vegas."

—Barry Manilow

"Vegas is everything that's right with America. You can do whatever you want, 24 hours a day. They've effectively legalized everything there."

—Drew Carey

"Vegas means comedy, tragedy, happiness and sadness all at the same time."

—Artie Lange

"What happens in Vegas stays in Vegas, but the rash doesn't.

—Ray Romano

"Las Vegas was such a teeny, tiny place."

—Eydie Gorme

"The winners are those who control the game, all the rest are suckers."

—Meyer Lansky, mobster turned casino operator.

CHAPTER 9

THE LAS VEGAS EXPERIENCE

The Las Vegas experience is everything, from the din of the slot machines to the green felt tables; from sexy and risqué shows and nightclubs to the ubiquitous escorts and legal brothels.

It includes the numerous and varied wedding options which gives it another title, "The Wedding Capital of the World."

The Las Vegas experience includes the acres of buffets, and numerous over-the-top and dazzling tourist attractions.

It also includes a dark side, touching the lives of compulsive personalities.

Keno and Slot Machines
Worst Odds In the House

Keno

You see them everywhere, scantily-clad women running about with Keno sheets and markers. Flashing number boards are conveniently posted in high vantage points. The reason for the "personal service" is that this casino game is for the "marks" and the house just rakes in money from them. Kinda like the mob's old numbers racket, only Keno is sanctioned by the casinos' bright lights.

But it's not bright lights, usually dim bulbs, who continuously shell out hard-earned money "hoping" to hit their numbers. Casinos love Keno, as they get to keep between 20 and 40% of all that is wagered, making it their best money maker. Plus, the house odds increase when more numbers, or spots, are picked. And if it's the best for the house, wouldn't players realize that it might be the worst for them?

Most players rarely think like that. Few attack Vegas with an analytical and determined approach, seeking out the best odds in their favor, and shunning games or venues that are not as favorable. Outside of a few, most visitors seem to be content just having fun.

Bingo

The second worst game might be an insult to all those blue-haired ladies at the local parlor, but Bingo, with its "all or nothing" opportunity to win, is a poor bet. It might be a great way to pass the time, and one can sit for a long time on a determined gambling budget, but the popular game has horrible odds.

Wheel of Fortune

Another bad bet is the Wheel of Fortune, a longtime "carnie" attraction. Why do you think that big wheel is right at the casino entrance, with attractive smiling attendants? Because that sucker bet brings in from 11 to 24% of every dollar played, all day, every day. That's why.

Slot Machines

"One-armed bandits," the mainstay of every casino, offer a variety of types and coin denominations. They can be mechanical, video, or touch screens. There are three to nine reelers, crisscrosses, multiples, progressives, and specialty machines to keep folks plucking in money.

Slot Machines

In the past 30 years, the slot machine bottom line has doubled for casinos. In the 1970s, slot machines generated 35% of the average casino's revenues. Today, they are responsible for a whopping 70%. Needless to say, the casinos want you to play them, making them as user-friendly and seductive as possible.

Slots are fun. Slots are easy, most requiring little thinking or strategy. Millions of tourists find playing slots the most enjoyable and relaxing form of gambling. It's random, it's fun, it's pure entertainment, and usually there's enough of a payback to keep it mesmerizing.

The problem with playing the slots is:

1. They are set so the house wins most of the time, and:

2. How much the house wins varies. Las Vegas slot machines are only required by law to pay out 75% of the money that goes into them, although most are set at over 90%.

Aha. So where are the best odds? My observations are that most slot players don't care. As stated, they just want to have fun. I once tried to explain to a friend that the casino next door offered better odds, but I was given the brush-off because he "liked the casino where he was."

Even if you realized (while awaiting that big jackpot) that you're donating so much of every dollar wagered to the house, wouldn't it still make sense to extend your play as long as possible?

Consider this: You're playing a $1.00 machine for an hour, making 600 wagers, or spins. At a 98% payout machine, that will cost you $12.00. If you were playing an 80% payout machine, you would have lost $120.00. Big difference. At the higher percentage payout, you could sit a lot longer giving you a much greater chance to hit that jackpot.

Where are the best machines? Generally speaking, the higher the denomination the better the payout. On the Strip for example, $1.00 machines average about 95% payout, while 5-cent (nickel) slots average about 90%.

Where you play is a major consideration. Shun the airport and 7-11 stores; they have the worst payouts. The downtown casinos generally have better, higher payouts than the Strip. Even slightly better than downtown are the more "out-of-the way" local casinos in North Las Vegas and on the Boulder Highway.

Nickel slots overall pay back between 86.9 to 92.8% of what they take in, averaging about 90% on the Strip, and 91.5% Downtown. It's a bigger (about 2 percentage points) difference for 25-cent (quarter) machines, with Downtown returning around 95% to the Strip's 93%. During one recent year, the $1.00 slot machines ranged from 94.67% average payout on the Strip, to 95.35% Downtown, to 96.48% on the Boulder Strip, to 97.21% in North Las Vegas. Avoid the progressive machines too. The appeal of Megabucks loses a little luster when you consider the huge potential jackpot forces a regular payout of only about 89%.

Seek the loosest machines, those with the most favorable odds. Even within a given casino slot machines are not equal.

Avoid Tight Machines

If you can't find "loose" machines, maybe you can avoid the "tight" ones, those with the worst payouts. Casinos tend to place their tightest machines in more secluded areas that generally don't attract slot players.

Other Slot Tips

Play the maximum. Most machines reward you for playing more coins. You don't want to miss big bucks for the lack of a coin. Remember, one pull of a slot handle is completely random and independent of the previous and next pull. Therefore a machine is never "due to hit." A machine can go for days without a decent payout and then have several large payouts in a short period of time. That said, there are many "table game" enthusiasts who would never consider the poor odds and randomness of the slot machines. But the slot machines bring in the money to keep the places going. They provide many hours of entertainment and remember—somebody's gotta win.

Roulette

Playing roulette is random fun with the spinning ball eventually settling on a number. If there were no green zeros, players betting either red or black, or odd or even, would have a 50-50 chance of winning. But when a zero comes up, all bets on the layout (except those on zero) lose. The two green zeros on a 36 number roulette wheel are what give the house its advantage.

Most wheels in Europe usually have only one zero, while the majority of American wheels have two. The casino edge for the standard double-zero game is 5.26%. Yet a single-zero wheel can cut that edge in half, lowering it to 2.7%.

Single-zero roulette wheels are not common in Las Vegas, but they do exist; the Monte Carlo Resort & Casino Hotel, for example, offers single-zero tables.

Most puzzling to me is seeing people play at a double-zero roulette table when a single-zero one is nearby. When told about it, the players generally don't want to be bothered.

Many types of people go to Las Vegas to gamble; the vast majority to be entertained, to have fun, and hopefully get lucky.

Craps, Baccarat and Blackjack

There are several games where the astute and skilled player can make the odds close to even. The craps table only has a 1.4% player disadvantage while playing the pass/don't pass line. If the player adds the "odds" bet, that casino edge can drop to less than 0.2%.

Baccarat, once considered a "James Bond-type" white dinner jacket high stakes game, has relentlessly pursued market share in recent years, and its percentage of gambling revenue has skyrocketed. The casino disadvantage can be trimmed to 1.17% (Bank) or 1.35% (Player). To some, the gambling is a challenge. They want the odds whittled down as much as possible in their favor, and they expect to win. They are disciplined and leave immediately if they've lost their allotment, and more importantly, leave when their target goal is met. According to Dr. Marvin Karlins, author of *The Book Casino Managers Fear The Most*, casinos are carefully designed to make you lose and keep you there as long as possible knowing that the longer you're there, the more you'll lose. That's why you'll never see a wall clock in a casino, and exits are hard to find. Karlins also discusses the powerful currency-devaluation ploy, in which chips just don't seem like real money, and credit is easy to get.

It takes knowledge and awareness to avoid the casinos' ongoing manipulation. The disciplined gamblers usually play the table games, like the more highly skilled game of poker, and they often play blackjack. Blackjack features the players against the dealer, based on fixed rules. A skilled player, following the basic game strategy, can reduce the house odds to under 1%. Understanding blackjack has almost become a cottage industry. It deserves its own chapter.

Books on Blackjack
BEAT THE BANK

Unskilled blackjack players have casino management salivating. They are why casinos still offer the game. The object of blackjack is for each player to get closer to "21" (as the game is sometimes called) than the dealer, by drawing more cards, without going over, or "busting." The dealer and the players each get two cards, but one of the dealer's cards is "down," or unseen. Even though there are usually up to seven players at each table, it is not team play, but each player against the dealer. Thus in the same hand, one can be a winner while the next person can lose.

The primary house advantage is that if the player "busts" he loses, even if the dealer subsequently "busts." The dealer "must" hit anything below 17, while the players do not have to. Thus, for example, a player can "stay" or "sandbag" with a 13, especially if the dealer is showing a 4, 5, or 6. Chances are the dealer will "bust" or "go over" with those cards. That is one facet of the basic strategy. Poor or new players often don't understand the significance of the all-important dealer's visible card and hit indiscriminately, giving the house an enormous edge. Conversely, a skilled player with a good understanding of what has become known as the "basic strategy" or "basic game" which dictates when to hit, stay, double, or split, can cut the house edge to less than 1%. Furthermore, card counters, shuffle trackers, and others who legally employ various mathematical methods can even shift the game's odds from the house to the player.

Blackjack Strategy

The skill and mathematical possibilities began to appeal to a number of players, and by the 1950s several strategies and books came out, beginning with Roger Baldwin's 1956 *The Optimum Strategy in Blackjack*. Many have since refined Baldwin's work and have used the subsequent strategies to "break the bank."

Of course, through the years the casinos have countered each strategy, making the most popular methods harder and harder to do, by using multiple decks, moving up shuffle points, and adjusting rules like the dealer "hitting soft 17 (Ace-6)," which alone boosts the house edge 0.2%. Hey, every little bit helps.

Blackjack is one of the few casino table games that can be beaten legally and with some consistency by a skilled player. Beyond the basic strategy of when to hit and when to stand, individuals who can "card count," that is determine what's left in the deck by what has been played, have a definite advantage. Card counting is legal in Las Vegas, but casinos take a very dim view of successful counters, banning them from ever setting foot again in their establishments. Stories abound about card counters being detained, interrogated, and even beaten by casino employees.

Blackjack has intrigued cheaters too, and hidden cameras, special computers built into shoes, trick cards, teaming up with crooked dealers, reflective lenses, and all sorts of other ingenious methods have been employed and discovered. Notwithstanding, most Blackjack experts attack the game legally.

By the 1960s, several pioneers had honed the basic game, published books, and won enough money to encourage a stampede of gamblers to Las Vegas intent on "breaking the bank."

The Blackjack Hall of Fame

Those early blackjack pioneers, most of whom were eventually barred from Las Vegas casinos, have been idolized by Barona Casino in California which created the Blackjack Hall of Fame in 2002. Of course, Barona just "honored" them; that doesn't mean they'll let them play against the house. They're no dummies.

Those 14 honored Hall of Famers really "wrote the book" on Blackjack. They are: Roger Baldwin, Edward O. Thorp, Lawrence Revere, Stanford Wong, Julian Braun, Ken Uston, Al Francesco, Peter Griffin, Arnold Snyder, Tommy Hyland, Max Rubin, Keith Taft, James Grosjean, and Johnny Chang/ Massachusetts Institute of Technology (MIT) Team.

Former MIT mathematics professor Edward O. Thorp, who authored the 1962 classic *Beat the Dealer*, is sometimes considered The Father of Card Counting. Testing his theories he went to Las Vegas and won $11,000 the first weekend before being kicked out by casino security. Current shuffling rules at casinos are a direct result of Dr. Thorp's success.

Lawrence Revere, author of *Playing Blackjack as a Business*, headed for Las Vegas after getting a mathematics degree from the University of Nebraska in 1943. By the 1960s, while banned from casinos, he was considered the preeminent blackjack expert. He died in 1977 but his book is still a popular seller and people using his techniques are still winning.

Stanford Wong (A pseudonym for John Ferguson) earned a PhD. in finance from Stanford in 1970 and wrote the 1975 classic *Professional Blackjack*, which popularized a technique known as "Wong-ing." It was the first instance of players keeping count and only placing a bet after the count had become positive and then stepping out again. It proved so popular that casinos now usually bar this style of play if detected.

Julian Braun, who had advanced degrees in both mathematics and physics, was a computer programmer at IBM and later authored 1980's *How to Play Winning Blackjack*.

Ken Uston, a Yale University and Harvard MBA graduate, authored *Million Dollar Blackjack* and *The Big Player*, which tells the secrets of the card counting teams; of course that encouraged other teams to evolve. Uston was a skilled card counting member of Al Francesco's team, the basis for *The Big Player*.

The team approach utilizes trained players at various tables in the casino counting cards and when a count becomes extremely positive, team members would flag down the designated Big Player (BP) who would then make significant bets. After Uston's book was published, Al Francesco and his team were barred from playing in Las Vegas. Tommy Hyland was manager of one of the longest-running (more than 25 years) Blackjack teams.

Johnny Chang/Massachusetts Institute of Technology (MIT) Team

Former team manager of the exalted MIT Blackjack Team, Johnny Chang is the "Mickey Rosa" character in the 2008 movie "21," itself patterned after the book *Bringing Down The House* by Ben Mezrich. The MIT Blackjack Team of 10 mostly students started in 1980 with a total stake of $89,000. Ten weeks later, using the team and Big Player (BP) approach, they more than doubled their original stake. John Chang, an MIT undergrad, joined the team in 1981 and took over as manager from Bill Kaplan. In 1992 Chang organized the team into a professional legal business entity called Strategic Investments. Unfortunately, the Griffin Investigations agency hired by the casinos was at the height of their power then and noticed most of the suspected counters had Boston addresses, were of college age, and attended MIT. They were harassed enough to disband in 1993, although they were all reported to have made between $1-$10 million each!

Computer analyst and professional player James Grosjean was the author of the classic *Beyond Counting*. The former math major at Chicago University became endeared to card counters everywhere after winning a lawsuit against the hated Griffin Agency.

The members of the Blackjack Hall of Fame did not go to Vegas for "a good time." They were highly educated, analytical, and went to win, often sharing their successes later through their publications. The Basic Strategy itself is not that difficult. In fact most casino gift shops sell a small laminated card which you can usually take out of your pocket to make a decision at the table. Card counting, however, is a lot harder. It takes a quick brain with almost instant recall, but it can be learned.

Today, many players inspired by these Blackjack pioneers are out there in the casinos on a constant quest to "break the bank" themselves.

It Stays in Vegas...

Sex in The City

L as Vegas is called "Sin City" for a reason. Vice, gambling and sex are constantly in your face, front and center, not sequestered to a small "red light district" like some cities. The Entertainment Capital of the World is way more than world class entertainment—it is an "anything goes" mindset, and SEX leads the list. The refrain "What Happens in Vegas, Stays in Vegas" refers more to sex than anything else, and everyone knows it. From merely catching a bawdy topless act, to seeing nudity at a strip joint, to acting out one's fantasies, Las Vegas is where it's at. It's no surprise that the "Most Photographed Sculpture in

Crazy Girls sculpture in front of Riviera

Las Vegas" is of the bronze molded tushes of the "Crazy Girls," a longtime semi-nude showgirl revue. The life-size butts grace the Riviera entrance right on the Strip sidewalk to be photographed, compared to, or affectionately patted. There are so many tantalizing "sexy" venues in Las Vegas to amp up your libido, we'll save the more out-and-out obvious prostitution for its own chapter. But remember, in Vegas anything often goes and one can find a willing, or for-hire partner anyplace the sexual energy is charged up.

Bachelor/Bachelorette Parties

With over 100,000 couples tying the knot in Las Vegas every year, it stands to reason that Sin City is also the World Capital of Bachelor/Bachelorette Parties. There are scores of pages of web sites for bachelor and bachelorette party packages offered in Las Vegas.

The options are endless. For example, many companies have packages (usually running from $100 to $200 per person) that feature a night on the town including something like: limo service, champagne, VIP entrance to a hot nightclub or strip joint, and a bottle or two of booze.

Male and female strippers can also be made available, either through the package, through one of the clubs, or independently.

For a lascivious good time, the girls have several male strip joints to choose from, beginning with the classic "Chippendales," an ongoing male revue show at the Rio Hotel billed as "the ultimate girls' night out." But there are many more in Vegas, where even more sedate women get caught in the frenzy and allow inhibitions to go out the window. Some even join the boys on stage, something they certainly wouldn't think of doing back in Omaha.

A newer show is the interactive and hot all-male revue of buffed "blokes" from Australia, "The Thunder from Down Under" at Merlin's Theatre in the Excalibur Hotel & Casino.

There's also "American Storm" at the Miracle Mile Shops' V Theater. "American Storm" was named "Best Male Strip Show 2008" by the *Las Vegas Review-Journal* and the "Sexiest Show on the Las Vegas Strip" by *Where Magazine*.

"Men of Sapphire" at the Sapphire Las Vegas ladies-only showroom specializes in attracting Bachelorette Party Packages and offers "the largest amount of sexy Las Vegas strippers you can find," to quote their publicity, which continues, "It's down to your final few days as a single, independent woman and you want to celebrate them guilt-free with a limo-full of your most loyal friends—Sapphire Las Vegas."

Another ladies' choice is "Sin City Strippers," which offers "the hottest male entertainers in Las Vegas…and will insure the bachelorette and her guests have a really hot night!" They claim to have gathered only the best looking, best built, most talented, and most experienced male exotic entertainers in Las Vegas. What a way to end the single life!

Stripper 101

Where else can a devoted wife learn how to perform an exotic and sexy striptease without becoming a stripper? Las Vegas, that's where. "Stripper 101" at Miracle Mile Shops' V Theater is a private strip tease demonstration by current and former exotic dancers designed to teach ladies how to get their men drooling.

No men are allowed in class, so lap dances are performed to empty chairs. Props like wispy boas are available and women are encouraged to get comfortable with their fantasies.

The "Stripper 101" stage parallels a real strip club atmosphere, replete with effective lighting, the ubiquitous pole, and bump and grind music. "Stripper 101" has become an erotic setting for bachelorette or other "girls' night out" parties, and graduates from 18 to 80 years old, of all shapes and sizes, have exhibited their sexy side to learn the moves. Each graduating student receives an official license certifying them as a "genuine Las Vegas stripper." Photos are available to purchase after the class, and special packages for parties of six or more women are available.

It's another way for the Las Vegas visitor to get naughty. However, the skills learned at Stripper 101 need not necessarily "stay in Vegas." They may, however, leave a little of their "behind" behind as it's a 75-minute workout that burns off between 300 and 500 calories.

Strip Clubs

There's plenty for the guys. "Night Out" packages also exist for the Bachelor Parties, and limos are constantly discharging groups of rambunctious revelers at any of the city's numerous strip clubs. There are plenty to choose from, too, from small and intimate to large and brassy, with prices from only slightly expensive to "say what?" Don't forget to add the tips.

Some of the current favorites include: Badda Bing (which even has its own TV show, plus you can get married there), Can-Can Room, Cheetah's

A gentlemen's club beckons
Glitter Gulch tourists

Topless Lounge, Club Paradise, Crazy Horse III, Déjà Vu Erotic Ultralounge, Déjà Vu Showgirls, Diamond Cabaret, Eden Gentlemen's Club, Girls of Glitter Gulch, The Library, Little Darlings, Olympic Garden Cabaret, Palomino Club, Play It Again Sam, Rick's Las Vegas, Sapphire, Sheri's Cabaret, Spearmint Rhino, Talk of the Town, and Treasures.

One example of a major strip club is Spearmint Rhino, an 18,000-square-foot nightclub with a large center tipping stage offering great "views," two smaller go-go stages, and another sit-down tipping stage. Spearmint Rhino, open 24 hours, has a $30 cover for non-residents (locals free), and charges an extra $30 for people arriving by limo or taxi. Say what? Ladies must be escorted by a gentleman, and topless lap dances run from $20 to $400 (The $400 is a full hour with champagne, of course). They've got an extensive food menu, and two ATM machines for those guys who've indulged in too many lap dances.

Las Vegas Sexy Shows

The major Las Vegas theater shows have come a long way in sexiness since 1957, when Vegas showgirls first bared their breasts. Outside of the specific strip clubs and shows listed above, there are about a half-dozen Las Vegas shows that are a whole lot more risqué than what most people will find "back home." Here are some of the popular ones:

X Burlesque

This show at the Flamingo's Bugsy's Cabaret features the X Girls, six beautiful and talented topless dancers, upbeat choreography, and creative props in one sexy show.

Jubilee!

The big production "Jubilee!" at Bally's features about 85 statuesque and beautiful performers, many of whom appear on stage topless. The 1,000 elaborate costumes, made with 8,000 miles of sequins and rhinestones, are dazzling. Even headpieces weigh up to 35 pounds.

Zumanity

Cirque du Soleil's "Zumanity" show at New York New York offers a very sexy show with imagery, aerialists, and sultry dancing. This highly eroticized, cabaret-style spectacular has no story line, just various performers each themed by different elements of sexuality.

Crazy Horse Paris

French import "Crazy Horse Paris" at the MGM Grand is a small intimate cabaret show, an exact replica of its Parisian counterpart that was created in 1951. When the Crazy Horse Paris celebrated its 50th anniversary, the show La Femme, renamed MGM Grand's Crazy Horse Paris, came to Las Vegas. All 12 of the female dancers previously performed in Paris.

Fantasy

"Fantasy," the Luxor Hotel's sexy topless revue, is a fast-paced, sensual show with beautiful women, and an exotic soundtrack. "Fantasy" stars Angelica Bridges from *Baywatch* and *Playboy*.

Bite

"Bite" at the Stratosphere is different—a little more risqué than the traditional Vegas topless shows. This topless "vampire" show offers real variety with provocative dancers, aerialists and more.

Peepshow

Holly Madison of E! TV's *The Girls Next Door* and *Playboy* fame stars in "Peepshow" at Planet Hollywood. Along with Holly are some of the hottest dancers and singers on the Strip.

Sin City Bad Girls

"Sin City Bad Girls" is a topless review at the Las Vegas Hilton featuring singer Lorena Peril and eight seductive dancers with the accompaniment of an eclectic live band.

Nightclubs, Casino Lounges and Bars

Las Vegas nightclubs have a new/old look these days. Along with the interactive music and dancing, many feature burlesque shows, a nostalgic romp of strip tease like that which excited old grandpa many years ago. Several places have added the bump and grind action and one of the most risqué is Forty Deuce

Dancer at Planet Hollywood Pleasure Pit

at the Mandalay Bay. Tangerine nightclub at Treasure Island also has three very sexy burlesque shows nightly. Some of the most "in" spots in casinos are not only the nightclubs, but the casino lounges and bars, many right on the casino floor. At Mandalay Bay, "Eyecandy Sound Lounge & Bar" is in the center of the casino and features interactive table technology. You can send your "flirts" to others there—well, you get the idea. At Luxor, the bar "Flight" on the casino floor has been a non-stop (24 hours) party since it first opened in 2007. "Liquidity," also on the Luxor casino floor, features fiber optic images projected onto a massive water wall with the spray of 4,000 nozzles that pulsate in tune to the music. The "Heart Bar" at the Planet Hollywood casino is part of the Pleasure Pit which features black leather clad go-go dancers hovering over the gaming tables. "Centrifuge" at MGM Grand is another party bar right in the heart of the action on the casino floor.

Topless/Nude Pools

The topless craze is not reserved for Las Vegas stages anymore. Borrowing from European culture, topless sunbathing has hit the desert. Sin City is a long way from the ocean, but they've got pools, don't they? Las Vegas pools are all about seeing and being seen. Instead of nightclubs, they're called "beach clubs," and of course, it's "day life" as opposed to night life. To keep everyone charged up, the hotels have shifted all sorts of entertainment poolside.

Maybe too much entertainment. The adult Sapphire Pool, one of the four Rio Hotel pools staffed by ladies from the Sapphire Gentlemen's Club, was shut down indefinitely in July 2009 after a raid which busted eight women for prostitution and three other people for illegal drugs. Tao Beach at the Venetian Hotel is another topless sunbathing pool. Raising pool-side activity way beyond reading the latest Jackie Collins novel while discretely glancing about, this adult-oriented pool features European-style sunbathing, food from Wolfgang Puck, and luxury poolside cabanas that even have plasma TVs, gaming consoles, and a DVD library.

Topless/nude sunbathing takes on a new meaning at the Bare pool at the Mirage. This venue offers spa-type amenities and pampering to include iced towels to abate the summer heat and chilled cucumbers to soothe the eyes. Complimentary services are offered to guests who have rented daybeds and cabanas. Moorea at the Mandalay Bay Hotel is an upscale alternative to topless sunbathing. The private pool area (frosted glass) has views of the Beach below and turns into a hip ultralounge at night. Venus at Caesars Palace is more than a topless, European sunbathing experience with 12 poolside cabanas available for rent. It is a mid-day version of Las Vegas nightlife. There's great music and attentive service on the 4½-acre Garden of the Gods Pool Oasis. The adult Beach Club 25 at the Stratosphere on the 25th floor is a less expensive version of topless sunbathing, but a lot less pretentious than those on the Strip that charge $30 and $40 to go poolside. The Wynn Las Vegas also offers topless sunbathing in one of its luxurious pools set in beautiful inviting gardens.

Steve Wynn pulled out all the stops in June 2010 when he opened the most opulent beach club of all at the Encore. He actually tore out the hotel's Strip entrance for the beach club. If you think the others are pricey, cabana rentals at the Encore go for $1,500 to $5,000—a day! Rehab at the Hard Rock Hotel is not a 12-step recovery program. In fact, it has been considered to be the ultimate in hedonism. Sunday parties in summer are world renowned, with live music and regular poolside concerts. Rehab, which even denies local women discounts, is big, has a great layout and lots of bodies. However, it got so out of hand with nudity, etc., by 2010 the Gaming Control Board was forced to issue a warning for the resort to clean up its act. It was no surprise to see party animal Paris Hilton in April kicking off the 2010 season.

Each year more Las Vegas venues are offering topless and outdoor lounge areas. The envelope keeps getting pushed often enough and fast enough that people were not surprised about the "bust" at the Rio's pool. Early on, most of those folks who shed their suits were Europeans, Australians, and others from less-inhibited societies. In fact, the Flamingo Vegas has had a "European" pool for years. Today however, more and more Americans are joining them.

One wag who tried the topless pool at the Flamingo not only raved about the obvious "scenery," the music, and the service, but he was most vocal about the refreshing absence of kids.

Alternative Lifestyles

Las Vegas has plenty to offer everyone, and gays, lesbians, transsexuals, swingers, and others can find plenty of entertainment geared for them.

There are 15 or so gay nightclubs and bars, many of them located along a strip of Paradise Road north of Tropicana. In addition, the Blue Moon Resort Hotel in Las Vegas is exclusively for gay men.

Favorite lesbian haunts include: Candy Bar, FreeZone, and the 8½ Ultra Lounge and Piranha Nightclub.

Swingers/BDSM/Sex clubs

There are also clubs for "swingers" and those who seek other various erotic fetishes. The swingers clubs usually provide a venue for consensual sex between couples and/or singles, charging an entry fee, with unescorted males paying a bit more. The fetish clubs are similar and provide environments for various non-traditional sexual activities.

An example might be the Fantasy Social Club which advertises, "Admission is $40 for couples and $60 for single men. Single women are free. Fantasy Social Club is a place where consenting adults play out their fantasies in a relaxed atmosphere with theme and private rooms, including a dungeon, doctor's office and more. 18 and over."

Obviously, acting out unlimited fantasies abound. Other similar clubs are "The Green Door," "The Red Rooster," and "Hush, The Club." As another example, "Hush, The Club" even advertises, "The club has private dance rooms, an orgy room with view, a couples lounge with view, VIP lounge, swing sex room, dance floor, pool table, uni-sex showers and lockers, gift shop. Couples and singles are welcome." Wow! Not much to the imagination.

There's something for everyone in Las Vegas. After you learn about all the sexual possibilities, somehow grabbing that pole at "Stripper 101" sounds pretty tame. And we haven't even got to the escorts and hookers yet!

Brothels, Escorts and Hookers
WOMEN FOR SALE

Sex is everywhere in Las Vegas. You can ignore it but can't escape it. The lure dangles in front of all. Provocative photos of semi-nude women gracing small flyers are constantly thrust into tourist hands by a small army of touts all along Las Vegas Boulevard. The sidewalks become littered with their colorful entreaties: "Call Angel," Call Vikki," "Call Holly," they implore, offering "escort service," their nakedness taunting promises even from their trod-upon pavement perches. Newspaper racks burst with more papers and flyers of similar "come on" ads than they do mainstream newspapers. It's a visual cornucopia. From every indication, sex is wide open and legal in Las Vegas. But actually, prostitution is not legal in Sin City. In other parts of Nevada, yes—but not Las Vegas.

Nevada is the only state with legal prostitution, but for various perplexing reasons, the legislators outlawed it in counties with a population greater than

250,000. And that's only Clark County, home to Las Vegas, and Washoe County, home to Reno. Supporting the decision, in recent polls 64% of Las Vegas residents oppose legalized prostitution. So Reno and Las Vegas "johns" have several choices. They can either commission an escort, find a hooker on their own, or go outside the county. Not a problem in Reno, where two "legal" counties border the metropolitan area.

In Las Vegas, the ubiquitous "escorts" can offer a litany of services beyond eye-candy companionship. While most of "the more" is illegal, the law generally looks the other way; there are a lot more problems in Vegas to deal with than chasing down every one of thousands of "escort-transactions." Most of the time there is no problem, but with prostitution being illegal, there is little recourse if a tourist is ripped off, robbed, or cheated, and that does happen to many out-of-towners every year.

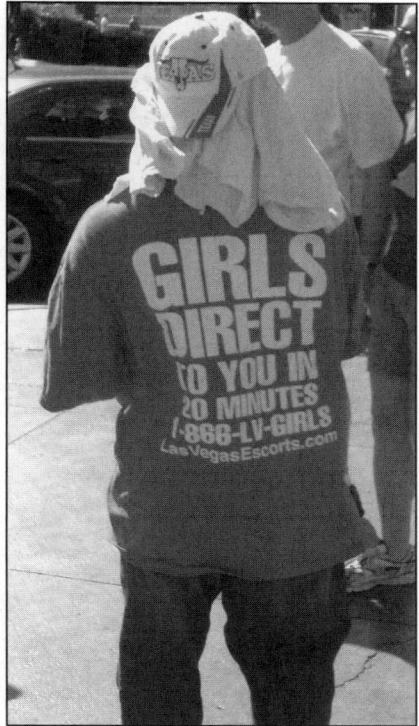

Tout passing out escort flyers

The Las Vegas Metropolitan Police Department vice squad admits that 99% of these "yellow page and flyer" escorts are prostitutes. They also advise that these "freelancers" are not checked medically like they are in the out-of-county brothels.

Las Vegas has far more than its fair share of prostitutes working within the city, so if you are willing to take the risk and you know where to look you should have no problem finding one, or at least someone who wants your money.

Las Vegas has everything from $20 "crack" whores hanging out around East Fremont Street to ex-porn stars who might charge up to $2,000 per hour. And everything in between. A lot of working women ply the bars and casinos along the Strip, and if a person wants to get connected, it is not hard to do.

The Legal Brothels

There are presently around 30 legal brothels in Nevada, most of which are in the northern part of the state near Reno and Carson City. All of these licensed bordellos are regulated by the state of Nevada and their employees must submit to frequent medical examinations. In addition to health issues, there is security in knowing that these licensed establishments would not condone

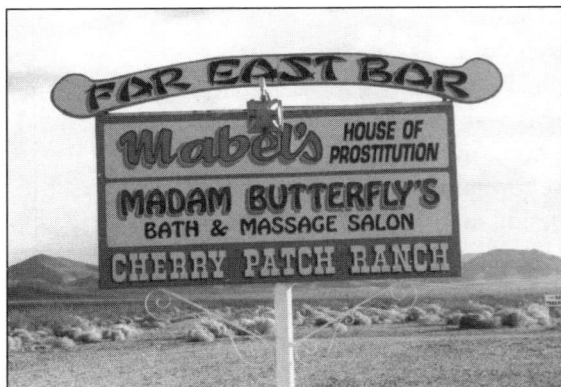

Cherry Patch brothel sign at county line

fraud, deception, theft, or anything that might risk them loss of their all-important state license.

From Las Vegas the closest state-licensed brothels are in either the vast Nye County, or Lincoln County. Nye County's largest town, Pahrump, is about 60 miles northwest of Las Vegas, and is home to two of the more famous legal brothels, the Chicken Ranch and Sheri's Ranch. Other small towns a little farther away that have legal brothels are Amargosa Valley, Beatty, Crystal, Death Valley Junction, and Scotty's Junction. North of Vegas on route 95 are the Cherry Patch Ranch, Mabel's Ranch, and the Cottontail Ranch.

The Chicken Ranch

The Chicken Ranch brothel has operated at 10511 Homestead Rd. in Pahrump since 1976. There are 17 beds and three extensively decorated, themed "bungalows" in a separate building. The ranch also has a collection of memorabilia from the original "Chicken Ranch" near LaGrange, Texas. The brothel also houses the Leghorn Bar which has a separate entrance.

Sheri's Ranch

Down the road from the Chicken Ranch, at 10551 Homestead Rd., Pahrump, is the newer and more upscale Sheri's Ranch, a "resort" with tennis courts, spa, swimming pool, volleyball court, and a sports bar. There is also a Bachelor's Party Room with stripper poles and a foam machine. Lora Shaner, a former madam of the brothel, wrote a book about her experiences there in *Madam: Chronicles of a Nevada Cathouse* (1999). In January 2001, Sheri's Ranch was purchased by Chuck Lee, a retired police officer and car dealer from Las Vegas.

What to Expect in the Legal Brothels

It starts with the line-up. Clients enter a lounge area where the girls are asked to line up and introduce themselves. After the "john" chooses and they've paired up, in her room they privately negotiate a price for the services requested.

The "unofficial" minimum price may be $100, but $200 to $300 is the common minimum for most of the girls for intercourse for about 30 minutes. Former and current porn stars sometimes base themselves at the brothels for a week or two at a time, and they can charge $1,000 or more. Guests should negotiate everything up front if they have something special in mind. The "john" is asked to pay in advance, and the girl takes the money to the cashier first. Tips are extra, but often expected as the prostitute shares the negotiated price 50-50 with the brothel. Bartenders and taxi and limo drivers also get a cut of the action.

"Prostidude"

During 2009 a Beatty, Nevada brothel, the Shady Lady Ranch, hired the state's first male prostitute, a muscular college dropout who abandoned a brief stint as a porn actor in Los Angeles to become the only legal gigolo in the United States.

After Nevada health officials approved a method to test men for infectious diseases, the Shady Lady successfully won state and county approval to clear the way for the "prostidude," as Nevada's newest sex worker was tagged. The male prostitute—known as "Markus"—has quickly become the center of attention in Nevada's brothel industry. Enter George Flint, a retired Assemblies of God minister who incongruously became executive director and lobbyist for the Nevada Brothel Owners Association. Flint, who for 25 years has balanced his beliefs in religion and prostitution, reluctantly and guardedly agreed to the male prostitute. He said, "We've worked hard for years to make the traditional brothel business in this state socially acceptable and something we can be proud of that most Nevadans accept."

Flint also owns several wedding chapels in the Reno area. Somehow there must be a connection. Preach about the weakness of the flesh and then provide the flesh. This whole scenario might cause puzzlement with a lot of people, but in Nevada it hardly raises an eyebrow.

The First Red Light District

Wide-open Nevada seems to have always been amenable to vice, namely drinking, gambling and prostitution, and officials have either looked the other way, or abetted the practices.

Integral to the initial plan for Las Vegas, on May 15, 1905 the railroad set aside two blocks in the northern section, Blocks 16 and Blocks 17, as the only places where liquor could be sold without licensing restrictions.

Block 16 soon evolved into the town's red light district, infamous throughout the West with wide-open prostitution.

Up until 1912, brothels, or simply "cribs" were located in rear rooms at The Arcade, Double O, and Star Saloon, all on the east side of First Street between Stewart and Ogden. Las Vegas featured six hotels and eleven saloons at Block 16 in 1909.

Other Block 16 bars without brothels included The Gem, Red Onion Club, and the Arizona Club, considered the town's finest saloon. But in 1912, when the Arizona Club at 219 North First Street was sold, the new owner built a second floor to house a bordello and the saloon became known as the "Queen of Block 16."

The pressure to change was not altruistic, but economic. By 1941, the U.S. Army, in locating facilities near Las Vegas, told city leaders the town would be off-limits to military personnel if prostitution remained at Block 16. City officials hastily decided they better do something rather than lose the military presence. So they set up the raid.

On December 2, 1941, Block 16 was raided and 22 women were arrested on prostitution charges. After posting $50 bail each, nearly all of the women returned and the brothels reopened. But several weeks later, in January 1942, city commissioners voted to cancel the liquor and slot machine licenses for all of the block's saloons. That was the death knell, and it wasn't long before the saloons and the brothels of infamous Block 16 closed.

The Hookers

The money thrown around in Las Vegas can be tempting, like fresh blood for sharks. It's so tempting it attracts many to compete with the sharks, and the jackals, and the vultures, and other bottom feeders who milk Las Vegas visitors of all the cash they can get.

Some of the Las Vegas hookers are married, many have legitimate professions. Some leave their Orange County or Los Angeles offices on Friday afternoon to make more money over the weekend than they would in two months at the office.

The dismal economy that began in 2008 affected the Nevada prostitution business big time. Not only is there less money out there for people to pay for sexual diversions, but more and more women want to get into the act, exacerbating the supply-demand squeeze. According to a *Las Vegas Sun* article in December 2008, one escort agency owner reported getting about 40 interested applicants each and every day. Others "in the business," especially in the mid-price range ($400-$700), reported that their income has been seriously curtailed, in many cases halved. One said she now had to do "more for less." Lower-end hookers ($100-300) were not as severely affected, nor have the high-end girls lost much. Apparently, there are always rich guys.

Occasional streetwalkers "on the track" or escort or outcall service providers would give the brothels a try, but few stayed. The house rules, obligatory confinement, and lack of independence dissuaded many. Conversely, fewer than 50% of the brothel girls sell sex outside.

Author Alexa Albert in writing *Brothel: Mustang Ranch and Its Women*, was granted access to a Nevada brothel and reported that one common trait among the girls there was perceived financial hardship. Women were often there to provide for loved ones, either a lazy husband or other family members. One's mother "turned her out" so she didn't have to work. Another's mother-in-law announced that she had freeloaded off her son's family long enough so she drove her to the "ranch" to get a job. Pimp boyfriends also were high on the list of those who benefited from the brothels.

It's hard to tell how many women are in the Las Vegas prostitution business but a good guess by academics who must know about such things figure about 3,000-3,500 indoor working prostitutes at any given time. That's a lot of sex in a county where it's supposed to be illegal.

Wedding Capital of the World
GETTING MARRIED WITH ELVIS

Invite Elvis Presley to your wedding—thousands do. Have him administer the vows. Or maybe have the "King" escort the wedding party down the Las Vegas Strip in a Cadillac convertible? Anything is possible in Las Vegas.

Las Vegas "Elvis" weddings are so popular, and by far the most requested, there's no shortage of work for his impersonators there. At the Viva Las Vegas Wedding Chapel, for example, for an additional $250 you can hire the King of Rock 'n' Roll to add a memorable element to "your day" as he rolls out his guitar and enlivens the place with his major hits, even swiveling his hips in the mannerisms of the famous entertainer.

There are all sorts of Elvis wedding packages to tickle your fancy, or put a shine in your "blue suede shoes" at the Viva Las Vegas chapel. There's an Elvis Blue Hawaii wedding package, featuring lush tropical sets and hula girls dancing to The Hawaiian Wedding Song! You can even have a "Priscilla" impersonator be your Matron of Honor. You get the idea. In addition to Elvis and his Pink Caddy

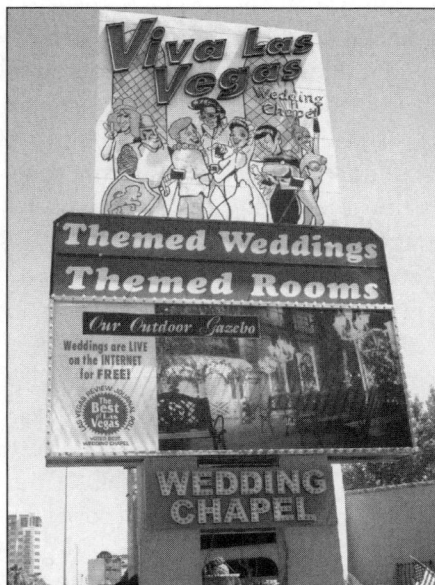
Viva Las Vegas Wedding Chapel

weddings, you can also tie the knot outdoors, in helicopters hovering over the Strip or the Grand Canyon, or in other outdoor venues like Red Rock Canyon (all with or without Elvis). Some places, like Viva Las Vegas, will also post your wedding live on the internet.

Or for the guys who prefer women in strip joints, the Badda Bing Gentlemen's Club offers its Chapel of Lust, and you can get married surrounded by topless beauties. You can get divorced there too, the owner says.

The competition to provide weddings to throngs of visitors intent on leaving town with a mate is intense, all offering something different or special, hoping to grab some of the business of the many thousands of Las Vegas weddings.

120,000 Couples a Year

The wedding business is huge in Las Vegas, adding approximately $1 billion to the local tourist economy annually. Over 5.5% of all U.S. weddings take place in Sin City each year, as over 120,000 couples (that's 240,000 people) tie the knot there. Over the decade 1999-2009, the percentage of all U.S. marriages performed in Las Vegas remained consistent, ranging between 5.1 and 5.7%, with an average 118,700 annual licenses. During the year 2004 alone, Las Vegas issued 128,250 marriage licenses. That's 256,000 people, or the total populations of both Topeka, Kansas and Columbia, South Carolina.

In addition, each year about 40,000-50,000 couples enjoy their mates so much they renew their wedding vows in Las Vegas. Another Nevada city, Reno, is a distant second from Las Vegas' annual 120,000 weddings with 25,000 total, and Hawaii places third with 10,000. During the 50 years between 1956-2005, nine million people got married in Nevada! That's more than the populations of Ireland and New Zealand—combined.

Las Vegas was not yet a city when the first wedding took place there in 1909. Then in 1912, California enacted what became known as the Gin Law, making couples wait three days after filing to ensure they were not too drunk to get married. Many solved that eloper's hurdle by crossing the border to Nevada. No blood test was required, and that is still the case.

Wedding Chapels Everywhere

Wedding chapels sprung up along Las Vegas Boulevard faster than timeshare offices do in today's resort locations. There are still more than 50 wedding chapels in Las Vegas and some of them have long and fascinating histories, including those in virtually all of the resort hotels. For example, The Wedding Chapel at 513 S. Fifth St. (now Las Vegas Blvd.) performed its first wedding in September 1933, and is still going strong. The Wee Kirk of the Heather was a residence transformed into a chapel in 1940, and is still hitching up people. So is the catchy-named, longtime Hitching Post, also on Las Vegas

Boulevard. Others include Cupid's Wedding Chapel, Little Chapel of the Flowers, Little Church of the West, Vegas Wedding Chapel, and Little White Wedding Chapel, all with enticing chapels or white gazebos, and "bags" full of extra "goodies" enamored folks might want. For example, the Little White Wedding Chapel offers 24-hour drive-thru service in their Tunnel of Love. Signs indicate that for $40 you can get their "plain vanilla" wedding ceremony; for $60, you also get a red rose and a Polaroid photograph; for $80, it's the "Limo Lovers Lip Lockers Special" which enlarges the red rose to a "presentation of flowers," makes it two Polaroids, and throws in a garter to boot. The $100 "Cherubs Chariot" adds a video and a third Polaroid to the Lip Lockers Special. Whatever you want.

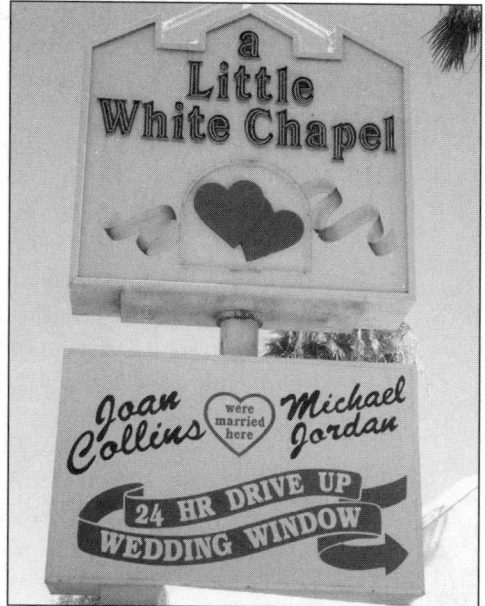

Little White Chapel

The Little White Wedding Chapel's "2ELVIS" Caddy convertible is white, in contrast to the pink one of their competitors. A sign indicates that both **Joan Collins** and **Michael Jordan** were married there. (They were: Joan Collins and Peter Holm in 1985, and Michael Jordan and Juanita Vanoy in 1989).

Chapels that now line the boulevard have attracted movie stars and big names since the celebrated 1931 nuptials between "it girl" actress **Clara Bow** and Rex Bell. Celebrities rule in Las Vegas even more than elsewhere, and many of them have performed their nuptial vows in Las Vegas. Even before Clara Bow, in December 1930 **William Boyd** (Hopalong Cassidy) and actress **Dorothy Sebastian** repeated the marriage vows in a Las Vegas hotel room.

The long list of celebrity Las Vegas weddings had begun and for decades it became the favorite place to get married. There are also those who got married enough times there they probably had the chapel's number on their Rolodex. For younger folks, that's the forerunner to today's speed dial. Nobody can top actor **Mickey Rooney,** who went to the Las Vegas altars with seven of his eight brides, getting married in 1944, 1949, 1952, 1958, 1966, 1967, 1969 and 1978.

Actor **Tony Curtis** got married in Las Vegas—several times. After he and **Janet Leigh** divorced, he took his second wife in 1963 at the Riviera, his third wife at the Sahara, his fourth someplace else, and his fifth wife at the MGM Grand in Las Vegas.

There are Las Vegas celebrity marriages that have stood the test of time. Hollywood's **Paul Newman** and **Joanne Woodward** were married on January 29, 1958 at the El Rancho Vegas. While the El Rancho no longer exists, their marriage lasted over 50 years!

Las Vegas celerity weddings through the years reads like the "A" list of Hollywood. A brief, partial list includes:

Rita Hayworth & Dick Haymes, 1953
Kirk Douglas & Ann Buydens, 1954
Joan Crawford & Alfred Steele, 1955
Carol Channing & Charles Lowe, 1956
Steve Lawrence & Eydie Gorme, 1957
Janet Leigh & Bob Brandt, 1962 (Sands Hotel)
Mary Tyler Moore & Grant Tinker, 1962 (Dunes Hotel)
Barbra Streisand & Elliot Gould, 1963
Betty White & Allen Ludden, 1963 (Sands Hotel)
Jane Fonda & Roger Vadim, 1965 (Dunes)
Xavier Cugat & Charo, 1966 (Caesars Palace)
Elvis Presley & Priscilla Anne Beaulieu, 1967 (Aladdin)
Ann Margret & Roger Smith, 1967 (Riviera)
Wayne Newton & Elaine Okamura, 1968 (Flamingo)

The May 1967 Elvis Presley/Priscilla Beaulieu wedding was nowhere near as flamboyant as many performed by his impersonators. Because he rarely carried cash, he borrowed the $15 weekend license fee and they repeated the vows in Room 246 at the Aladdin Hotel. The low-key affair was arranged by Colonel Parker, Presley's manager. Elvis and Priscilla flew from their Palm Springs retreat to Vegas before dawn, got their license at 7 a.m., and rushed to dress for the 9 a.m. ceremony. The wedding itself was attended by close family and friends, but over 100 guests celebrated at an elaborate breakfast banquet.

'Til Next Week Do Us Part

In contrast to Paul Newman and Joanne Woodward and their 50-plus years together, there have been many celebrities whose marriages did not endure—some only lasting hours.

Frank Sinatra and Mia Farrow

Frank Sinatra, then 50, married Mia Farrow, then 21, in a private ceremony at the Sands on July 19, 1966. Come divorce time, Frank had her divorce papers served publicly on the set of "Rosemary's Baby," further stunning the actress. Their divorce was final in 1968.

Axl Rose and Erin Everly

Guns N' Roses front man Axl Rose wed Erin Everly, daughter of rocker Don Everly, on April 28, 1990, at Cupid's Wedding Chapel. He reportedly said in a "romantic" 4 a.m. proposal, "Marry me or I'll kill myself," so Erin drove straight to Vegas. After only three weeks, Rose filed for divorce. But all was not over. The couple reconciled only to end the union less than a year later.

Dennis Rodman and Carmen Electra

Basketball player Dennis Rodman married "Baywatch" beauty Carmen Electra at the Little Chapel of the Flowers on November 15, 1998. After conflicting reports of the Chicago Bulls star's inebriation and their being madly in love, the couple put an end to the rumors and their marriage just nine days after exchanging vows.

Darva Conger and Rick Rockwell

Darva Conger, a reality show "winner" on "Who Wants to Marry a Multimillionaire," wed Rick Rockwell, a man she hardly knew, at the Las Vegas Hilton in front of a live television audience on February 15, 2000 at the end of the show. When news of her "groom's" shady past came to light, the honeymoon was over. She filed for an annulment in March, and it was finalized on April 5.

Billy Bob Thornton and Angelina Jolie

Actress Angelina Jolie, then 24, wed co-star Billy Bob Thornton, then 44, on May 5, 2000, at the Little Church of the West. They both wore blue jeans for the solemn occasion, and she had her groom's name tattooed on her arm. The marriage ended in divorce in 2003.

Nicky Hilton and Todd Andrew Meister

Socialite Nicky Hilton wed financier Todd Andrew Meister at 2:30 a.m. on August 15, 2004. Nicky was in town with sister Paris for a celebrity poker tournament when a chapel beckoned. Adding to the eccentricity, Paris' dog Tinkerbell wore a tiara and toted the ring pillow. The bride wore a thigh-length, blue halter dress. The wedding was annulled in less than two months.

Britney Spears and Jason Allen Alexander

Singer Britney Spears and childhood friend Jason Allen Alexander celebrated an impromptu wedding at the Little White Wedding Chapel at 5 a.m. on January 3, 2004. The "blushing" 22-year-old bride wore an ensemble of blue jeans and a baseball cap and her groom was in a sports shirt. The couple signed annulment papers later that afternoon ending an "enduring" 55-hour marriage.

Ross Geller and Rachel Green

TV sitcom show characters "Friends" Ross Geller and Rachel Green wed in a fictional Las Vegas chapel in an intoxicated, shotgun wedding. Other characters in the show, Monica Geller and Chandler Bing, considered having a quickie Vegas wedding, but ex-lovers Ross and Rachel beat them to it. Ross' third marriage did not last.

Clark County is used to being in the marriage business. The county clerk's Downtown Las Vegas office is open from 8 a.m. to midnight, including holidays, with a justice of the peace for civil courthouse weddings available until 10 p.m. The marriage license fee is now $60.00 (cash, money order, certified check, or credit card—no debit card and $5.00 more for credit card) and applications can be filled out online.

If you'd rather not leave your hotel for a small chapel, most of the resort hotels can accommodate you with their myriad of on-site chapels and amenities. Most charge from $250.00 to $1,000 for a nice package. However, if money is no object, you might try the Bellagio and its $15,000 Costa Bella Wedding package. It includes side-by-side massages, dinner, show, chocolates, and breakfast in bed.

The biggest weekend by far for Las Vegas weddings is Valentine's Day, followed by New Year's Eve. There are long waits for licenses on those dates and chapels turn over their facilities so fast a big crowd out front might actually be for four or five different weddings. On Valentine's Day 2006 there were 1,228 marriages, and on the same date the following year, 935. On February 14, 2008, there were 968 marriages performed in Las Vegas.

One of the most popular wedding dates of all time, 07-07-07 was a huge day in Las Vegas due to its implied luck and good fortune (it's the ultimate jackpot!) and the fact that it landed on a Saturday. A record 4,450 marriages were performed that day.

The gambling city of Las Vegas, the undisputed Entertainment Capital of the Word, is also rightfully the Wedding Capital of the World. No other place even comes close.

The Las Vegas Food Frenzy
FROM GLUTTONS TO GOURMETS

Las Vegas skews the old adage that the way to a man's heart is through his stomach. They don't care so much about your heart as they do your pocketbook, and casino operators have long known that food, lots of it and at good value, will keep their gambling tourists from wandering off down the street. Heck, if done right, food can be the draw to get more gamblers.

Ergo, for decades some of the best values in the desert town were food-related. From shrimp cocktails, junk food, fast food, food courts, fine dining, and romantic dining to the ubiquitous buffet, Las Vegas has a lot to offer its patrons and keep them fat and happy.

Shrimp Cocktails

A true Las Vegas legend was begun in 1959 when the Golden Gate Hotel & Casino downtown began to offer a shrimp cocktail for 99 cents at its San Francisco Shrimp Bar and Deli. The Golden Gate held that price until 2005 and served over 30 million cocktails in that time.

The price is now $1.99, but is still a value with a zesty sauce in a large tulip glass brimming with succulent bay shrimp.

Other casinos have got into the shrimp business and made Las Vegas the Shrimp Capital of the United States, as if it needed another "capital" designation. Over 60,000 pounds a day—that's over 22 million pounds a year—are consumed in Las Vegas, way more than the rest of the country combined!

Most of the other downtown casinos offer shrimp cocktails ranging in price from the super bargain 99 cents at the Fremont Hotel to $1.99 at most of the other places, although quality varies with some places offering smaller shrimp pre-refrigerated in a plastic cup with lettuce. According to *Las Vegas: The Best of Glitter City*, the top venues for shrimp cocktails are: Golden Gate Hotel & Casino, California Hotel & Casino, Four Queens

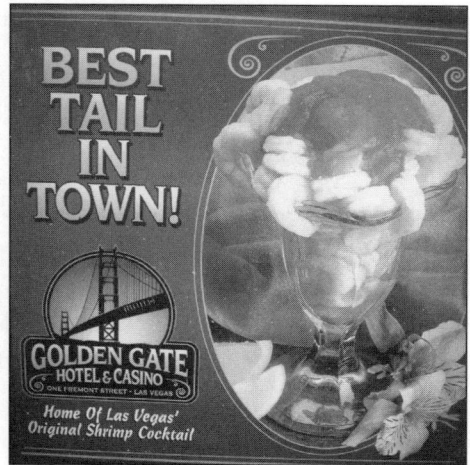

Golden Gate shrimp cocktails

Hotel & Casino, Fremont Hotel & Casino, Las Vegas Club Hotel & Casino, O'Shea's Casino, Riviera Hotel & Casino, Silverton Hotel & Casino, and the Westward Ho Hotel & Casino.

Fine Dining

Inexpensive fast food, food courts, in-casino buffets, and other bargain dining became the trademark of Las Vegas eateries. It's been good for the casinos to keep the people playing, and also good for the players to nab the bargains.

But something happened along the way. With the new breed of upscale casino that began arriving in the 1990s (Bellagio, Monte Carlo, Mirage, Venetian, Wynns, etc.) came a more discriminating tourist. New fancier restaurants, often celebrity-chef driven, opened and as a result some of the restaurants themselves are the draw. As an example, Picasso within the Bellagio Hotel and Casino is the most honored. It is a recipient of the AAA Five Diamond Award and continually leads several of the Zagat surveys, notably decor and food quality. It overlooks the famous eight-acre lake and water show.

Other top-notch Las Vegas restaurants include Bellagio's Aqua, Andre's at the Monte Carlo, Aureole at Mandalay Bay, the Eiffel Tower Restaurant at Paris Las Vegas, Renoir at the Mirage, Rosemary's Restaurant at the Rio, and Emeril's New Orleans Fish House at the MGM Grand. With the opening of CityCenter in December 2009, several of the country's top chefs have opened restaurants in the complex. Among ARIA's 16 new restaurants are Jean Georges Steakhouse and the uniquely designed American Fish, which looms out over the atrium like a banded mushroom.

There is no end of high-end dining in Las Vegas, the type various guide books would flag with four little $ signs. There are also endless ethnic, theme, and specialty restaurants, from Indian food (Gaylord India, or Original India), to Moroccan delicacies (Marrakesh). Like everything else, whatever you want you can find it in Las Vegas.

For the highest view, try the Top of the World at the Stratosphere Hotel & Casino. This off-Strip hotel restaurant gives a skyscraper view from 800 feet above Las Vegas, and takes 80 minutes to revolve a full 360° circle.

Local Favorites and Bargain Meals

There are so many inexpensive meal options in Las Vegas, a frugal person could eat well on a limited budget. Coupon books, "Two-Fer" specials, throw-away flyers, and newspaper and magazine ads constantly scream out for tourists to enter their establishments for bargain-priced food.

Buffets

Nothing defines eating in Las Vegas as its buffets do. There are approximately 50 Las Vegas area buffets offering incredibly wide selections at incredibly inexpensive prices. Most offer three meals a day with prices rising modestly from breakfast to lunch to dinner. But there is so much to choose from most folks learn that pigging out at a buffet trough only twice a day is quite sufficient.

The quality varies from "wow" to "it's been under a heat lamp too long." Some of the most popular are crowded but turn the food over much faster.

The World's Largest Buffet (surprise, surprise) is in Las Vegas, at the Excalibur, where the Roundtable Buffet feeds 3,000 to 4,000 people each and every day from four separate stations in a huge dining hall. As buffets go, it is an outstanding value (Breakfast $8.99, Lunch $9.99, Dinner $10.59) and the food is surprisingly good.

Many people have elevated Buffet Dining to their own personal art form. They know the best values. They have their favorite buffets, and have learned that weekends (Friday and Saturday nights especially) can be the most crowded. They know to reconnoiter the food and head directly for the most exotic stuff. You can get a salad anywhere so you don't want to fill up on ordinary stuff, not when there's crab legs and caviar for the taking.

Bargain Food

There are several charts out there ranking the Las Vegas buffets, offering their Top Five or Top 10, or highest ratings. Lists like that are often subjective, but a number of buffets constantly score high on the lists. In no particular order the following buffets have been rated high in several surveys: Le Village Buffet at Paris Las Vegas, French Market Buffet at Orleans, The Buffet at Wynn Las Vegas, Spice Market Buffet at Planet Hollywood, The Buffet at Bellagio, Cravings Buffet at the Mirage, both buffets at the Rio (Carnival World Buffet and Village Seafood Buffet), Big Kitchen Buffet at Bally's, and Paradise Garden Buffet at the Flamingo Hilton.

Most buffets feature all-you-can-eat and going back for more or sampling numerous desserts is considered the norm. Most dinners (the most expensive meal of the day) are still under $20.00 with just a few exceptions. And that includes a beverage. As you get your own food, tipping is minimal. Most people leave a dollar or two per person for the beverage server.

From made-to-order eggs and omelets in the morning to hand-carved prime rib and succulent Alaskan crab legs at night, buffet food continues to attract Vegas visitors.

One online blogger offered, "When you can eat all day for $20 at the Circus Circus buffet, why would you bother going to a "real" restaurant?"

Why indeed, another quipped: "I have lived in Las Vegas for many years. The high-end, upscale restaurants are always popular with the "whales" (high rollers), but don't discount those buffets. They have improved greatly. The quality and variety is much better."

Kinda hard for many people to shell out over $100 for an upscale meal when they can get prime rib, lobster, and crab legs for under $20.00. Heck, I kinda like those shrimp cocktails, too.

Sin City Attractions
SOMETHING ON EVERY CORNER

I f in your trip to Sin City, you're not looking for, well "Sin," don't dismay. Along with non-stop gambling, in-your-face sex, and stuff-your-face food, there's such a plethora of activities that you'll learn the word "boring" is not even in the Las Vegas vocabulary.

Even the Strip has enough going on in front of and in the casinos that visitors can "ooh" and "aah" their way the entire four-mile length. Steve Wynn can be thanked for pedestrianizing the Strip in 1989 when he opened the first mega-resort, the Mirage Resort & Casino. Previous to that, all the resorts sat back from the highway and in essence were different variations of Thomas Hull's original formula for the El Rancho Vegas. Wynn's special attractions like the Volcano, the Pirate Show (Treasure Island), and the Bellagio Dancing Waters show brought entertainment right to the street. Caesars Palace then had to come out to the street with the Forum Shops to counter what Wynn was doing. The others followed suit and today's broad Strip is its own attraction.

Casino Attractions

The city's highest perch, the **Stratosphere Las Vegas** (at the Strip's far north end), takes the tower's thrilling views to another level of excitement. There's a roller coaster called Insanity–The Ride, and an adrenalin-pumping attraction called Big Shot that propels you 160 feet in the air in an astounding 2.5 seconds, rendering weightless sensations normally reserved for astronauts—all dizzyingly high above the city skyline.

The Stratosphere had to go even one better, using all that height to advantage. Opening in April 2010 was Sky Jump Las Vegas, an 855-foot free fall jump from the 108th floor. Jumpers reach speeds up to 40 mph tethered by a metal cable. The controlled freefall has already been listed in the Guinness Book of Records as the world's highest commercial decelerator.

When **Circus Circus Hotel & Casino** opened, it was the first time a casino actually played second fiddle to the attraction, in this case circus acts with high-wire aerialists, jugglers, acrobats, and unicyclists performing overhead above the casino floor. Included on the mezzanine is a 200-game midway. Out back Circus Circus has a huge pink Adventuredome with all sorts of thrilling rides for old and young alike.

Continuing south, **Treasure Island Hotel & Casino** has revamped its streetside pirate show. Now called "Sirens of TI," the 18-minute free show is a tad more sexy (read: scantily clad female pirates) than the earlier version.

The **Venetian Resort Hotel** across the street not only has the Grand Canal Shoppes and Gondola rides, but the hotel is also home to Madame Tussaud's Wax Museum.

The redesigned Volcano in front of **Mirage Resort & Casino** features water, sound, and lighting along with spurts of lava and flame, making it one of the most popular free attractions along the Strip. The hotel is also home to a lush Secret Garden, Dolphin Habitat, and white tiger exhibit.

The fountains in front of **Caesars Palace** are huge and impressive, but the upscale Forum Shops and inside attractions continue to dazzle. For example, the Fall of Atlantis and Fountain Festival Show in the Forum Shops offer special effects using lifelike animatronics figures. It's a bit startling seeing those Roman statues come to life—but hey, it's a free show.

The **Imperial Palace** across the boulevard is home to The Auto Collection which features a rotating display of 300 classic cars, a mechanical nirvana destined to keep car fanciers in a state of automotive bliss.

The **Flamingo Las Vegas** next door has an oasis out back called the Wildlife Habitat which features over 300 species of birds along with turtles, fish, the only species of penguin that can live in a hot desert climate, and a few other animals. While you're out in the garden, note the Bugsy Siegel Memorial, a bronze plaque honoring the legendary gangster who originally opened the Flamingo. His secret tunnel escape route was discovered near the rear of the resort several years ago during a construction project.

The Dancing Waters show at **Bellagio Las Vegas** has been a big hit that tourists line up to view all evening. Water soars as high as 460 feet from 1,214 spouts into an 8.5-acre lake. The free show is every half hour, and every 15 minutes at peak times. The Bellagio also houses one of the West's finest art collections in the Gallery of Fine Art.

Across the street at the **Paris Las Vegas**, the Eiffel Tower offers fine views of the waterworks at the Bellagio from almost 50 stories above the Strip. About half the size of the French original, the tower is one of the city's romantic destinations.

The huge **MGM Grand Hotel** has a lion habitat at the rear of the casino where lions are rotated in from a nearby ranch for free viewing by guests.

Bellagio Las Vegas fountains with Paris Las Vegas
in foreground

New York New York Hotel & Casino across the street from the MGM Grand is its own attraction as the casino is modeled after the Manhattan skyline. But inside is the intense 4,777-foot-long roller coaster, featuring a drop of 144 feet, and attaining speeds of 67 mph. Not for the faint of heart.

Near the south end of the Strip is **Luxor Las Vegas**, a pyramid-shaped hotel that looks like it was just transplanted from the Nile Valley. One attraction is fittingly King Tut's Tomb with numerous Egyptian artifacts. The Luxor seems fixated by death as one bizarre attraction there is Bodies—The Exhibition. It could be called "Med school comes to the masses" as 21 bodies have been saved in a polymer preservation. The exhibit does feature lungs from smokers and non-smokers, so graphic only the most addicted would light up afterwards. Luxor also offers an exhibit with over 300 artifacts about the ill-fated Titanic.

Shark Reef

Many consider the Shark Reef at the **Mandalay Bay Resort & Casino** to be the Strip's finest attraction. Shark Reef opened in 2000 and is the only accredited aquarium in Nevada. While there are plenty of sharks, there are a total of more than 1,200 different species of marine life including exotic fresh and saltwater fish, a 300-pound sea turtle, and even a crocodile. You enter through a tunnel which houses five species of sharks and the aquarium's largest animals. It is designed to look like a sunken shipwreck and contains 1.3 million gallons of water.

Downtown Fremont Street

Downtown is the Fremont Street Experience, a dazzling display of lights and sounds that puts on a free show every hour on the hour. There are also two stages that feature constantly changing entertainment.

Old Mormon Fort State Historic Park

Not far from downtown, in fact just a few blocks north at 500 E. Washington Ave., is where the desert city got its start. Much of the old fort established by Mormons in 1855 has been reconstructed and one original and still standing adobe building now houses the visitor center. It's a quiet and reflective refuge in a loud and changing city.

Natural History Museum

Las Vegas has grown so fast it has often obliterated or at least ignored its history, but next door to the Old Mormon Fort on the Las Vegas Boulevard side (900 N. Las Vegas Blvd.) is the delightful Natural History Museum. Only a few years old, it was established and is still provided for by private funding. Along with fossils and dioramas, there are hands-on exhibits and other interactive displays.

Vegas Indoor Skydiving

Billed as "The Ultimate Experience of Freedom," Vegas Indoor Skydiving is at 200 Convention Center Dr. (behind the strip mall next to the Riviera). Built in 1982 and formerly known as Flyaway, it was the country's first indoor skydiving facility and uses a vertical wind tunnel to create the body flight sensation.

Atomic Testing Museum

An Atomic Testing Museum opened in 2005 at 755 E. Flamingo Rd. in Las Vegas to enlighten people about the Nevada Test Site and its impact on the nation and world.

It includes an 8,000-square-foot exhibit hall with artifacts from the Smithsonian Institution, Lawrence Livermore Laboratory, and pieces of the Berlin Wall and World Trade Centers. It is an interactive experience, with touch screens, motion sensitive plasma TV presentations, and audio interviews with former workers from the test site.

Neon Museum

The Neon Museum downtown is a collection of classic neon signs from the 1940s to the present day. The museum currently features 11 refurbished, vintage neon signs on display downtown at the Fremont Street Experience. There is also The Neon Boneyard, a nearby three-acre outdoor site viewable by appointment that features other historic signs.

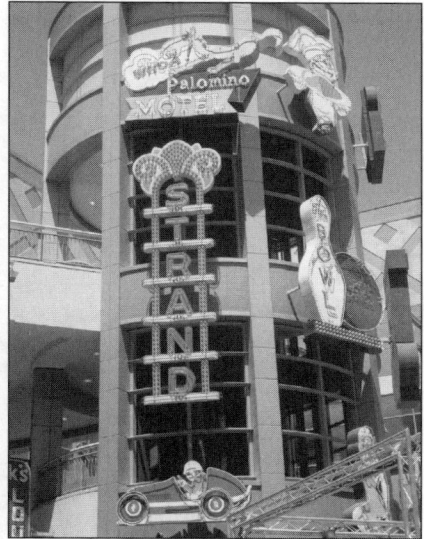
The Neon Museum

Erotic Heritage Museum

Las Vegas's newest museum, the Erotic Heritage Museum, or Sex Museum, is a 24,000-square-foot display featuring permanent exhibits designed "to preserve the erotic imagination as depicted through artistic expression"—as if Las Vegas visitors need the impetus. Guests can explore the vast array of sociocultural perspectives including the unfolding of the twentieth century's American Sexual Revolution. Well, Las Vegas has been a big part of that revolution.

The Las Vegas Museum of Law Enforcement and Organized Crime

The planned "Mob Museum," as it is called, is covered in another chapter (Glamorizing Gangsters). It will be interactive and provide an authentic view of organized crime and its impact upon Las Vegas. The controversial museum, which Mayor Oscar Goodman insists will not glamorize gangsters, will be located downtown in the former federal courthouse and United States Post Office building.

Fire a Machine Gun

In my era we joined the army, but if you've got an itchy finger to fire off a few bursts from a machine gun, Vegas is the place for you. The Gun Store at 2900 E. Tropicana has an indoor range where you can act out your own mobster fantasies. They've got Uzis, AK-47s, Thompsons, and Greaseguns. Anything you might want to fire.

A competing firm, Discount Firearms, Inc. is at 3084 S. Highland, and also offers instructors in safety and firearms, including certifications. While you're there, you can even rent a handgun for only $35.

World's Largest Gambling Superstore

Having a store as a top attraction may seem strange, but this is no ordinary store. It's a fascinating array of everything for the gambler: how-to books, custom poker chips and playing cards, blackjack tables, slot machines, and roulette wheels. There are over 5,000 items, many of which "you can't get back home." The 8,000-square-foot Gamblers General Store is located at 800 S. Main Street and they also have an online catalog.

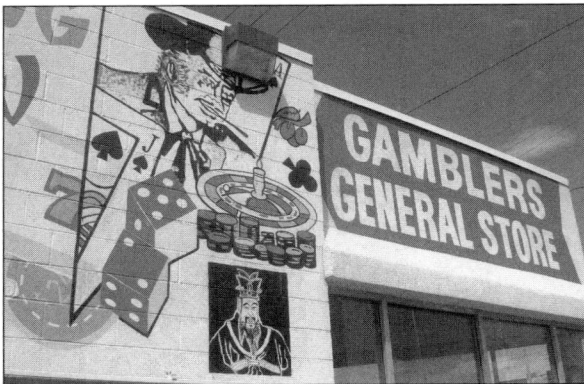

The Gamblers General Store

As mentioned, there is always something in Sin City; and attractions can even be visited more than once as exhibits rotate, and new things are constantly being added to keep Las Vegas changing and charged. If you can't find what you want in Las Vegas, keep looking. It's there.

Las Vegas Tunnel Dwellers
Lost People Underground

There are as many stories about Las Vegas as there are residents and visitors. A long-standing joke was about the guy who arrived in a $20,000 car and left in a $200,000 bus.

For every success, there are numerous examples of defeat. The fast pulse of the city tends to sap one's energy, not to mention one's pocketbook. To remain in Vegas, some indigents often do whatever it takes: panhandle, dumpster dive, credit hustle, scrounge recyclables, become prostitutes, and/or deal drugs or otherwise engage in criminal behavior. An inevitable step for those down-and-out folks is to scale down their lodgings. How low can you go in scaling down lodging? How about underground? Some people, after departing the cheapest apartments and temporary lodging and trying to "make it" on the streets, have found refuge underground. Yes, literally underground.

Like ancient Rome, the catacombs of Paris, and the extensive New York Subway system, Las Vegas too has an elaborate underground. There are 350 miles of flood channels coursing throughout the bowels of the city, much of which is directly below the glittering Las Vegas Strip. The underground community, however, is void of glitter. It's a dark, damp, and dirty existence for about 700 denizens who make their homes there, directly under some of the world's largest hotels. The tunnel dwellers have collectively fallen on hard times, but surprisingly little of it from gambling. While most of the tunnel residents gamble when they can, the "knock-out" punch for most of them has been addiction to alcohol and drugs.

The recession and dismal job outlook for those who want gainful employment has also combined to keep some of the residents down, and under. Many had worked in the hotels over their heads but lost their jobs due to downsizing, or heroin or other addictions. One admitted to a reporter that he would like to leave the tunnels but couldn't because of two outstanding arrest warrants from old drug possession charges. In the meanwhile, they make their "homes" as comfortable as possible. Many have scrounged and assembled pretty elaborate "digs" for a storm tunnel. Beds and other simple furnishings either came from dumpsters or outside apartment complexes where property from "skips" has been ingloriously placed hoping someone might cart it away. That's gold to the sewer rats. Of course, a lot of their makeshift furniture has to be raised on blocks or crates lest the dampness and occasionally flooding carry the furnishings away. Despite scrambling from a desert deluge once in a while, and avoiding ill health from the dampness, not to mention sidestepping venomous spiders like black widows, some of the people have been there for 2, 3, and 4 years and are content with living there. One said, "It's not a terrible place to be if you're homeless. It's much cooler than on the streets, we get a breeze coming through and the cops don't really bother you. It's quiet and everyone helps each other out down here."

To eke out livings, even in their rent-free society, the temporary moles generally surface each day to do what they do best. Emerging into the Strip hotels and casinos, some go dumpster diving, some beg, and almost all of them go credit-hustling.

"Credit hustling" is an art form to hundreds of people, even little old ladies who live above ground. It involves prowling the casinos, checking out slot machine after slot machine for money or "credits" inadvertently left by drunken or careless gamblers.

The hustlers usually follow a pattern, working their way either up or down the Strip. One admitted to finding $500 a couple of times, but usually quits for the day after picking up about $20 or so. Matthew O'Brien, author of *Beneath The Neon*, went from reporter to activist as he has been trying to help find housing and health and drug counseling for the tunnel people. He discovered a strong resistance to help, with many unwilling to give up their addictions. "They like their freedom and that no one is telling them what to do."

Living in the tunnels has been precarious. When a desert thundershower strikes Las Vegas, roadways and underpasses quickly fill with water, rendering many thoroughfares impassable. That's nothing compared to what happens below, where all that water goes. It's not often, but those tunnels fill up and there have been 20 drownings in the past two decades, many of them the tunnel people. One tunnel couple admitted they came to Las Vegas for jobs, bright lights and all the excitement the city has to offer. After discovering jobs scarce, they've lived in the tunnels for two years. They found the bright lights in the tunnels pretty dim, and "excitement" for them is finding a big slot credit.

Gamblers Anonymous
The Dark Side of Gambling

Humans being humans, there will always be those who have a hard time living within established societal parameters. Many compulsive personalities are ravaged by substances that often have a lesser effect on others. Abuse of alcohol, drugs, tobacco, food, and, yes, even gambling can send those afflicted "out of control."

Las Vegas is perhaps the worst place to be for a compulsive personality— but the casinos love you. While they would never tacitly admit it, they like compulsive people. Like the National Rifle Association's (NRA) mantra, "Guns don't kill people, people do," the casinos contend that it's not the casinos' fault if people overdo it. Yeah right, but it's okay to exploit their weaknesses.

Compulsive people are, well, compulsive. They like to smoke, drink, eat, and gamble, often to excess. The casinos, cognizant of this and desirous of not offending a large percentage of their gamblers, seem to go out of their way to appeal to them. Smoking is rampant and encouraged in the casinos, even in the restaurants.

Buffets are designed for compulsive people. That all-you-can-eat approach has a definite appeal to all those folks who waddle in three times a day to gorge themselves. Compulsive people tend to have multiple disorders. Alcohol is most decidedly encouraged. A few free drinks or drink specials not only gives the players a good feeling about where they're playing, but, hopefully, relaxes them enough to make mistakes. Which leads us to the most obvious Las Vegas compulsion—gambling. The old prudent saying, "Never gamble more than you're afraid to lose," is good advice, but unfortunately that's hard to do, nearly impossible for many people.

Players visit casinos for different reasons. As mentioned in other chapters, some learn the skills and approach the games with purpose, goals, and discipline. Most folks, however, go for entertainment. Playing is an enjoyable experience and the lure of winning money adds to the excitement. Many players enjoy the adrenaline rush and some experience a high that accompanies the thrill when they risk money. This feeling can be so seductive and alluring that, unfortunately, some succumb to the darker side of gambling—addiction.

Canadian author Lorne Tepperman, in his book *Betting Their Lives: The Close Relations of Problem Gamblers*, estimates that 1 in 50, or 480,000 Canadian adults have a gambling problem. The same equation for the U.S. population would total over 4 million Americans with a gambling problem. A national survey conducted by the California Council on Problem Gambling (1-800-GAMBLER) boosted the scope, noting that problem gambling affects 3.7% of the U.S. population. Addiction is a compulsive need. What starts as a pleasurable experience turns into an uncontrollable destructive craving. When the thrill of the game outweighs everything else, the player has crossed over the line from player to addict. Gambling, like all addictions, can be devastating for the person and his/her family.

The addiction is pervasive. Katie Cunningham's 2005 fiction book *Nicotine Dreams: A Story of Compulsive Gambling* is based on her true-life problems. One online reviewer called the book "...the most frightening and real depiction of a descent into 'gambling hell' I have ever read..." Author Josh Axelrad vividly describes the subtle fall from disciplined card counter on a professional team to a compulsive poker player in his book *Repeat Until Rich*, (The Penguin Press, 2010). In a similar vein, *Gripped by Gambling* by Marilyn Lancelot (2007) echoes a true-life battle of the compulsion. Lancelot has been "gambling free" for over 16 years and has helped found several chapters of Gamblers Anonymous.

Which brings us to the obvious question: Are you a problem gambler? **Gamblers Anonymous (GA)** is a twelve-step program, patterned after Alcoholics Anonymous (AA), or Narcotics Anonymous (NA). They offer this 20-question quiz to those who think they might have a gambling problem:

Twenty Questions

1. Did you ever lose time from work or school due to gambling?
2. Has gambling ever made your home life unhappy?
3. Did gambling affect your reputation?
4. Have you ever felt remorse after gambling?
5. Did you ever gamble to get money with which to pay debts or otherwise solve financial difficulties?
6. Did gambling cause a decrease in your ambition or efficiency?
7. After losing did you feel you must return as soon as possible and win back your losses?
8. After a win did you have a strong urge to return and win more?
9. Did you often gamble until your last dollar was gone?
10. Did you ever borrow to finance your gambling?
11. Have you ever sold anything to finance gambling?
12. Were you reluctant to use "gambling money" for normal expenditures?
13. Did gambling make you careless of the welfare of yourself or your family?
14. Did you ever gamble longer than you had planned?
15. Have you ever gambled to escape worry or trouble?
16. Have you ever committed, or considered committing, an illegal act to finance gambling?
17. Did gambling cause you to have difficulty in sleeping?
18. Do arguments, disappointments, or frustrations create within you an urge to gamble?
19. Did you ever have an urge to celebrate any good fortune by a few hours of gambling?
20. Have you ever considered self destruction or suicide as a result of your gambling?

Those questions require that you give brutal answers. And the test only works if you're totally honest with yourself. Most compulsive gamblers will answer yes to at least seven of these questions. If you're in that category, you might seek out GA.

GA began in Los Angeles in 1957 and by 2005 there were over 1,000 GA meetings in the United States, plus more around the world.

At last count, there were 148 weekly meetings of Gamblers Anonymous in Nevada—107 of them in the Las Vegas area. There are a wide variety of options, meetings every day and night of the week, some Spanish speaking, some "Open" (anyone, friends etc.), and others "Closed" (Just the gambler). That's a lot of support out there for Las Vegans should they seek help.

Many of the Las Vegas meetings are held at the Unity Club in an older, primarily Asian strip mall on East Karen St. One wall sign inside the club bluntly addresses the problem gambler, "One Bet Is Too Much, and Many Bets Are Not Enough." Tables are set up meeting-style so participants can interact. Awaiting a meeting to commence one evening, several talked about their problem, even their gambling games of choice.

The 13 people in attendance that night were a mixed group, all ages, six females, four blacks. They solicitously welcomed the newcomer, offering the encouragement that comes from shared knowledge, experience, and agony.

Aside from financial insecurity, problem gambling has been shown to cause dysfunctional families, legal problems, employment difficulties, psychological distress, and higher rates of suicide and attempted suicide. Yet, fewer than 10% of those with gambling problems seek treatment. I kept thinking that there were many thousands times this group of 13 gambling away at the nearest casino.

The only requirement for GA membership is a desire to stop gambling. There are no dues or fees and GA is self-supporting through small contributions. A dollar or two each buys coffee and cookies for meetings. Controlling gambling (meaning still gambling, but only "a little") is an obsessive dream of compulsive gamblers, and most often a persistent illusion. Those successful in GA realize that abstinence is the only sure answer. In fact, control is such an illusion, fewer than 8% of those who initially attend GA remain in the program and abstain from gambling for over one year. So even GA is not a panacea unless one is willing to relinquish the control.

Gamblers Anonymous meetings are listed online, or you can find a meeting nearby by calling 1-800-522-4700. There have been online blog discussions debating whether or not the casinos should be held responsible for gambling addicts. Do they provide enough safeguards to prevent gamblers from gambling away all of their money? Should they? Or is it enough for them to declare that their guests are adults, responsible for their actions? After all, "Guns don't kill people...."

CHAPTER 10

FROM CASINOS TO MEGACASINOS

The end of the twentieth century brought a new type of casino, a Megacasino, ultra-expensive, huge, and luxurious.

Through the years, the power along the Strip shifted to just a few moguls who even battled each other to build the biggest and the best.

Even amid a difficult economic year a new concept, the large CityCenter project, opened in 2010 right in the middle of the Las Vegas Strip.

A Downtown Renaissance

Back in Glitter Gulch

By the 1990s, the Las Vegas Strip was growing so fast it was becoming wall-to-wall casinos, sucking up any land that had the audacity to remain vacant. In the minds of many, it became that the Strip *was* Las Vegas. And it looked like the Fremont Street area downtown was relegated to becoming a second class backwater.

From the late 1980s to the mid-1990s, there was some limited growth activity going on downtown: the Fitzgeralds and Main Street Station hotel-casinos opened, and the Horseshoe expanded into Binion's—but nothing like out on Las Vegas Blvd.

Fitzgeralds — 1987

Taking over a hotel at the corner of Fremont and Third Street called the Sundance, Fitzgeralds Casino & Hotel opened in 1987 with a "Luck of the Irish" theme. Fitzgeralds is a 34-story, 638-room hotel and casino, has a 42,000-square-foot casino, a race and sports book, and several restaurants.

Horseshoe/Binion's

Benny Binion, who had bought into the Las Vegas Club Hotel & Casino on Fremont Street with J. Kell Houssels Sr. in 1947, had opened his own casino, the Horseshoe Casino, in 1951. In 1970, Benny's son Jack began hosting the World Series of Poker (WSOP) at the

Binion's Gambling Hall and Hotel

Horseshoe, and it eventually became the largest poker tournament in the world.

In 1988, the Horseshoe expanded by acquiring the Mint Las Vegas, the high-rise hotel next door, and it became Binion's Gambling Hall & Hotel. That expansion provided room for Binion's first poker room. In 2004 the 366 hotel room, 81 gaming table, 800 slot hotel-casino was bought by Harrah's, and was sold again shortly thereafter, even though the name Binion's has endured.

In 2008 Four Queens Hotel & Casino owner Terry Caudill (TLC Enterprises) bought Binion's and replaced the $1 million that had been on display from the 1950s until 2000. Now, instead of rare vintage $10,000 bills, much smaller denominations make up a huge stack encased in an acrylic pyramid. The casino will take your photo next to the cool $1 million for free.

Main Street Station — 1992

Around the corner from Fremont Street, the Main Street Station Hotel & Casino was opened by Bob Snow in 1992, about two blocks north of the Plaza. It is linked by a skywalk to the California Hotel & Casino across the street. While not as luxurious as some, it has 406 hotel rooms and a 27,000-square-foot casino. Like its sister, the California, it caters to a large Hawaiian clientele.

Golden Nugget

The old (1946) Golden Nugget Hotel & Casino underwent a lot of changes, especially after Steve Wynn became a majority stockholder. In 1984 extensive remodeling made it the largest and most luxurious downtown hotel-casino (now 1,907 deluxe rooms and suites with its new tower that opened in 2009).

Capitalizing on its name association, in 1981 the Golden Nugget decided that what might attract people would be a real "golden nugget." So they acquired and put on display not just any but the world's largest gold nugget, a 27.21 kilo monster (that's 61 pounds or 875 troy ounces). Only superlatives for Las Vegas.

One would think the "The Hand of Faith" (it resembles a hand) nugget would be featured prominently. However, it innocuously sits on a turntable setting in a little-used corridor behind the casino floor. A few smaller nuggets (only about baseball size) accompany the monster.

Even with those few hotel additions, by the mid-1990s Downtown Las Vegas needed something to draw tourists. They came up with the Fremont Street Experience.

Fremont Street Experience

What's Las Vegas without lights? I remember Vegas during the 1973 oil crisis when the city's signature lights were turned off. Minimum lighting dimmed way down provided the only illumination. It was so unlike Vegas it was shocking. It made me think about how London must have been during WWII. Fortunately, those austere measures didn't last long, not in Vegas where neon gave the town its identity. Looking to lights, a cooperative venture of 10 downtown casinos owners got the first five blocks of the famous downtown "Glitter Gulch" closed to traffic and opened the now-famous Fremont Street Experience light show in December 1995.

Covering the 175,700-square-foot pedestrian mall for four blocks (1,500 feet long) is a huge rounded canopy imbedded with more than 12.5 million multi-color LED light bulbs, which replaced the original incandescent lights. The dazzling overhead animated display reaches a height of 90 feet and has 220 speakers capable of delivering 550,000 watts of sound.

It's been a success and people line up outside every hour on the hour each night to catch the free high-tech shows of color, sound, and lights, attracting 19 million visitors during a recent year.

Vegas Vic

There's also Vegas Vic downtown guarding the Fremont Street roost. Nothing was more iconic of Glitter Gulch's western heritage than Vegas Vic, the 40-foot neon cowboy placed at the entrance to the Pioneer Club in 1951. He waved his arm and his recorded voice blurted out "Howdy, Pardner" every 15 minutes. The Pioneer Club has gone to the big casino in the sky; a souvenir shop occupies its old space; and Vegas Vic, well the plug has been pulled on his animation but he's still there, mutely guarding the entrance. He no longer talks and waves, but he's still ablaze in colorful Vegas neon glory.

The pedestrian mall under the canopy tends to unify the area and there are always activities and shows in the two adjacent stages.

Fremont Street "Zoo"

Even with the attractions the Downtown Las Vegas hotels and casinos have offered in recent years, it has still been outpaced and out-casinoed by the glittery and glamorous Strip. Downtown still attracts a different clientele than the Strip, and in the opinions of many a somewhat sadder one.

For comparison, when a European arrives in the U.S., one of his or her most noticeable first images is the high percentage of obese American people.

They often comment about it. Then, when Americans go to Europe, most are startled at the high number of smokers there. Go to Russia and the numerous folks walking around sipping alcoholic beverages forms another cultural image. For poorly dressed people, go to any developing country.

For all of the above (large percentages of sloppily dressed, and/or obese people, walking around smoking and drinking), you can't go wrong going to Fremont Street. The tourists themselves become a side show almost every night, even though there is plenty going on around them. Scantily-clad "showgirls" compete for the tourist photo-op dollar with numerous Elvis wannabees, although I saw one "Elvis" who, at about 300 pounds, should hang up his stretched-out white suit.

Fremont Street

Most of the Fremont Street casinos have sexy gals in skimpy outfits dealing at the streetside blackjack tables, while others gyrate to music nearby. Women in little more than low-cut bras and bikini thongs cajole passersby from casino and strip club entrances. Meanwhile a few feet away drunks are stepping around baby strollers and kids eating ice cream. Alcohol reigns king as bars are set up along the pedestrian street and few revelers, outside the kids, are not carrying an alcoholic drink. It is more than a zoo; it is a happening.

Glitter Gulch continues to draw people, for the Fremont Street Experience and the Fremont Street "experience." For those who care, there's also the nearby Neon Museum, the humongous gold nugget, the more relaxed table play downtown, and the generally better slot odds, but the area's people-watching offers the most fascinating attraction.

Las Vegas Redevelopment Agency

The City of Las Vegas consists of more than Fremont Street. In 1986 the Redevelopment Agency (RDA) was formed to battle the urban decay downtown.

One major RDA achievement is the 150-store Las Vegas Premium Outlet center. With a lot of parking, the popular mall is between Bonneville Avenue and Charleston Boulevard, and sandwiched between the I-15 freeway and the Union Pacific Railroad tracks.

Another RDA project is the three-building World Market Center on Bonneville Ave. It features state-of-the-art showrooms in its massive five million square feet of space.

One of the most remarkable architectural oddities houses the new (July, 2009) Lou Ruvo Center for Brain Health, operated by the Cleveland Clinic. It looks like a pile of aluminum that caught fire and melted.

A Pioneer Trail for tourists has been established to highlight Las Vegas history, and the city has been partitioned for various types of development.

One project that might be an RDA challenge is the Fremont East District. Entrance signs have gone up and several neon signs grace the street to render a positive first effect. However, the seedy bars, loan shops, low priced hotels, and constant congregation of street people are grim reminders that more needs to be done.

Fremont East District

There's been a renaissance going on downtown. It's not complete, but Las Vegas—even Downtown Las Vegas—knows only one direction and that's forward.

1990s – 2000s
CASINOS OF THE CENTENNIAL

While downtown was struggling to attract gamblers and tourists during the mid-1990s, down south on the Las Vegas Strip, things were humming along.

In addition to the early '90s casinos already unveiled (Excalibur, Luxor, Treasure Island, MGM Grand), Bally's Hotel & Casino opened in 1993 on the site of the original MGM Grand, which itself was built upon where the Bonanza (1967-1973) once stood. Then opening in 1995, the hip Hard Rock Hotel & Casino off the Strip on Paradise Rd. was so successful it became a standard for other Hard Rock hotels in other cities.

The late '90s saw continued growth away from downtown. About midway between downtown and the Strip, Vegas World, an old landmark casino at the corner of Sahara and Las Vegas Boulevard, became history in 1996 to make room for an entrepreneur's dream.

The Stratosphere — 1996

The entrepreneur was Bob Stupak and his dream was the biggest. He built the most dominant feature of the Las Vegas landscape and the tallest observation tower in the U.S., the 1,149-foot Stratosphere Las Vegas. It's big; the hotel itself has 2,444 rooms and the 55,784-square-foot casino has 120 table games and 1,450 slots.

Stratosphere Las Vegas

The main Stratosphere attraction, however, is way up top next to a wonderful revolving restaurant, where a couple of rides, including a roller coaster, dangle thrill seekers over the city skyline. There's also Sky Jump, a dramatic new free fall attraction, that's the largest of its kind.

Stupak, who died of leukemia in September 2009, was himself a Vegas legend, a flashy promoter, and gambler who won a World Series of Poker title in 1989 and also won a $1 million Super Bowl bet. His largesse fit perfectly with his adopted city.

Monte Carlo — 1996

Another 1996 debut on the Strip was the Monte Carlo Resort & Casino, a joint venture between Mirage Hotels and Circus Circus. The understated European-style resort has 3,002 rooms and 256 suites. The 102,197-square-foot casino is home to 1,800 slot machines and 87 table games. There is a 1,200-seat auditorium that has featured the magician Lance Burton since its opening.

The Orleans — 1996

In December 1996, the Orleans Hotel & Casino opened off-Strip, out on Tropicana Ave. The hotel has 1,866 rooms, but the gigantic casino features a whopping 3,110 slot machines and 94 table games. The Orleans is popular with locals as it also has a 70-lane bowling alley, an 18-screen movie theater, and a 9,000 seat arena that is home to the Las Vegas Wranglers hockey team.

New York New York — 1997

In January 1997, New York New York Hotel & Casino opened on the Strip. The new casino featured a New York City skyline complete with a one-half-size (150-foot) Statue of Liberty. Along with a casino that houses 1,885 slots, there's a fun zone and a 67-mile-per-hour roller coaster that zips around the place.

Bellagio — 1998

Steve Wynn had opened the Mirage in 1989, and most insiders consider that the beginning of the megaresort era. But Wynn still had a few aces up his sleeve and a dream even bigger and better. Enter the Bellagio Las Vegas. Wynn had acquired the land just south of Caesars Palace where the

New York New York Hotel & Casino

Dunes Hotel & Casino used to be and originally was going to call his dream project the Beau Rivage. On an Italian vacation he was enchanted by a village called Bellagio which he learned meant "a place of elegant relaxation." He scrapped the earlier title in favor of Bellagio as he wanted his theme to be "pure luxury"—marble bathrooms, classical music and peaceful gardens.

Wynn pushed the casino envelope ever further and oversaw construction of the most expensive and fanciest Las Vegas casino yet. It opened in October 1998 with 3,933 hotel rooms, 512 suites, a 116,000-square-foot casino, and a record-setting cost of $1.6 *billion*. There are high-end retail shops, a Gallery of Fine Art, and a world-famous water show out front. The dancing fountains feature more than 4,500 lights and over 1,200 water nozzles.

By the time the Bellagio opened, Wynn was back-pedaling from his initial family-oriented destination mindset and initiated a policy barring persons under 18 years of age not registered guests of the hotel.

Mandalay Bay — 1999

The year 1999 again was a multiple-opening year for casinos on the Strip with the debuts of Mandalay Bay Resort & Casino, the Venetian Resort & Casino, and the Paris Hotel & Casino.

The glittering (gold leaf on windows) Mandalay Bay at the extreme south end of the Strip is huge (4,332 rooms, 2,010 slots, and 193 table games). There are 41 high-end shops and some fine restaurants; a new tower was added in 2004.

The old, longtime Western-themed Hacienda was imploded to make room for the Mandalay Bay. The Blues Brothers made the March 1999 grand opening memorable as actors Dan Aykroyd, Jim Belushi, and John Goodman led a parade of Harley-Davidson motorcycles through the front doors.

Circus Circus Enterprises, the company that built the hotel, even changed its corporate name to Mandalay Resort Group.

Venetian — 1999

In April 1997, Las Vegas Sands Inc. broke ground to build the $1.5 billion Venetian Resort & Casino on the grounds of the original Sands Hotel & Casino on the Las Vegas Strip. The venerable and historic Sands, which CEO Sheldon Adelson had owned for eight years, was imploded in November 1996.

The luxurious, all-suite (4,049 of them), 36-story Venetian, between Harrah's and The Palazzo, has a 120,000-square-foot casino, 19 restaurants, Grand Canal shops, and gondola rides with singing gondoliers. It was one of the most expensive resorts of its kind when it opened on May 3, 1999, and has been honored with architectural and other awards naming it as one the finest hotels in the world.

Paris Hotel & Casino — 1999

Closing out the decade, and the century for that matter, the last Las Vegas Strip hotel to open was the Paris Hotel & Casino in September 1999. Hilton bought Bally's Hotel & Casino in the late 1990s and continued the project Bally's was planning, another hotel and connecting promenade just south of the old MGM-Bally's. Called the Paris Hotel & Casino, it's Parisian theme includes a half-scale, 541-foot-tall replica of the Eiffel Tower, a sign in the shape of the Montgolfier balloon, a two-thirds-size Arc de Triomphe, and a replica of La Fontaine des Mers.

As Hilton then divested itself of all its Las Vegas properties, Harrah's Entertainment bought Paris and Bally's Las Vegas, which was linked by a promenade, and also the Las Vegas Monorail which runs from the MGM Grand to the Convention Center and the Las Vegas Hilton. The megacasinos had arrived and the Strip never looked back. Many of the original casinos that defined the town were gone, blasted into smithereens, the demolitions themselves even creating still yet more dramatic visual effects for Las Vegas visitors.

The new century awaited, and it hardly seemed possible that the world destination resort called Las Vegas was not yet even 100 years old.

Paris Hotel & Casino

Power on the Strip

Battle of The Moguls

W ith the advent of the megacasinos along the Strip came money, and with it power. Forget the mob; they were gone. Forget Howard Hughes; he was gone too. The new Raiders of Las Vegas were board-room sharks, and they went after prey like every day was a feeding frenzy. Vegas casino men like Jackie Gaughan, Sam Boyd, Jay Sarno, and Bill Bennett had watched over their empires, but were soon overshadowed by the new "Kingpins"—Kirk Kerkorian (a longtime old/new kingpin), Steve Wynn, Gary Loveman, and Sheldon Adelson. The head-to-head clash of the titans, Wynn and Kerkorian, was of significant interest, extending way beyond Vegas to cor-porate boardrooms everywhere.

Kirk Kerkorian

Kerkorian has been redefining Las Vegas resorts for over 40 years and many insiders conclude he has done more in transforming the mob-ruled des-tination into a modern city controlled by capitalism and mega-financial deals than anyone else.

Born in 1917 to Armenian-American immigrants, he became a pilot dur-ing World War II, saved his money, and bought Trans International Airlines after the war to shuttle gamblers to the fledgling town of Las Vegas. In 1962, for just under $1 million he bought the Strip land where the Caesars Palace now stands. He collected rent and finally sold it to Caesars in 1968, netting himself $9 million. In 1967 he bought 82 acres on Paradise Road and built the International Hotel (now the Las Vegas Hilton), the world's largest at the time.

In 1969 he bought MGM Studios in Hollywood and also opened his sec-ond "world's largest at the time" hotel, the MGM Grand Hotel & Casino in Las Vegas. In 1986 he sold that original MGM to Bally's for $594 million and later (1993) built the modern MGM Grand Hotel farther south on the Strip.

The second MGM Grand Hotel & Casino at Tropicana Avenue had a world-record 5,000-plus rooms, a 15,000-seat arena and a 330-acre theme park, his third "world's biggest hotel" when it opened, and the first hotel to cost $1 billion to build. Its 171,500-square-foot casino was almost double the size of most on the Strip.

In 1997, Kerkorian opened another hotel-casino across the street in part-nership with Gary Primm and Primadonna Resorts—the New York New York Hotel & Casino. He later bought out Primm's share, setting the stage for con-tinued buyouts. And he had his eye on some.

Steve Wynn

Steve Wynn was on a roll. His Mirage Resort & Casino (1989) set new standards in luxury. His Treasure Island Hotel & Casino (1993) was immensely popular, and he pulled out all the cards in opening the super-luxurious $1.6 billion Bellagio Las Vegas in 1998.

Steve Wynn was a major player. Born in upstate New York in 1942, Wynn took over his father's debt-ridden East Coast bingo operation. He made it profitable, paid off debts, sold it, and moved to Las Vegas in 1967 where he bought some land and a minor stake in the Frontier Hotel & Casino. In 1971 he parlayed profit from a land deal into controlling interest in the Golden Nugget Hotel & Casino, which he totally revamped, making it the largest and most successful downtown hotel.

The flamboyant and lavish Wynn has been known for spending lots of money to provide the finest in luxuries and amenities. That didn't work so well in Biloxi, Mississippi where his casino there, which opened in 1999, cost way too much and wasn't appreciated by the clientele they were able to attract.

Initially Mirage Resorts coated over that Southern mistake and the price of the corporation shares still rose. Wynn then announced plans to build in Donald Trump's backyard, Atlantic City, and this attracted money from Goldman Sachs, who bought 16.6 million shares of Mirage at $25 each.

The Deal

That was the high point for Mirage Resorts, as shortly thereafter Wynn warned that earnings would be roughly a third of what Wall Street analysts had predicted. Shares plummeted to the glee of the vultures circling overhead. Trump is even said to have crowed, "…Mirage is dead."

Wynn went to meet with financial gurus at an investment conference but his ego and Wall Street naïveté got in the way. Instead of answering hard, direct questions, he optimistically began to describe upcoming projects. They weren't impressed and the stock continued to drop.

Kerkorian started buying Mirage Resorts stock like mad, picking up 10 million shares for approximately $12 a share. Goldman Sachs lost a ton of money on its Mirage investment, and by 2000 Kerkorian and his MGM Grand Inc. initiated a bid to buy Mirage, starting at $17 per share. After a lot of scrambling and negotiating, The Deal was ultimately consummated in June 2000 for $6.6 billion ($21 a share) and MGM Grand became the new owners of the Mirage, Treasure Island, and Bellagio. (Nine years later MGM Mirage sold Treasure Island to K Hotels).

Wynn was losing his flagship hotels, but he was not out. He even said the deal doubled his net worth. Five weeks before the sale was closed (April 27, 2000) Wynn purchased the Desert Inn and its golf course for $270 million.

MGM Mirage Grows

Kerkorian renamed his company MGM Mirage, which became the world's second largest gaming company (to Harrah's Entertainment). In 2004, MGM Mirage then acquired Mandalay Resort Group to claim the "biggest" title.

At that time, Mandalay consisted of the following Las Vegas hotels and casinos: Circus Circus,

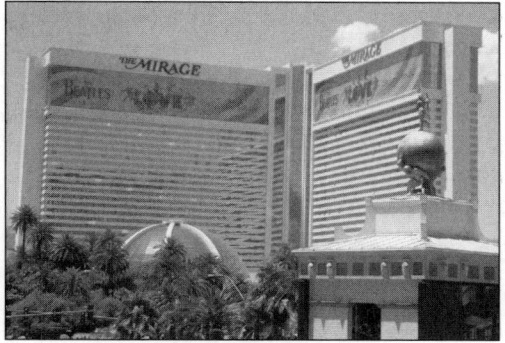

The Mirage

Slots-A-Fun, Excalibur, Luxor, Mandalay Bay, and Monte Carlo (joint ownership), as well as two in Reno, two in Laughlin (Colorado Belle and Edgewater), two in Jean, Nevada (Gold Strike and Nevada Landing), the Railroad Pass Hotel and Casino in Henderson, Nevada, and casinos in Mississippi, Illinois, and Michigan. Quite a package they picked up in one swoop.

That acquisition, worth $7.9 billion in cash and debt assumption, meant Kerkorian's company owned 10 major hotel-casinos in Las Vegas and with the others, surpassed Harrah's and become the biggest casino company ever, with nearly 30 properties worldwide, about 70,000 workers, and annual revenues of nearly $7 billion.

Mandalay Resort Group

The Mandalay Resort Group that MGM Mirage acquired had earlier sprung from Circus Circus Enterprises which went public in 1983. Circus Circus had developed the Excalibur Hotel & Casino in 1990, the Luxor in 1993, and the Mandalay Bay Resort & Casino in 2000 for which the group was renamed. Mandalay Bay was also a partner in the 1996 opening of the nearby Monte Carlo Resort & Casino.

Jay Sarno

The genesis of Mandalay Resort Group was the Circus Circus Hotel & Casino, the brainchild of Jay Sarno. Born in 1922, Sarno owned several high-profile hotels, creating both Caesars Palace and Circus Circus.

The World War II veteran got his start with borrowed money from Allen Dorfman of the Teamsters Union with which he initially built a small Atlanta motel.

Seeing opportunity in Las Vegas, he began building a hotel casino with a European flair and his opulent Caesars Palace opened in 1966. Three years later he and some partners sold it for $60 million to work on their new project, Circus Circus, which opened in 1968. The hotel at Circus Circus opened after the casino and circus acts had become popular. The Circus Circus was leased to William Bennett, a Del Webb executive, and his partner, Bill Pennington, who turned it into a money machine.

After retiring from the Circus Circus, Sarno spent the rest of his time tutoring hotel owner management, including one astute student named Steve Wynn. In 1984, Sarno died of a heart attack while gambling at Caesars Palace, a hotel he formerly owned. Sarno's vision and fanciful imagination set a relentless and productive pace for Las Vegas.

Gary Loveman

Another force to be reckoned with on the Las Vegas Strip is former Harvard Business School professor Gary Loveman, who took over Harrah's Entertainment (now Caesars Entertainment) in 2005. Harrah's has been a dominant player in the gaming world since William F. (Bill) Harrah opened a small Reno bingo parlor in 1937.

In 1990 former lawyer Phil Satre took over and instituted numerous innovations. In 1995 Satre became president of the new Harrah's Entertainment and the company was still growing, adding Players International, Harveys Casino Resorts, and Horseshoe Gaming Holdings to amass an astonishing total of 36 casinos and 42,000 employees. Phil Satre turned the reins over to the highly respected Loveman in 2003. The former professor was a practical, down-to-earth businessman, a unique fit in flashy Las Vegas, but using his business acumen Loveman soon became a very respected player.

After seeing MGM Mirage buy out the Mandalay Resort Group, he too looked for opportunity and saw it at Caesars Palace. He had considered building high-end casinos on the Strip for Harrah's clients, but it appeared the costs and time demanded were daunting. But an established class act would be irresistible. Within weeks of the MGM Mirage/Mandalay Resort deal, Harrah's made an offer of $9.3 billion for Caesars Palace. Loveman, one of the best minds in Las Vegas, had a challenge. Caesars Palace was showing a profit and some of its board members, like Barron Hilton, were loathe to part with it, seeing it as the end of an era. Others didn't want to lose the perks a board member enjoys. Loveman hammered away at them, and by June, 2005, the sale was concluded, not only making Harrah's again the world's largest gaming company (42 casinos), but giving the company its first big luxury presence in Las Vegas. Harrah's then owned five major Strip resorts, including the high roller Caesars Palace and 20% of the Strip's hotel rooms. When asked why he sought the merger, CEO Gary Loveman explained that as well-known and popular as the Harrah's brand is with recreational gaming enthusiasts nationwide, the company still lacked a luxury option in Las Vegas. "The acquisition of Caesars fills that void," he said.

Loveman has continued to lead Harrah's (renamed Caesars Entertainment in December 2010) growth, not only refining, but adding to the world's largest gaming company.

In September 2009, Harrah's bought the 2,500-room Planet Hollywood Hotel & Casino. That resort, on the site of the original Aladdin Hotel & Casino, sits directly south of Harrah's Paris Hotel & Casino, giving the company seven contiguous resorts on the east side of the Las Vegas Strip. Not to mention that iconic Caesars Palace across the street. Harrah's has a plan to link their casinos via a high-end pedestrian corridor with about 20 restaurants and bars called Project Link.

Sheldon Adelson

Sheldon Adelson, the Chairman and CEO of Las Vegas Sands Corp., was born in 1933 to Jewish immigrant parents. His father drove a taxi and Sheldon always worked, owning his first business at age 12. In 1979 Adelson and partners developed the computer trade show COMDEX, which became the defining computer trade show through much of the 1980s and 1990s.

Adelson purchased the Sands Hotel & Casino in Las Vegas in 1988, and the following year, constructed the Sands Expo and Convention Center, the only privately owned and operated convention center in the United States.

In 1991 Adelson imploded the venerable Sands and spent $1.5-billion to construct the Venetian Resort & Casino, a Venice-themed resort hotel and casino, a 4,000 plus all-suite, $1.5 billion hotel on the grounds of the original Sands.

In 1995, Adelson and his partners sold the Interface Group Show Division, including the COMDEX shows, to Softbank Corporation of Japan for $862 million; Adelson's personal share was just over $500 million. He vastly increased his net worth again in December 2004 upon the initial public offering of Las Vegas Sands by selling just 10% of the shares. Adelson led the drive to establish a casino in Macau, the former Portuguese colony that has become a major Chinese gambling city. The one million-square-foot Sands Macau opened in 2004 and Adelson made his investment back in one year.

Even though he lost much of his multi-billion-dollar fortune in the Great Recession of 2008-09, Adelson's Las Vegas Sands Corp. constructed a casino resort in Singapore. The new casino, Marina Bay Sands, opened in April, 2010 at a rumored cost of $5.4 billion.

The power on the Las Vegas Strip is now relegated to a few tycoons who have the skill and daring to play the high-stakes game. Forget the high rollers and the whales. They are but tenants in the houses of some very skilled and daring Monopoly players.

The Newest Casinos
STEVE WYNN ROARS BACK

The Wynn Las Vegas

S teve Wynn ushered in the megaresort age by building the Mirage, Treasure Island, and Bellagio. After selling them to MGM Mirage, he set his sights on even bigger things. He took Wynn Resorts Limited public in 2002, and became a billionaire in 2004 when his net worth doubled to $1.3 billion.

In 2000, Wynn purchased the 50-year-old Desert Inn and its 218 acres for $270 million. On the site he constructed the opulent Wynn Las Vegas, a tall sleek tower that houses 2,716 hotel rooms and an 111,000-square-foot casino. Bringing nature back to the Strip, out front is an 18-story man-made mountain, a rock-strewn waterfall, and a three-acre lake. Opened on April 28, 2005, it was the first new hotel on the Strip in five years. And to top off the hotel's upscale shopping options, there is a luxury Ferrari/Maserati dealership on premises.

Setting his sights elsewhere, in fact to the new gambling capital of the world, Macau, a brief jet ferry ride from Hong Kong, Wynn successfully bid on a franchise there. The Wynn Macau, the first Las Vegas-style integrated resort (casino/hotel) in Asia, opened in September 2006.

Encore

In April, 2006, Wynn Las Vegas celebrated its one-year anniversary by breaking ground on a second hotel tower next door. It was originally to be the Encore Suites as an expansion of the Wynn Las Vegas, but evolved into a separate full-scale resort. The 2,034-room Encore at Wynn Las Vegas cost $2.3 billion and shares resources with the Wynn Las Vegas resort. They are connected by an upscale shopping arcade. Despite the dismal economic situation at the time, the Encore formally opened on December 22, 2008 to large crowds. The Encore and Wynn sit side by side, their smooth copper finishes reflecting opulence in the desert sun, although at 63 floors, the Encore is three floors higher. The company has also completed construction of Encore at Wynn Macau, a further expansion of

Encore Suites

Wynn Macau. Encore at Wynn Macau added a fully integrated resort hotel to Wynn Macau with approximately 410 luxury suites and four villas, along with restaurants, additional retail space and additional gaming space. Encore at Wynn Macau opened in April 2010, costing approximately $600 million.

In October 2009, Wynn Macau, Ltd. had its ordinary shares of common stock listed on the Stock Exchange of Hong Kong Limited and sold 1.4375 billion (27.7%) shares of its common stock through an initial public offering. Net proceeds to the company as a result of this transaction were approximately $1.8 billion.

After all that activity, wonder what Steve Wynn will do for an encore? After all, Wynn Resorts enjoyed a 31.7% increase in revenue for the fourth quarter 2009 over the previous year.

The Palms — 2001

The "in" place to be these day is the Palms Casino Resort, or simply The Palms, a hip casino hotel well off the Strip on Flamingo Road. The main tower has 702 rooms and suites and contains a 95,000-square-foot casino, a recording studio, and a 2,200 seat showroom. The Palms opened in November 2001, and is owned by George J. Maloof Jr., owner of the Sacramento Kings (NBA) and the Sacramento Monarchs (WNBA). Maloof is a UNLV grad who studied casino management and successfully operated hotels and casinos in Nevada, California, and Colorado before building The Palms. Despite being off-Strip, The Palms has become a popular destination for many, especially with the younger crowd, athletes, and Hollywood celebrities.

The Palms hosts the annual CineVegas film festival, and is home to several top Las Vegas nightclubs, including Moon Nightclub, Rain Nightclub, and now the world's only Playboy Club. In October 2005, the "Fantasy Tower" opened at a cost of $600 million. The new tower offers a two-story, 10,000-square-foot suite that includes the world's only basketball court in a hotel suite. Some of the other "Fantasy" rooms include the G suite, the Pink suite, and the Playboy Villa. Even off-Strip, The Palms is where it's at these days.

South Point — 2005

It used to be that the Hacienda Hotel (which became the Mandalay Bay) was at the Strip's southern terminus. No more. Enter South Point Hotel, Casino & Spa, earlier called South Coast. And it's over two miles south of Mandalay Bay!

At opening on December 22, 2005, the South Coast was the first megaresort located south of McCarran International Airport and the Strip. Then, the hotel contained 662 rooms and 800,000 square feet of not-yet-finished casino and restaurant space.

In 2006, Michael Gaughan offered to sell all of his Boyd stock to Boyd Gaming in exchange for full ownership of the South Coast. After the deal closed, the South Coast was renamed South Point Hotel, Casino & Spa on October 24.

In 2008 the South Point added 830 rooms with a third hotel tower, a $95 million expansion. The hotel now has a total of 2,163 all-suite rooms and 160,000 square feet of meeting and convention space. They're so far from the Strip proper, they often offer great deals on hotel rooms.

To the Border

It appears that even as far out as South Point is, in a few decades it'll be considered more "central." Already the M Resort opened farther south and even it is in the midst of other buildings, apartments, and mini-malls.

The Strip is already lined with buildings all the way south to where you enter the Las Vegas Valley, and is destined to go beyond. Developers are in the wings, waiting for favorable financial winds, before they start construction anew.

The City of Henderson has annexed land along the east side of Interstate-15 to almost the California border. Someday the Strip will host building activity all the way to the border.

Red Rock Station Casino — 2006

In addition to Strip and highway casinos, Las Vegas is the only gambling destination in America with support for suburban casinos. The Station Casinos Group is by far the leader of the suburban and off-Strip casinos.

They built the Red Rock Casino Resort & Spa on 70 acres in Summerlin Centre, way west of the Strip. Known as a locals' casino, it is on Charleston Blvd. at the interchange of the I-215 Freeway. The resort is the flagship property of Station Casinos, and the company's corporate headquarters is located on property.

The resort includes a 198-foot hotel tower with 815 rooms, casino, meeting space, a 16-screen movie theater, a bingo hall, bowling alley, and 11 restaurants.

Aliante Station — 2008

Even North Las Vegas is enjoying a new casino as the Aliante Station Casino & Hotel was opened there by Station Casinos Inc. in November 2008. Popular with locals, long lines of people were waiting to enter on opening day. The Aliante Station has a similar interior design as the Red Rock Casino Resort & Spa.

Palazzo — 2008

The Palazzo Las Vegas, a luxury hotel casino resort reflective of modern European ambiance opened in 2008 as a sister hotel to the Venetian Las Vegas next door. The Palazzo is owned and operated by the Las Vegas Sands Corporation. The $1.8 billion resort features a lobby where guests from the street arrive beneath a 60-foot glass dome with a two-story fountain. Those approaching from the Venetian make the transition through a towering structure and garden topped by a glass-and-iron

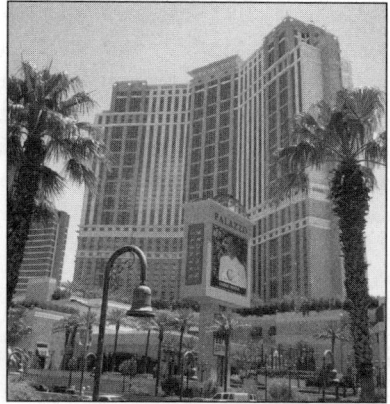

The Palazzo Las Vegas

dome. The all-suite hotel offers the largest standard accommodations on the Las Vegas Strip at 720-square-feet per guest room. In its first year of eligibility, The Palazzo was awarded the AAA Five Diamond Award for 2010.

Temporarily On Hold

Echelon—one of the largest Las Vegas Strip projects ever has been put on hold, with the overall economy to blame. Boyd Gaming Corporation, known for its local-popular casinos, reported another drop in profits at the end of 2009 and decided to put off completing its huge $4.8 billion Echelon Place.

Boyd's reported net income for the third quarter was $6.3 million, just seven cents a share. Boyd's development of its multibillion-dollar Echelon Hotel-Casino at the north end of the Strip has now been put on hiatus for several (3-5) years. It is slated to be a casino with four hotel towers, a shopping center and a convention center, and originally scheduled to open in 2010.

Construction on the 63-acre site for Echelon Place began in 2007 when the Stardust Hotel & Casino, which opened in July 1958, met its demise 49 years later.

Echelon Place is an ambitious multi-use project, planned with a 140,000-square-foot casino, four hotels providing 5,300 rooms, 25 restaurants and bars, the 650,000-square-foot Las Vegas ExpoCenter, and a 1,000,000-square-foot convention center, all sprawling over 87 acres. The Echelon Resort is to be a 3,300 room hotel owned and operated by Boyd. The other hotels are expected to be a Shangri-La Hotel, a Delano Hotel, a Mondrian Hotel, and the Echelon Tower.

Until construction resumes, the unfinished project just sits on the Strip, considered an eyesore by some. Others feel that Boyd had no choice, noting almost 14% local unemployment and the poor worldwide economy. In the meantime, Boyd has already put hundreds of millions of dollars into the construction—but it still needs a lot more money. Executives insist there won't be any costly wear and tear on what's sitting in the hole on the Strip because it's essentially just steel and concrete. The company acknowledged that with CityCenter opening down the Strip, Echelon couldn't have competed now, "but in a few years, it will be in the perfect position. When Boyd opens Echelon, it will be the newest supply for a numbers of years."

So until the economy improves, the once-ambitious Echelon will remain an eyesore.

Others on Hold

Echelon is not the only Las Vegas project that has been postponed. **Hilton Grand** delayed two of their four timeshare towers indefinitely. **Trump Towers**, which has built one 64-story $1.2 billion tower, has postponed the second tower until the economy improves.

Harrah's had a $1 billion renovation planned for **Caesars Palace**, including the 660-room Octavius Tower. They've put that off.

Fontainebleau Las Vegas LLC, owners of the **Fontainebleau Las Vegas**, declared Chapter 11 bankruptcy in 2009 on their 68-story, $2.9 billion hotel/condo/casino project that was being constructed on the site of the old El Rancho Vegas and Algiers hotels. Selling the condos to keep the project afloat just wasn't happening.

A Memorable Skyline

While some future growth is in a holding pattern, the Las Vegas Strip skyline that has emerged over the past few decades is one of the world's most memorable. Where else can you see the Empire State Building, the Statue of Liberty, the Eiffel Tower, a fairytale castle, a huge circus tent, an Egyptian pyramid, and other gigantic buildings of diverse architectural styles in one panorama?

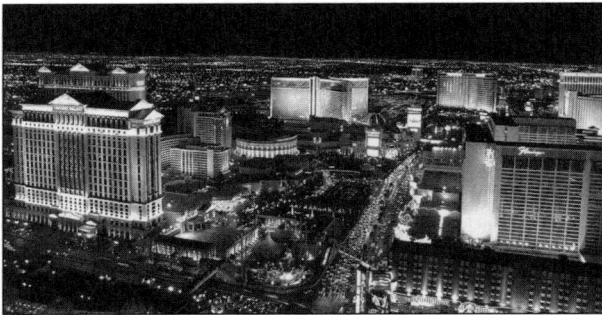

Las Vegas at night

From any direction, from the highways or from the air, the dazzling skyline mesmerizes and energizes. It is sometimes funky, sometimes breathtaking, always unique. From the shimmering Trump Tower, to the graceful curves of Wynn and Encore, to the stately Caesars Palace—it is Las Vegas.

CityCenter—A Dazzling New Concept
A "City" On the Strip

After Kirk Kerkorian and his MGM Mirage Corporation gobbled up the Mandalay Resort Group in 2004, they did not rest on their laurels. There were still deals to be cut in and out of Las Vegas.

And there was still opportunity along the famed Las Vegas Strip. With the Mirage Resorts package came the Boardwalk, a small carnival-themed casino that had earlier belonged to Holiday Inn, smack-dab in what was the center of the Strip. In fact its location was its best feature, sandwiched between the luxurious Bellagio and the European-themed Monte Carlo, and across the boulevard from the Paris, The Planet Hollywood, and the massive MGM Grand.

Thinking big, MGM Mirage had the Boardwalk imploded in 2006 and partnered with Dubai World to begin construction on what would be the Strip's crowning glory—CityCenter.

CityCenter, six glass and steel towers covering 67 acres, which opened in phases beginning in December 2009 and throughout 2010, is a new community concept combining resorts and resi-

The 67-acre CityCenter in the heart of the Strip

dences to make it one of the largest sustainable developments in existence. The $8.5 billion project houses 6,300 hotel rooms in four hotels and 2,400 condos. Bobby Baldwin, president and CEO of CityCenter, said in a report, "CityCenter bridges the vitality of Las Vegas with the experiences travelers seek when they visit great cities around the world, whether London, Hong Kong, or San Francisco—spectacular architecture, culturally significant art, great public spaces, sophisticated hotels, unique restaurants, and incredible amenities."

CityCenter includes ARIA Resort & Casino, a 61-story, 4,004-room gaming resort; luxury non-gaming hotels including Las Vegas' first Mandarin Oriental and Vdara Hotel & Spa; Veer Towers, the development's only strictly residential buildings (2,400 residences); and Crystals, a 500,000-square-foot retail and entertainment district.

Eight internationally acclaimed architectural firms are responsible for breathing life into the massive project. CityCenter was expected to have approximately 12,000 permanent employees, making it the country's single largest hiring effort in 2009.

CityCenter offers complimentary valet as well as self parking. In addition a tram, able to transport 5,000 guests an hour, runs through CityCenter from both Monte Carlo and Bellagio.

Throughout the buildings that comprise CityCenter is a Fine Art Collection, about $40 million worth, showcasing works by world-acclaimed artists.

ARIA

ARIA Resort and Casino is massive. The 150,000-square-foot casino offers never-before-seen technologies. For example, slot machine bases house air conditioning units, cooling from the bottom up rather than from the ceiling. It is the project's only new casino. Within ARIA's 4,004 guestrooms, including 568 suites, panoramic floor-to-ceiling windows, guests find modern décor, cutting-edge entertainment, and next-generation technology. The amenities are pricey—$35.00 a day just for *access* to the gym and spa, for example, but they are top-notch. In ARIA's 80,000-square-foot, two-level spa are 62 treatment rooms, a full-service salon, and an advanced fitness center. ARIA's 215,000-square-foot pool deck is a tropical oasis, featuring three primary pools, and the adults-only pool Liquid, which often has a line to get in.

The hot and already popular new show at ARIA is Viva ELVIS™ by Cirqúe du Soleil which celebrates the music and life of Elvis Presley. For Elvis "spotters," there's even a bronze bust of "The King" in front of the showroom. The resort also has 10 upscale bars and lounges, including HAZE Nightclub by The Light Group.

Vdara Hotel & Spa

Vdara is a 57-story all-suite hotel and spa designed for those who prefer an exclusive, non-gaming and smoke-free environment. Physically connected to Bellagio and adjacent to ARIA, Vdara offers access to all of the entertainment, gaming, shopping, dining and nightlife at CityCenter and in Las Vegas, while also providing a retreat from it all. The sleek, shimmering Vdara has 1,495 modern hotel suites, including 250 corner-end units, ranging from approximately 500 to 1,650 square feet, and a plethora of amenities.

Crystals retail and entertainment district

What's a community without shopping? Crystals houses more than 500,000 square feet of sophisticated retail and dining in a unique upscale atmosphere. A central element of Crystals is the three-story sculptural treehouse that reaches 70 feet from the ground level. Central to the atrium at Crystals is the unusually shaped Ocean Club restaurant jutting out over the shops.

There are numerous one-store only retailers as well as some of the world's top names. The largest Louis Vuitton store in North America, as well as flagship stores for Tiffany & Co., Prada, Gucci, Roberto Cavalli, and Ermenegildo Zegna are located at Crystals. Restaurants debuting their first Las Vegas locations at Crystals include Eva Longoria Parker's Beso (already a place of controversy as an Israeli co-partner got ejected for threatening staff and customers), and the aforementioned Ocean Club, which serves a great Chilean sea bass.

Mandarin Oriental

Mandarin Oriental is a 47-story, non-gaming hotel with 392 rooms and luxurious suites and 225 residences, all featuring Oriental design, state-of-the-art, environmentally conscious technology, and cutting-edge entertainment systems.

According to *Conde Naste Traveler* magazine (May 2010), "...the 392-room hotel is a study in calm sophistication—nary a fanny pack nor a bachelor party in sight." Open less than a year, by late 2010 The Mandarin Oriental and ARIA Resort and Casino had both garnered the coveted AAA Five Diamond Award.

The Residences at Mandarin Oriental have a private residential entrance. Owners of these 225 luxury condominiums enjoy full access to hotel amenities—including housekeeping, in-room dining, concierge, and The Spa & Fitness Center.

Veer Towers

Veer Towers, CityCenter's most unique residential development, consists of two 37-story glass towers inclined at five-degree angles, although it looks like a greater tilt. They have been the talk of the town, called everything from "drunken tourists" to "swaying dancers." Tower architect Helmut Jahn admitted he wanted to create a "wow" effect, and it appears he succeeded. He definitely added a bit of whimsy to the super-functional and often rigid CityCenter.

Each tower houses approximately 335 modern condominium residences ranging from 500 to nearly 3,300 square feet, available in studios, deluxe studios, one-, two- and three-bedroom residences, and penthouses.

A Green Vegas

While CityCenter can definitely be considered lavish, it is not wasteful. Bucking the bright lights and neon trend, CityCenter is eco-correct, making use of natural materials, such as recycled wood, stone, and concrete. Six of the buildings have received gold status in the Leadership in Energy and Environmental Design (LEED) Green Building Rating System. Opening in a difficult economic market was a gamble, but that's what they do in Las Vegas. During the early months of 2010, the city waited and watched, many competitors hoping for success, hoping it might help jump-start the Las Vegas economy. Even competitor Steve Wynn admitted, "We've got our fingers crossed that it's a success and that it grows the market."

Wynn later expressed dissatisfaction by stating that the 6,300 additional new rooms at CityCenter depressed Las Vegas room rates so much, he was having a hard time making a profit.

Kirk Kerkorian

Kirk Kerkorian, well, even at age 93, he has showed no signs of slowing down; he had formed his own private investment company Tracinda Corporation (named for his two daughters Tracy and Linda) and it in turn owns MGM Mirage stock.

Kerkorian has had his fingers in a lot of pies through the years, including Ford, Chrysler, MGM studio, and more. In 2005, he sold the studio to Sony Entertainment, the cable TV firm Comcast, and other investments for $5 billion, netting him a personal profit of $1.8 billion. One of the world's richest men, his net worth was put at $16 billion (#41) by Forbes in 2008.

In May 2009, following a $1 billion dollar stock offering by MGM Mirage, Kerkorian and Tracinda lost majority ownership of the gaming company, dropping from 53.8% to 39%. Even after pledging to purchase 10% of the new stock offering, Kerkorian is still a minority owner. By 2010, Kerkorian was among those hardest hit by stock market recession as his net worth tumbled to $3.1 billion. He dropped from number 41 to 307 on the world's richest person list. It might be hard for someone hoping to hit a $100 jackpot to say "poor guy," but then again, everything is relative.

Kerkorian and the other shareholders are hoping to fatten their pocketbooks back up, and that should happen if CityCenter does what has been envisioned for it.

Chapter 11

Around Southern Nevada

During the Cold War, Nevada became the scene of nuclear testing at a desert test site north of Las Vegas.

There are a few mysteries in the deserts around town. The "Lost City" is an old Anasazi village, and many believers are convinced that the secretive place known as Area 51 is sure to house flying saucers and aliens.

The other towns and cities around Las Vegas also have interesting histories: from Laughlin on the river, to the gold town of Searchlight, to Boulder City, the only place in Nevada where gambling is illegal.

Another thing people may not realize about Las Vegas—there are numerous and varied outdoor activities just outside of town.

Nuclear Testing
WHEN THE DESERT SHOOK

The war with Japan ended in dramatic fashion with the dropping of two atomic bombs. The world hoped to never experience such weapons again, but that didn't mean that once the demon was released, it would go away. Arsenals had to be developed and maintained—and tested.

On the morning of January 27, 1951, Las Vegans were abruptly introduced to U.S. nuclear testing by a window-rattling, ground-shaking boom that could even be heard in Los Angeles, over 300 miles away. The pre-dawn blast triggered a brilliant flash and giant mushroom cloud that lit up the sky, scaring animals, most notably anxious humans, many of whom thought it was war all over again. The desert would never be the same again.

There was public outrage and media hounding, but the U.S. Atomic Energy Commission initially denied that anything unusual had occurred. After all, the two earlier post-war tests were done on remote atolls in the Pacific (Bikini and Eniwetok). But that first nuclear explosion in Nevada, code-named "Able," made it hard for them to deny. Playing coy word games, officials initially maintained that nothing happened at the Indian Springs Air Base about 40 miles northwest of Las Vegas. Technically that was true—the blast actually exploded 25 miles farther north at what would become the Nevada Test Site. They finally had to come clean.

The atomic secret didn't last long—especially when they were commencing a total 235 above-ground experiments conducted at the Nevada Test Site (originally called the Nevada Proving Grounds), roughly one every three weeks for the next 12 years. Finally, on April 22, 1952, the government invited the media to the Test Site. Numerous print and TV reporters, including commentator Walter Cronkite, hunkered down at a location 10 miles away to watch and film live. At detonation, a momentous blast created a giant mushroom cloud that dominated the skies above their vantage points at Frenchman and Yucca Flats, demonstrating the power and awe of nuclear weapons to the public.

The Nevada Test Site occupies a huge chunk of the state, running about 30 miles wide by about 50 miles in length. It is buffered on three sides by federal land, over 4,120 square miles of it a gunnery range from the Nellis Air Force Base, and a smaller Tonopah Test Range. The entire 5,470 square miles (2.9 million acres) is one of the nation's most unpopulated areas, yet the southwestern most point is only 65 miles from Las Vegas. It's not entirely isolated. The test site has over 1,100 buildings: housing, offices, hospital, laboratories, warehouses, law enforcement, security, cafeteria, and post office. Most of the time there are also over 3,000 employees contracted by the government on site.

In October 1958, immediately following a large test series, the United States, behind President Dwight D. Eisenhower, entered a unilateral testing moratorium with the understanding that the former Soviet Union would also refrain from testing. After initially honoring this agreement, the Soviets blasted off an immense nuclear testing campaign in September 1961. Before the month was over, U.S. testing resumed in Nevada. President John F. Kennedy and Soviet Premier Nikita Khrushchev then signed a treaty banning above-ground bombs, so all nuclear weapons tested after July 1962 went underground.

The actual number of the 928 total experiments conducted in Nevada would not be revealed until the 1990s. Even today, tests go on, albeit underground. In 2004 there was a test to study how plutonium behaves under pressures generated by explosions. In 2010 the U.S. and Russia were still trying to come to a pact on reducing their respective arsenals.

While the blasting might have shaken many from a good night's sleep, the testing definitely helped the economy. Nearly 100,000 men and women worked at the Nevada Test Site, the state's second largest employment source behind mining for many years.

Nellis Air Force Base oversees the huge complex which includes Creech AFB (Creech specializes in fighting the War on Terror). In total, the bases employ 9,227 military personnel and 3,748 civilians (2008 figures). Adding to the Las Vegas metropolitan area economy are the 27,615 military retirees in the area.

The Las Vegas Chamber of Commerce began early-on to capitalize on the nuclear testing phenomenon and promoted the atomic tests as a tourist attraction, offering postcards, atomic cocktails, atomic hairdos, and even sponsoring "atomic beauty pageants."

From the nervous days of the cold war where nations brandished weapons as deterrents, as threats, and as shows of strength, the gauntlet has been withdrawn and nuclear testing in Nevada only remains as an important part of the state's history.

The Atomic Testing Museum, an affiliate of the Smithsonian Institution, today sheds a lot more light on America's atomic program. Located at 755 E. Flamingo Rd. in Las Vegas, it goes into detail about the Nevada Test Site and its impact on the nation and world. One highlight is the Ground Zero Theater where you can experience what an atomic explosion was like.

The nuclear testing and large area of adjacent government controlled land spawned more activity—so secret and suspicious that it caught the attention of the UFO crowd. It is called Area 51—and it has become a real "Las Vegas Legend."

The Extraterrestrial Highway
Close Encounters with Aliens

U FO buffs come in droves. They regularly patrol Nevada's Extraterrestrial Highway, cameras at ready, scanning the skies and adjacent desert, hoping to spot the aliens they are sure are there. To an area rife with folklore, the addition of UFOs and visiting aliens is a natural.

Area 51, a top secret military installation north of Las Vegas, has provided the fodder for Nevada's "Great Martian Chase." The very intense secrecy of the place, which the U.S. government barely acknowledges even exists, fed the fuel that to believers meant "something's going on."

Stickers blanket Extraterrestrial Highway sign

Area 51 is part of the vast Nellis Air Force Base north of Las Vegas. It is centered at Groom Lake, a large secretive airfield, in the heart of the immense 2.9 million-acre Nevada Test and Training Range and surrounding federal lands.

There are other names for Area 51, (Dreamland, Paradise Ranch, Neverland, and Groom Lake), or simply "The Box" as the pilots refer to it. At first the government refused to acknowledge the base existed. Finally in 1990, after all sorts of stories began running rampant, they acknowledged that the Area 51 base is to support development and testing of experimental aircraft and weapons systems—no tremendous revelation there.

Tongues wagged about what perhaps the "real purpose" was, and ideas and theories, from plausible and possible to "say what?" abounded. Conspiracy fanatics had a fresh new palette for their paint brushes. While a lot of the theories were correct—yes, the U-2 and other spy planes were tested there—many others slipped into the realm of fancy.

The current wave of "UFO-tourists" began in November 1989 when Las Vegas resident Bob Lazar announced on a local TV station that aliens had arrived there. He said he saw nine flying saucers in a hangar built into a hill-side, and that he helped work on one's propulsion system where the government was trying to "reverse engineer" the craft to see how it worked.

Lazar said he even brought some friends to a desolate area along Highway 375 called Tikaboo Valley, some 25 miles south of the hamlet of Rachel, Nevada to observe the saucers in flight as they were tested on Wednesday nights. The sensation-driven medium of television did its job—soon the area was swarming with watchers.

Many came to believe that Area 51 is a site where the government retrofits these alien aircraft. A prevailing theory is that the flying saucers and bodies were taken to Area 51 after they "crashed" at Roswell, NM.

With so many UFO-tourists, by 1996 U.S. Highway 375 was officially renamed the "Extraterrestrial Highway, or "ET Highway" for short. The area where sightings are supposed to occur, usually on Wednesday nights, is about 150 miles one way from Las Vegas, and is in the middle of nowhere. As desolate as the moon, it inspires unworldly thoughts.

The only landmark along the lonely out-of-the-way road in Tikaboo Valley was a "black mailbox," so that became ground zero for watchers. From there, people soon gravitated toward the Rachel Bar and Grill, 20 miles north of the sacred mailbox. The mailbox, on the west side of the highway, has since been painted white. Perhaps by Aliens?

Rachel Bar and Grill owners Pat and Joe Travis saw a good thing drop into their lap, maybe not an actual Martian, but the crowd drawn by them. They changed the name of their establishment to the Little A'le'Inn (pronounced Little Alien) and it quickly became the unofficial headquarters for all things UFO. From originally being skeptics, the Travises soon got into the fever of the alleged sightings and would tell a visitor, "Why, just the other night..."

The bar and grill now stocks all sorts of items for "watchers," such as t-shirts, cups, and other souvenirs imprinted with aliens. Joe passed away in

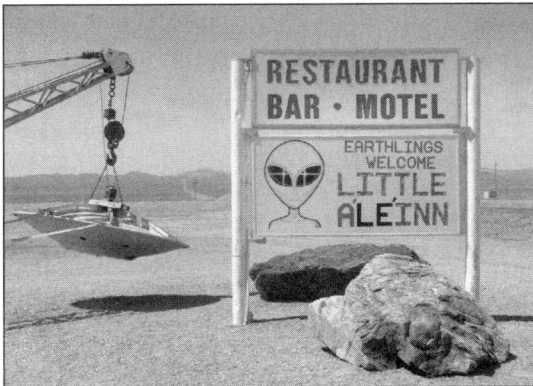

2003, and Pat has remarried. Her daughter Connie, grandsons Cody and Ryan, and her new husband Bill help run the busy place. Despite absolutely nothing (no towns, businesses, or even trees) in either direction for miles and miles, the restaurant was crowded on an April weekend.

"When was the last sighting?" I asked Pat.

Sign at Little Ale'Inn

Nearby other diners at the counter snapped to attention to hear her straightforward answer, "About 2 ½ months ago, is the last one that sounded real. There were a couple of others since then, but I really don't think they saw anything." She sounded so convincing, even dispelling obvious cranks and mistakes to render her words greater authenticity.

After the restaurant cleared out, I mentioned I was a writer and was fascinated by the story. I said, "There are a lot of believers out there. Non-believers, too."

She grinned and said, "I really don't care, as long as they all come." And come they do. They sold more hamburgers on one Saturday afternoon than they would have in a month to the locals or occasional traveler. The gravel parking lot features a mock spacecraft, a "self parking" sign with a picture of a spacecraft, and numerous memorabilia that designates the place as unworldly, including signs that say, "Earthlings Welcome."

Others in the hamlet of Rachel got into the act. One offered that the UFO mystery is most likely related with the "New World Order," a worldwide conspiracy involving the U.S., the United Nations, and others to suppress individual rights, interpreted to mean that somebody wants to take away their guns—scary words to many stubborn Westerners.

One Rachel resident, Glenn Campbell, wrote a book about his claims. Called *Area 51 Viewer's Guide,* his 115-page book contains just enough facts to make it palatable. He found a hill bordering the restricted area about 25 miles south of Rachel where one could legally peer into the Groom Lake area. He called it Freedom Ridge and in June 1993 he blazed a 4-wheel-drive road to its summit, creating another spot where watchers hoped to be rewarded by sighting flying saucers hovering over the desert floor.

The Air Force got miffed and tried to make Freedom Ridge and another hill off-limits. Their action was the impetus Campbell needed to tell the world. He sent out press releases which stirred up incredible publicity. Major media, including ABC News, CNN, *Wall Street Journal, The New York Times*, and *Popular Science* descended on the area creating a UFO circus wild even by Nevada standards. Even television impresario Larry King joined the stampede. There seemed to be more newspeople than dedicated watchers—or little green men for that matter.

The Pentagon has steadfastly admitted that there are no aliens on the site, but why let that ruin a good story?

Besides, could aliens exist elsewhere? There was even an expensive government program (NASA's Search for Extraterrestrial Intelligence, or SETI project) established for the scientific search of extraterrestrial civilizations. Numerous scientists including Dr. Carl Sagan and several Nobel Prize winners supported the study, but Congress squelched it.

"Alien" guards museum on ET Highway

Senator Richard Bryan (D.-Nev) led the opposition, offering, "The Great Martian Chase," he said, "may finally come to an end. As of today millions have been spent and we have yet to bag a single little green fellow. Not a single Martian has said 'take me to your leader,' and not a single flying saucer has applied for FAA approval."

While the government may not offer any definitive proof, or even sate your interest, you can check out the area yourself. Head up the desolate spaceship-friendly Extraterrestrial Highway (U.S. Highway 375) to Rachel. Wednesday nights are best, they say. Stop at the Little A'le'Inn for an Alien Burger, the new Saucer Burger, or a "Beam Me Up Scotty" cocktail, and talk to the other watchers. After all, "Just the other night…"

From Primm To Laughlin
AROUND SOUTHERN NEVADA

While the destination resort city of Las Vegas and its adjoining Strip dominate, there are other towns in Southern Nevada (Clark County) that have been luring the tourist dollar with hotel casinos and other attractions.

Back in the 1960s when my sister lived in Eldorado Canyon, for a night on the town we'd go all the way to Henderson. Boulder City was dry, and Railroad Pass was little more than a gas station casino. The old mining town of Searchlight had two small bars with slots, but usually only one blackjack table between them would be open at any given time, if at all. Laughlin was just a small landing on the river where a few retirees lived. That has all changed big time.

Henderson

Abutting Las Vegas to the southeast is Henderson, which has grown from almost being sold as U.S. Army surplus after World War II to becoming the second largest city in Nevada with a population of over 250,000.

Henderson, named for Nevada Senator Charles B. Henderson (1918-1921), actually came into being in 1941 when manufacturer Howard Eells was looking for a place to establish a magnesium plant to aid the war effort. He found large deposits of magnesite and brucite in Nevada and convinced

Nevada and federal authorities that the area midway between the Las Vegas rail yards and the generating facilities of Hoover Dam would be ideal. It helped that his ally Senator Henderson was chairman of the Reconstruction Finance Corporation at the time.

On July 5, 1941, Eells' Basic Magnesium Inc was formed and would be the largest magnesium plant in the world. Dwarfing the Hoover Dam project which had 5,250 workers, the number of employees at Basic Magnesium had swelled to 13,618 (or about 10% of Nevada's population at the time) by July 1942.

Eells soon sold the operation to Anaconda Copper, which promptly broke production records and also started to establish a town site. Numerous women were employed at the plant and "Magnesium Maggie" was Nevada's answer to the war effort's "Rosie the Riveter."

Magnesium demand dropped abruptly after the war and the plant suspended operation. A few employees settled in the Las Vegas area, but most drifted away. Henderson was an eyesore. School enrollment was reduced by two thirds, and well over half the workers' houses went vacant. In 1947 the United States War Asset Administration actually offered Henderson for sale as war surplus property. The state stepped in and saved the day by purchasing much of what remained. New firms were found to use portions of the plant. Other businesses arrived and the town began to swell again. The city of Henderson incorporated in 1953.

While much of Henderson has in recent years become residential, with neighborhoods ranging from modest to mid-range to upscale, there are still the ubiquitous casinos, about 30 of them. Right downtown are the Rainbow Club & Casino, El Dorado Casino, and Emerald Island Casino. Also in town are Terrible's Town Casino, Lake Mead Lounge & Casino, Mystic Lodge Casino, Fiesta Henderson, and Skyline Restaurant & Casino. Railroad Pass Casino is actually south of town on the Boulder Highway. Also on Boulder Highway is the Clark County Museum, 25 acres of history including trains, a collection of historic homes, a resurrected ghost town, and Paiute village.

Henderson's Lake Las Vegas is just a few miles east, and only 17 miles from the Las Vegas Strip. The 320-acre man-made lake is the focal point for an upscale community of resort hotels, gourmet restaurants, golf course, and elegant homes. Henderson has definitely come a long way from the auctioneer's block.

Boulder City

Boulder City is an anomaly, the only Nevada city that does not allow gambling. Thirty miles southeast of the Las Vegas Strip, on the way to Lake Mead, Boulder City was built in the 1930s to house Hoover Dam construction workers and their families.

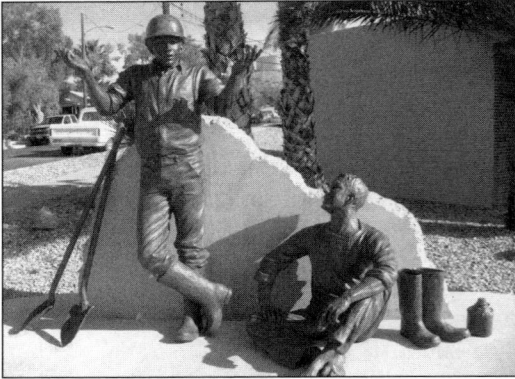

Bronze statue of dam workers in Boulder City

By March 1931 when construction on the dam commenced, the government had yet to build Boulder City so men were forced to live in a makeshift Ragtown. Workers rioted, and by early 1932 dam manager Frank Crowe personally laid out the town and the tents of Ragtown were vacated. While Boulder City became a nice place to live, workers had to go to Las Vegas to blow their paychecks. Gambling, drinking alcohol, and prostitution were not permitted in Boulder City during the period of construction. In fact the sale of alcoholic beverages was not legal in Boulder City until 1969. I well remember celebrating that liberating event with my sister and brother-in-law.

Responsible for much of the restrictive laws was a hard-nosed, righteous totalitarian named Sims Ely, who in 1931 at age 69 was given broad power by the Secretary of Interior in becoming Boulder City city manager (1931-1941). Called a dictator by some, he imposed his moral values on the town even after the dam was finished. He ruled by iron fist, and fired workers, denied business applications, revoked permits, disallowed home purchases, and even scolded children, based on his ideas of right and wrong.

One former dam worker even complained, "He was a little Hitler." After Ely finally retired at 79, the Bureau of Reclamation, which remained in control until 1960, abolished the title. Today there is a city manager, but one with conventional powers.

While there are no casinos, Boulder City's historic Old Town district is worth a visit, home to many quaint shops and bronze sculptures on every corner. Visit the historic Boulder Dam Hotel, a 33-room Dutch Colonia-style building built in 1933 to house VIPs who came to visit and oversee the construction of Hoover Dam. The hotel's vintage restaurant still offers fine meals in the dining room and on the terrace outside.

The Nevada State Railroad Museum in Boulder City is like a step back in time. It features a seven-mile, round-trip excursion train ride on Pullman Coaches along its vintage Boulder Branch Line.

Mesquite

Mesquite, Nevada, 80 miles up I-15 from Las Vegas at the Utah border, was founded in 1880 by Mormons who called the area on the Virgin River Mesquite Flat.

The Peppermill Casino opened in the 1970s and others followed. Mesquite hotels and casinos today include the Virgin River Casino, CasaBlanca, Eureka Casino Hotel, and Stateline Casino & Motel. Today the town of about 20,000 has golf courses and is home to many retirees.

Primm

Those who drove I-15 from California years ago recall the couple of gas stations at the edge of Ivanpah Dry Lake, straddling the Nevada border. Only 40 miles from Las Vegas the few slot machines would be either the first or last ones encountered and as such, people stopped.

Today, what was once called State Line now houses three big casinos, Buffalo Bill's Resort & Casino, Primm Valley Resort & Casino, and Whiskey Pete's Hotel & Casino, as well as a large outlet mall, Fashion Outlets of Las Vegas. As seen from the Nipton cutoff

Whiskey Pete's, Primm

10 miles south, the casinos rise like a whimsical village, their phantasmal hulks floating over the dry lake mirage.

The Desperado Roller Coaster dominates the view at Buffalo Bill's, and it's a good one for those who seek thrills. It has a 225-foot drop which attains speeds of 80 mph.

The community hotels also get the overfill when Las Vegas hosts major conventions. All of Primm's residents are employees of the properties and their families. In 2004, under MGM Mirage ownership, 52 apartment buildings were constructed in Primm to serve as housing for employees at the three casinos.

Primm is the source of a great Nevada legend. In the 1920s Pete "Whiskey Pete" MacIntyre owned a gas-station at the state line, and supplemented his income by bootlegging. When Whiskey Pete died in 1933, legend has it that he wanted to be buried standing up with a bottle of bootleg in his hands so he could watch over the area. Many years later, while workers were building the bridge over I-15, Whiskey Pete's unmarked grave was accidentally exhumed. The body was moved and is now said to be buried in one of the caves where Pete cooked up his moonshine.

Primm is named after casino owner Ernest Jay Primm. Another Primm note of interest is that the convenience store on the California side of the border is the entire state's highest-selling location of California State Lottery tickets.

Jean

Twelve miles from Primm, the small hamlet of Jean has added a few casinos to the area that only had a Nevada Highway Patrol substation and the female minimum-security Jean Conservation Camp. Jean's first casino, Pops Oasis Casino closed in 1988, and the MGM Mirage closed its Nevada Landing Hotel & Casino in 2008. Today only the Gold Strike Hotel & Casino still draws the travelers.

You might find the nearby mining town of Goodsprings more interesting. It's six miles west of Jean nestled against Mt. Potosi. The old Pioneer Saloon there is the real thing; in fact it's where the distraught Clark Gable awaited word about his wife Carol Lombard's nearby fatal plane crash.

Searchlight

The hometown of Senate Majority Leader Senator Harry Reid (D.-NV), the old mining town of Searchlight is well off the beaten path. When the main road from California to Nevada and Utah changed in 1927 from Highway 95 and Searchlight in favor of Highway 91 (now I-15), the town's population was reduced to only 50 hardy souls. Between 1907 and 1910 the gold mines produced $7 million in gold and other precious minerals and the town had a population of about 1,500.

In 1909, when Clark County was formed, Searchlight was a larger town than Las Vegas and was initially slated to be the new county seat. According to Senator Reid, who has written extensively about his hometown, the town received its name in 1897 when George Frederick Colton was looking for gold and he supposedly said that it would take a "searchlight" to find gold ore there. Of course, shortly thereafter he found gold, which led to the area's boom.

Today there are two small casinos, both open 24 hours, the Searchlight Nugget Casino (98 machines, three table games), and Terrible's Casino (75 machines).

On March 27, 2010, the little hamlet of Searchlight swelled tenfold from its fewer than 1,000 hardy souls to over 9,000 when political aspirant Sarah Palin and right wing Tea Party advocates invaded the place where Reid still owns property. Arriving in 42 city busses, the activists called for the ouster of Democrats who supported the health care overhaul, starting with the Senate Democratic leader.

Reid shrugged off the intrusion in a statement, "I'm happy so many people came to see my hometown of Searchlight and spend their out-of-state money, especially in these tough economic times." Senator Reid was re-elected in November 2010.

Now people outside Nevada know where Searchlight is.

Laughlin

The biggest development in Southern Nevada outside of the Las Vegas-Henderson area is Laughlin, near the southern tip of the state on the Colorado River across from Bullhead City, Arizona. It's easier to drive to from Phoenix and also a shorter distance for many Southern Californians.

Laughlin receives five million tourists each year, Nevada's third (after Las Vegas and Reno) most-visited destination. A lot of people, especially older ones, prefer the more laid-back resort that offers considerably more inexpensive lodging than Las Vegas. Laughlin has nowhere near the vitality, energy and nightlife as does Las Vegas.

Some 10,000 to 15,000 "snowbirds" descend on Laughlin each year from their colder climes to make Laughlin one of the top five destinations for American RV enthusiasts.

Laughlin's name comes from Don Laughlin, owner of the 101 Club in Las Vegas, who bought much of the southern tip of Nevada, then called South Pointe, in 1964. He opened what would become the Riverside Resort, beginning with 12 slot machines, two gaming tables, and eight motel rooms (although half of the rooms were occupied by family). His main attraction was 98-cent, all-you-can-eat chicken dinners. Laughlin personally wanted to call the community "Riverside," but the post office opted for Laughlin instead.

The Riverside Resort grew in stages (new rooms in 1972, the high rises in 1986), and the river location began to attract other developers. By the 1980s other casinos opened up. In 1987, Don Laughlin fronted $3.5 million to build a bridge over to the Arizona side and the many businesses in the larger Bullhead City. Today there are nine big casino hotels in Laughlin. These are: Aquarius, River Palms Casino Resort, Tropicana Express, Harrah's Laughlin, Avi Resort & Casino, Colorado Belle, Edgewater, Riverside Resort Hotel & Casino, and the Golden Nugget Laughlin.

Most of the Laughlin hotels offer riverboat cruises, watercraft rentals, and much more. Plus, most of them have rooms priced as low as $30.00 a night, with only a couple exceeding $100 even for the most expensive rooms. There are a lot of people who eschew the bright lights and dynamic action of Las Vegas to make their regular treks to Laughlin along the Colorado River.

The Great Outdoors
Beyond The Glitter

O utdoor activities don't normally come to mind when people mention Las Vegas—but there's plenty to do outside the casinos. Day trips from the heart of the Strip can immediately transplant you into a whole different experience. You can enjoy placid desert scenery, colorful craggy canyons, rugged pine-scented mountains, a broad lake, an amazing dam, ghost towns, ancient petroglyphs, and several world-class national parks.

For the more adventuresome, there's quality rock climbing, mountain biking, boating, river rafting, kayaking, and ATV tours. The area's natural attractions are so spectacular, many have been protected, and the man-made ones are historic, and for the most part unique to the area.

Red Rock Canyon

Red Rock Canyon is the closest natural wonder near Las Vegas. Just keep driving west on Charleston Blvd. until you run out of town and you're there. Only 15 miles west of Las Vegas, the dazzling bright red rock formations are the result of a 3,000-foot thrust fault escarpment.

Red Rock Canyon

Most popular is the one-way, 13-mile scenic loop road through the colorful canyons that features several overlooks and parking areas. Nineteen different hiking trails (mostly easy and moderate) take off in every direction from the parking areas. For climbers there are several multi-pitch routes.

Run by the Bureau of Land Management, there are picnicking areas, and a new visitors center to greet the approximately one million visitors each year.

Open to the public year-round, you always see bicycles (there's even a bicycle pavilion rest stop) and joggers on the road, and hikers and rock climbers on the trails. You'll almost always spot wild animals too—wild burros, feral horses, coyotes, bighorn sheep if you're lucky, and a colorful variety of desert plant life, especially in the spring.

Red Rock Canyon is a wonderful outdoor destination, especially when you consider it's less than a half hour from the Strip.

Spring Mountain State Park

From the Red Rock Canyon loop, continue south on Highway 159 a few miles to get to Spring Mountain State Park. This historic 520-acre ranch was a stopover for travelers on the Mormon and Spanish trails, but its more recent history is quite interesting as it had been owned by Howard Hughes when he was buying up Las Vegas. It was also owned by radio personalities Lum and Abner, and German munitions heiress Vera Krupp. Spring Mountain State Park is today the site of seasonal outdoor theater and concerts. The park is open year-round and offers guided tours as well as day use areas.

Bonnie Springs Old Nevada

Bonnie Springs Old Nevada is an Old West town in Red Rock Canyon near Spring Mountain State Park. There's a motel, shops, and the obligatory Western shootouts. Bonnie Springs was originally built in the 1840s as a cattle ranch and watering hole. Today, along with the gunfights, are horseback riding, a children's petting zoo, and mini-train rides.

Mt. Charleston — Spring Mountains National Recreation Area

Only 35 miles from Las Vegas, the Mt. Charleston (11,918 feet) area affords skiing in winter, picnicking, hiking, horseback riding, and communing with nature. To escape the desert heat, the Spring Mountains National Recreation Area is an average of 20 to 30 degrees cooler than Las Vegas. In addition to year-round hotel accommodations and tours, full-service camping and self-contained RV camping is also available from May through September.

The Spring Mountains National Recreation Area is accessed north of Las Vegas off of Highway 95, via one of two canyons (Kyle Canyon and Lee Canyon which do connect about 17 miles up the canyons, offering a scenic loop). There are also private vacation and year-round residences.

Kyle Canyon emerges from the desert floor through quaking aspens and pine trees to terminate in a beautiful natural mountain bowl. A popular trail is from the end of the pavement 1.2 miles to Mary Jane Falls. The Las Vegas Ski and Snowboard Resort is at the end of Lee Canyon.

Tule Springs — Floyd Lamb Park

About 15 miles north of Las Vegas (off Durango Drive on I-95) is a park at Tule Springs, little-known outside the area. While familiar to scientists as an important Pleistocene paleontologic site, Tule Springs was a watering hole for Indians and early travelers. The city of Las Vegas purchased the property from private owners in 1964. There's an historic ranch, and shady trees surrounding several small lakes for picnickers.

Valley of Fire State Park

Valley of Fire State Park is 55 miles from Las Vegas (north on I-15 and then east at Crystal), and offers dazzling scenic landscapes of hidden canyons, unique rock formations (including Elephant Rock and the Beehive), numerous petroglyphs, and remains of ancient Indian civilization. It is Nevada's oldest state park and is so named because of the effect of bright sunlight reflecting off the red sandstone. Dazzling red rocks jut up from the desert floor.

Stone cabins, Valley of Fire

There are lots of hiking trails as well as picnicking and camping facilities. One easy trail is a half mile round trip to Mouse's Tank, a water catchment basin named for a renegade Indian who hid out there in the 1890s. But the hike itself is a fine destination, with numerous petroglyphs on the rock walls high above the trail. They were not defaced as badly as the ones at nearby Atlatl Rock, which is accessed by an 85-steel-step climb.

Valley of Fire State Park also has three cabins built of native stone by the Civilian Conservation Corps (CCC) in the 1930s to provide shelter for travelers.

Administered by the Nevada State Park Service, there is a visitors center, art gallery, and guided tours available.

Hoover Dam (See Chapter 2)

Hoover Dam is an engineering wonder 34 miles southeast (I-93) from Las Vegas. This historic man-made creation harnessed the Colorado River and created Lake Mead, North America's largest man-made lake. The 726-foot-high, arch-gravity dam is 660 feet thick and was instrumental in providing power and water to a parched West. On-site tours of the dam are available to the public throughout the year and feature two high-speed elevators that descend 520 feet.

Lake Mead National Recreation Area

The Lake Mead National Recreation Area's closest point to Las Vegas is 25 miles. The massive lake created by Hoover Dam is 110 miles long and has more than 550 miles of shoreline. The Las Vegas metropolitan area gets 88% of its water from Lake Mead.

Administered by the National Park Service, the lake offers swimming, water skiing, camping, boating, fishing, and six marinas. At the Las Vegas Boat Harbor you can rent fast boats, ski equipment, family fun boats, and personal watercraft.

Mojave National Preserve

For real communing with a desert environment, you can visit the Mojave National Preserve, 60 miles southwest of Las Vegas (in California). This 1.6-million-acre preserve, which protects one of the most diverse environments in the world, abounds with sand dunes, volcanic cinder cones, Joshua tree forests and mile-high mountains. The preserve's visitor centers are located in Baker and Needles, California.

Desert Tortoise Conservation Center

The Desert Tortoise Conservation Center (DTCC), just southwest of Las Vegas, serves as a haven for lost, injured, and unwanted pet desert tortoises. It also helps those desert tortoises moved off of development sites throughout Clark County, Nevada.

In Spring 2009 the Nevada tortoises got further assistance when the famous San Diego Zoo became directly involved in their safety. The Zoo's Institute for Conservation Research partnered with U.S. Fish and Wildlife Service, the Bureau of Land Management, and the Nevada Department of Wildlife to operate the center.

The 250-acre DTCC is home to about 1,000 desert tortoises. Current operations include care and maintenance, quarantines as needed, and health assessments to ensure diseases are not transmitted back into the wild populations once they are released. Students from the Nevada State College in Henderson and other volunteers have been assisting in the project.

The National Parks (Death Valley, Grand Canyon, Bryce and Zion)

There are several world-renown national parks within a day or two of Las Vegas that definitely merit a visit.

Death Valley National Park, the lowest elevation in North America at 282 feet below sea level, is in eastern California, 135 road miles from Las Vegas and a 40-minute plane ride away.

The Grand Canyon in northwestern Arizona is approximately 300 miles or a one-hour flight from Las Vegas. Over millions of years, the Colorado River carved this natural wonder that is one mile deep and 277 miles long. Sightseeing air tours and ground tours of the Grand Canyon depart Las Vegas daily for half-day, full-day and overnight excursions. Grand Canyon West, at the Grand Canyon's western rim, features The Skywalk, a cantilever-shaped, glass, 70-foot walkway suspended more than 4,000 feet above the canyon's floor. The Skywalk is located 120 miles east of Las Vegas at Grand Canyon West's Eagle Point.

Zion National Park is 158 miles north of Las Vegas (I-15) across the Utah border. The Virgin River has carved deep and colorful sandstone canyons. It's also good for rock climbing.

Bryce Canyon National Park is located in Utah, 210 miles northeast of Las Vegas (I-15). Bryce features unique rock formations with imaginative names like Pink Cliffs, Silent City, and Cathedral.

Skydive Las Vegas

Adrenaline junkies can head for the Boulder City Airport where a full-time skydiving school operates. They offer the ultimate thrill ride—a tandem free-fall/parachute jump from 15,000 feet above sea level.

Bootleg Canyon Flightlines

For those zipline thrill seekers, a major adventure awaits in Boulder City. This isn't a treeline zip, but a free fall "soar" reaching speeds of up to 50 mph while you're dangling 1,000 feet above the ground, from the top of Red Mountain to the desert below. You can drive to Boulder City or they will pick you up from the Excalibur Hotel in Las Vegas.

Raft the River

Black Canyon River raft tours are available that depart from just below Hoover Dam. Contact Black Canyon River Adventures for guided raft trips that shuttle from Las Vegas hotels.

Awesome Adventures

Awesome Adventures Las Vegas is one company offering active outside adventures. They have mountain biking trips around the Hoover Dam/Lake Mead area, kayaking on Lake Mead, ATV tours in the desert and the Valley of Fire State Park, horseback riding, and sightseeing tours into Eldorado Canyon.

Pink Jeeps arrive at Techatticup

Pink Jeep "Experience the Natural Side of Las Vegas" Tours takes clients in air-conditioned comfort to their outdoors adventures. I saw them discharging tourists at Techatticup Mine in Eldorado Canyon for both mine tours and river kayaking adventures.

Check with your hotel as there are other companies offering similar or other unique adventures. For example, at Big Dig, you can relive your sandbox days by operating giant excavators, tractors and bull dozers.

There's a lot to do in the Las Vegas area out of town; those who prefer the outdoors to the busy and crowded environs of a casino might be surprised to discover a lot of memorable options available.

Nevada's Lost City
WHERE DID THE ANASAZI GO?

Before "Sin City" ever recorded its first transgression, another intriguing city dominated the southern Nevada landscape. Called the "Lost City," it is a series of Anasazi Indian ruins at the northern end of man-made Lake Mead, continuing up the Muddy River and Virgin River valleys for approximately 30 miles.

Like many of today's casino resorts, the "city" was built and developed by one group, lived in and utilized later by others, and then abandoned. They didn't implode buildings back then, just walked away. And like casinos, there were rich pickings in those days too, the area great for farming and hunting.

The over 150 recorded sites of the Lost City were initially occupied by the Anasazi (the earliest group called the Basketmakers) sometime after the first century. Later, from 700-1150 A.D., the Puebloans moved in. Some of the sites were also reoccupied by the Paiute Indians; experts are not sure exactly when, but sometime after year 1000 A.D. The Basketmakers lived in subterranean pit houses and hunted local game with spears. They used baskets, mostly as storage vessels, hence their name. The later Puebloans lived in above ground multi-room pueblos

Part of the Lost City Museum in Overton

(stick and adobe structures). Culturally more advanced, they developed bows and arrows for bagging their food, and manufactured ceramic vessels for storage and cooking.

In addition to farming (corn, beans, squash, and cotton) and hunting, the Lost City Anasazi mined salt and turquoise, both for personal use and for trading.

The Lost City ruins were originally noted by explorer Jedediah Smith back in 1826-27. He reported finding stone tools in salt caves along the Virgin River where Lake Mead stands today. It would be almost 100 years later before Smith's report generated any interest. In 1924, two brothers from Overton, Nevada, John and Fay Perkins, announced their "discovery" of the ruins. Nevada's Governor James Scrugham then arranged for M.R. Harrington, a noted New York archaeologist, to investigate.

Harrington named the complex the Pueblo Grande de Nevada, "grande" because of its large scope. However the media, knowing the public's infatuation with more intriguing names, labeled the find the "Lost City."

Harrington began excavations of the Lost City in 1924, fortunately just a few years before they really would have been "lost." The Hoover Dam project was slated to inundate the priceless archaeological finds with the rising waters of Lake Mead.

Some of the artifacts were moved and are now housed in The Lost City Museum at Overton, about an hour's drive from Las Vegas. Built in 1935, the museum (run by the State of Nevada since 1953), is a worthwhile tourist attraction, welcoming more than 50,000 visitors a year. Why did the Anasazi vanish? Some archaeologists believe that a severe drought forced relocation to a more habitable area. Other theories suggest that malaria-laden mosquitoes, overpopulation, or the aggression of neighboring tribes decimated the ancient Anasazi. But no one really knows, adding another unsolved web of intrigue to the Las Vegas area. The departure of the ancients left the world a puzzle. Even the petroglyphs and art left in the area merely signify the existence of the Anasazi. What they were all about continues to stump experts today.

Hoover Dam Bypass Bridge
Spanning The Colorado

I t's big—even overshadowing the historic Hoover Dam just 1,500 feet up canyon. The massive new Colorado River Bridge spanning Black Canyon ceremoniously opened to traffic in October 2010, replacing the winding, narrow circuitous route over the dam. Like the dam itself, and so much more in Southern Nevada, the project was huge, with a dramatic 1,060-foot-twin-rib concrete arch spans the centerpiece of the 1,900-foot-long bridge that soars 900 feet over the river below.

The impressive Hoover Dam Bypass Bridge opened in October 2010.
(Photo courtesy the Hoover Dam Bypass Project).

The bridge immediately became a necessary river-crossing route, removing through-vehicle and truck traffic from the top of the dam. This new route eliminates the narrow road with sharp turns, inadequate shoulders, poor sight distance, and low travel speeds of the dam route. U.S. Highway 93 had used the top of Hoover Dam to cross the Colorado River. It has been the major commercial corridor between the states of Arizona, Nevada, and Utah, and is also on the North American Free Trade Agreement (NAFTA) route between Mexico and Canada. Thus U.S. 93 was identified as a high-priority corridor in the National Highway System Designation Act of 1995.

The bottleneck congestion caused by the inadequacy of the old U.S. 93 across the dam had imposed a serious economic burden on the adjoining states. More than 17,000 vehicles a day traveled over the Depression-era Hoover Dam's two-lane roadway. To spur the action, it was projected that traffic volume would increase 50% over the next 20 years for this section of U.S. Highway 93.

Then, following the devastating September 11, 2001 terrorist attacks on the U.S., more than 2,000 trucks a day have been diverted 23 miles away from the dam, going through Laughlin, costing consumers some $30 million annually in added fuel and delays. Since the diversion, Highway 95 (from Boulder City, through Searchlight, and to the state border where Highway 163 leads to the Laughlin Bridge) has been widened to four lanes, as has Highway 163. It's better for the truckers but still farther out of the way. There was always the potential for a dangerous situation. A major catastrophe could occur, involving innocent bystanders, millions of dollars in property damage to the dam and its facilities, contamination of the waters of Lake Mead or the Colorado River, and interruption of the power and water supply for people in the Southwest. Thus additional objectives of the bridge project were: to protect Hoover Dam employees, visitors, equipment, power generation capabilities, and Lake Mead and Colorado River waters; to eliminate possible interruptions in electricity and water delivery; and provide improved dam operating conditions.

Originally called the Colorado River Bridge of the Hoover Dam Bypass Project, it has officially been named the Mike O'Callaghan-Pat Tillman Memorial Bridge by the United States Congress. Its name honors Mike O'Callaghan, a former Nevada Governor, community leader, and businessman who died in 2004, and Arizonan Pat Tillman, who played professional football for the Arizona Cardinals, joined the Army, and was killed in Afghanistan in 2004.

Getting it Done

The Central Federal Lands Highway Division (CFLHD) led the Project Management Team (PMT) in overseeing the design and construction of the bridge project. The PMT had representation from each of the major project stakeholders including the Federal Highway Administration, the States of Arizona and Nevada, the Bureau of Reclamation (BOR), the Western Area Power Authority (WAPA), and the National Park Service (NPS). The total Hoover Dam Bypass design and construction budget was $240 million. The Obayashi Corporation and PSM Construction USA, Inc., a joint venture partnership, was awarded the contract to build the Colorado River Bridge portion with a bid of $114 million and a completion date of June 2010. Onsite construction of the bridge began in late January 2005.

Problems and Scandals

The project was not without its problems and, being Nevada, its share of scandals.

In early 2006, local concrete supplier Casino Ready Mix Inc. was found to be unlicensed, causing a four-month delay.

Originally slated to be finished in 2008, the bridge then underwent a major delay when, in September 2006, the critical cableway system set up 780 feet above the river to shuttle materials between Arizona and Nevada had totally collapsed under 55 mph winds.

While the cableway system was being replaced, Obayashi/PSM mobilized a 330-ton crane on the Nevada side and a 135-ton crane on the Arizona side to build columns, pier caps, box girders, and arch segments. The new cableway system went into operation in January 2008. Replacement costs and accident details have not been disclosed because legal action is still pending between American Bridge and Obayashi/PSM.

The project's troubles continued. On November 24, 2008, ironworker Sherman Jones, 48, of Las Vegas, was killed while adjusting an alignment cable on the twin arches. Jones was using hydraulic pumps on the strand jack when the cable snapped. The U.S. Occupational Safety and Health Administration (OSHA) found Jones died from blunt-force trauma injuries and ruled the incident an accident, and no fines were levied.

Along with problems was a scandal. The scandal actually wasn't directly related to the project but involved the parent company of one half of the joint venture, Tokyo-based Obayashi Corporation. In 2007 the company CEO/President had to step down after his adviser and two other employees were arrested on the suspicion of rigging bids.

It was the second time that same year that Obayashi employees were arrested on bid-rigging charges. In the first instance Obayashi and four other builders were temporarily barred from Japanese government contracts after being indicted for price rigging on a Nagoya City subway extension project. By this time, their U.S. subsidiary was hard at work over the Colorado River.

No toll

The new bridge and total 4.3-mile access highway are free to use. As rugged as the site of the crossing is, the approaches were no easier to construct than the bridge itself, with harsh terrain, abrupt drops, jutting rock surfaces, and uneven contours.

The present roadway will remain open to Hoover Dam visitors. However, through traffic and truck traffic will not be permitted on the dam. During the past few years only select tourist busses had been allowed, and they, along with all passenger cars had to undergo an inspection.

The new four-lane asphalt highway follows a winding route in Nevada just south of existing U.S. 93. It crosses over the existing roadway twice before crossing the Colorado River past Sugarloaf Mountain, then tying into U.S. 93 in Arizona.

It's big, it's important, and like Nevada itself, it's dramatic; but if you've got acrophobia, when you're crossing that monster just don't look down.

Chapter 12

Las Vegas Today

The Las Vegas of today is very much a product of its past. There have been tragedies and fires, a history of dirty dealing, and numerous movies and television shows that have highlighted the fantastic, almost unreal place.

In a return to its railroad beginning, competing companies are now hoping to bring high-speed trains to Las Vegas.

There are challenges that Las Vegas faces; the economy, Indian and riverboat casinos, Macau (where gambling has already surpassed Las Vegas), and Internet gambling, to name a few. Las Vegas has proven to be resilient and its future will depend on how it weathers these challenges.

Kiel Ranch
A Ranch of Ignominy

M aybe if you look the other way, it will go away. Now, is that any way to treat a Historic Place? Especially if that place is a ranch house considered the oldest structure still standing in Nevada?

The Kiel Ranch, 200 West Carey Ave. (at Washington), North Las Vegas, is an integral part of the history of southern Nevada, but it might have been imploded like a worn-out old casino for all the care it's received.

The Kiel Ranch (sometimes misspelled Kyle) was developed from the old Indian Farm established by the Mormons in the 1850s to teach agricultural practices to the Paiutes. The site was a spring about two miles north of the Mormon Fort, and the Indians helped the settlers build an adobe ranch house structure there that still exists today.

The Indian Farm was later developed into a ranch by Conrad Kiel who arrived in the valley in 1875. Kiel Ranch, run by Conrad Kiel and his sons, Edwin and William, soon developed deserved notoriety for harboring horse thieves and criminals. The ghosts of the ranch are witness to three murders, neighbor Archibald Stewart, and Erwin and William Kiel.

Kiel Ranch House, 1988 *(Library of Commerce, Department of Interior)*

The original Old Mormon Fort itself had become the Las Vegas Ranch, and in 1882, the Stewart Ranch, run by Archibald Stewart and his family.

Meanwhile, the 240-acre Kiel Ranch was sold in 1903 to the San Pedro, Los Angeles & Salt Lake Railroad. Subsequent owners included Edwin Taylor (1924-39), and Edwin Losee (1939-58), who developed the Boulderado Dude Ranch there, primarily used for divorce seekers to establish Nevada residence. There were several other ownership changes and acreage spinoffs before bureaucracy intervened.

To Protect and Preserve

Citing flag-waving historic preservation opportunities, in 1976 the City of North Las Vegas (site of Kiel Ranch) and its Bicentennial Committee jointly purchased the ranch and its 28 remaining acres.

Despite promises to protect and improve the site and buildings, the project has been bungled, and bungled so badly, you have to wonder whether it was decades of just stupidity and ignorance, or whether there were ulterior motives.

Consider: Initially the city accepted federal and state money to protect and preserve the historic ranch and signed an agreement that it could not be used for private purposes. City planners and preservationists began drawing up blueprints for a public park, equestrian trails, and an old Western town. But nothing happened.

In 1983, the North Las Vegas city council decided that the best way to get the funds for the promised park was to sell off much of the land. So they sold 21 acres of the historic 28-acre property at a bargain to a local businessman who had friends on the council. He agreed to make it a "park," only somewhere the translation must have got garbled, because he immediately paved the acreage and added a bunch of drab warehouses on the site in his "industrial park." Hey, it's a park. The remaining historic seven acres have been neglected, although through the years council after council announced they were going to do something. A 1992 fire destroyed the ranch's largest building that had been built for the Boulderado Dude Ranch.

About half of the original fund money had been spent, and the only significant improvement is now a chain-link fence around the existing buildings. Some money went toward building a parking lot, fencing, and a now-decaying canopy meant to protect the adobe structure. The city also used some of the funds to complete street improvements adjacent to the ranch's parking lot.

The place has been allowed to deteriorate into an eyesore. It's covered with trash, homeless people regularly squat there (you can see where they piled up boxes and tree limbs to scale the wall), and the historic spring itself is hard to find in the weed-choked, overgrown lot. Most of the important buildings dating from the Kiel era have either burned in mysterious fires or crumbled from the elements.

By 2006, the Kiel Ranch had become a source of problems with water runoff from the spring and wetlands flowing into the industrial park. It was fortuitous that the city's misguided plan to destroy more of the site to divert the water was uncovered and luckily met with opposition.

More negligible is the fact the ranch has also been used as a dump, and not by private parties seeking to evade recycling fees—but by the City of North Las Vegas itself—potentially destroying much of its value as an archaeological site and historic place. That's not just negligent, but some would call that unconscionable.

What became a "Say What?" decision to observers was a few years ago when the city turned down $2.4 million in U.S. Bureau of Land Management funds meant to spruce up the ranch and rehabilitate its pond. The city said they refused the money because they couldn't find any partners to help with the rest of the financial burden. They felt that it would be a statewide benefit and questioned why North Las Vegas citizens should bear the full responsibility of restoration, operation, and maintenance. "The concern is whether the BLM funds were earmarked for restoration only and could not be used for operation or maintenance," said city spokeswoman Brenda Johnson.

Opportunities came and went. In their minimal defense, the current City of North Las Vegas officials say they have been working on a plan to preserve Kiel Ranch. At this point, it's still a lot of talk with ongoing committees and focus groups. The Kiel Ranch Comprehensive Development and Preservation Master Plan has been formed and held several community workshops, asking residents to share their ideas for improving the plan.

Meanwhile, all that remains are buildings near collapse and a parking area, built at a cost of $500,000, that is closed.

Old is equated with "bad" to a certain mindset that is quite prevalent in Nevada. People who have attended grand openings at glittering new casinos have later stood back and watched that same "old" casino blasted to smithereens a couple

Kiel Ranch House today

271

decades later. With what they've seen, it appears they have not been conditioned to appreciate the past.

Kiel Ranch is in North Las Vegas, but there are "historic venues" all over southern Nevada. It sometimes seems Las Vegas only reveres and worships at the altars of the glittering and the new. The city is only 100 years old and has already destroyed much of its past. If you want old buildings and a sense of history, well, you best go to Europe; you won't find much of that in the Las Vegas area.

Las Vegas Endures

A History of Dirty Dealing

Las Vegas has rightfully earned its sobriquet, Sin City. Along with the hedonistic practice of excessive living and the flaunting of compulsive behavior, Las Vegas has also always endured in-fighting and dirty deals. It has become part of the psyche of the city itself, and has been since the days of the original Mormon Fort.

The early Las Vegas Mormons even fought among themselves for local leadership, the loser banished from the area by the alpha male victor. Then came the miners, who were constantly killing and maiming each other. They fought over mining claims, over women, over cards, over insults real or imagined, over drunkenness, even over which side of the Civil War one supported. Sam Gay, the first Las Vegas sheriff, even commented that especially between 1905 and 1910, there were always bodies to be removed from town on most Sunday mornings.

After the railroad auction launched Las Vegas in 1905, other area settlements were thwarted from development because precious water was withheld from them by the railroad people. The city began its fabulous march to prominence with gloves on, fighting to keep others from prospering. There have been and still are many examples of "dirty dealing" associated with Las Vegas.

The mobsters didn't invent dirty dealing, just refined it and made it their credo.

Nevada today has one of the most effective gambling control systems in the world. State authorities knew they had to make sure the gambling was as clean as possible. In that regard, they created the Black Book and other safeguards to minimize cheating and theft, keep the industry as honest as possible, and of course collect taxes.

In Las Vegas, even today it seems that unless it has to do with the sanctity of the casinos, it's almost accepted practice to condone cheating and dirty dealing. The casinos are heavily self-governed and widely scrutinized. But elsewhere,

272

authorities often look the other way. Like a rattlesnake in the desert, unless you do something to really tick it off, it will leave you alone.

That laissez-faire policy is what works, and is what seems to hold the Las Vegas economy together. The authorities know that most of the escorts, models, and dating services are fronts for prostitution. Each weekend they will arrest anywhere from 200-300 of them to curtail the activity. It's a presence, but as one cop said, "Sometimes it's like pissing in the wind." Unless there is a reason, they generally do not mount a wide-scale attack on their activities. They look for underage girls, for drug use, and often find themselves spending their time as counselors.

They know people live in the tunnels, but it's easier to just leave them be. If they commit a crime up above, bust them, but otherwise, leave things alone.

Today, the power in Las Vegas rests with the corporate boards of those companies that own most of the casinos. Their objective is no different than those who came before them. Like the miners and Mormons who sought pockets of ore in the hills and deserts, the casino owners of today are finding new and different "pockets of ore" to mine. If it's out there, they want it.

That attitude is well expressed in the preface of the John L. Smith book *Sharks in the Desert*, when publisher Lyle Stuart noted: "From the made men to the corporate tough guys—they're all here. Things only appear to have changed. The corporate hard-asses have the same goal as the mobsters who preceded them: to make as much money as possible without regard to who gets destroyed in the process."

Casino owner Bob Stupak, who died in 2009, unabashedly and directly admitted, "I target everybody. I'm in the business of taking their money. It makes no difference to me if it's a Social Security check, a welfare check, or a stock-dividend check. It's our duty to extract as much money from the customers as we can and send them home with smiles on their faces."

Cities tend to have personas and reputations. Washington D.C. thrives on *power*; the denizens of New York's Wall Street are seemingly fueled by *greed*; Los Angeles is perceived as being more concerned with *image* and *vanity*. And Las Vegas—well, the word *excess* comes to mind. Everything is over-the-top, even dirty dealing.

Desert Tragedies
FIRE AND TERROR

N o city is immune from tragedies as both the forces of nature and the vagaries of man can periodically render great harm. Being a major city Las Vegas has had its share. Occasional thunderstorms have rendered roads impassable and flooded business and residential areas. Even before the city was incorporated in 1911, two major floods (1907 and 1910) wiped out railroad tracks isolating the town, and the school house even burned down in 1910.

Fire is always to be dreaded in cities with high-rise buildings, and Las Vegas has had crippling and horrible hotel/casino fires even in the days before the high-rises made their presence.

The low-rise El Rancho Vegas, the Strip's first resort, caught on fire in June 1960. The fire started in the kitchen and left the main building a charred shell. No one was injured.

In 1980 the worst fire in the city's history occurred and it was a tragic one.

MGM Grand (Bally's) Fire

The worst disaster in Nevada's history was the fire that engulfed the MGM Grand Hotel & Casino (Now Bally's Las Vegas) on November 21, 1980. The tragedy took the lives of 87 people, most of whom succumbed from smoke inhalation.

The MGM Grand was a 26-floor, 2,000-room luxury resort with approximately 5,000 people in both the hotel and casino at the time. A fire broke out in a hotel restaurant called The Deli just after 7 a.m. and smoke and fire quickly spread through the building. Along with the 87 people killed, another 650 were sent to the hospital, including guests, employees, and 14 injured firefighters. The fire itself was mostly confined to the second floor casino and adjacent restaurants, yet most of the deaths occurred on the upper floors due to smoke inhalation. It seems that the vertical shafts caused by elevators and stairwells acted as conduits to allow the toxic smoke to go up.

Seventy-five of the deceased died from smoke and carbon monoxide poisoning, four from smoke alone, three from burns and smoke, one from burns alone, and one head trauma caused by jumping from a high window. Three died later from injuries sustained in the fire. There were valuable lessons learned from the tragedy, including the fact that smoke inhalation is the most serious threat in a fire. Building construction codes and fire prevention measures have been changed in the aftermath.

Las Vegas Hilton Fire

Only three months (90 days) after the tragic MGM fire, on February 10, 1981, the Las Vegas Hilton was set on fire by an arsonist employee, killing eight people. The toll could have been much worse, but the hotel and firefighters had learned from the MGM conflagration. At the time, the Hilton was in the process of being retrofitted with modern fire safety equipment. Then as part of a new plan, firefighters used local television networks to notify people to stay in their rooms and not go out to the halls and stairwells. Because of the lessons learned, only eight people died in this fire. In 1982, a man named

Philip Crane was sentenced to eight life sentences for his role in starting the Hilton fire.

Learning from Experience

In the long run, the MGM Grand and Hilton fires in Las Vegas led to momentous reforms. In 1981, the Nevada legislature required all new buildings above seven floors to have built-in sprinklers and all older buildings had to be retrofitted.

Within a few years, the entire Hilton chain retrofitted all of its high rise hotels in the United States, and other chains followed suit. By 1990, the safety trend had gone global based on the Las Vegas experience and other deadly fires elsewhere.

Gold Spike Fire

In 2001, at the six-story Gold Spike Hotel & Casino downtown, a man and a woman reported their mattress was on fire. The most extensive damage was confined to that third floor room, but thick, black smoke from their room filled the hotel hallways, panicking some guests into jumping out windows. Seventeen people suffered minor injuries.

Monte Carlo Fire

Passersby noticed billowing black smoke rising from the roof of the 32-story Monte Carlo Resort Hotel before the hotel and guests were aware of it. The late-morning January 2008 fire had started on the roof where there were no fire alarms.

Calls to the fire department promptly had the hotel issuing evacuation orders over ceiling speakers, in what was described as "measured and patient words."

The fire was the result of a welding incident. Although there were no injuries, the fire caused severe damage to the hotel's 32nd floor. Dislodged hotel guests meanwhile settled in at other MGM Mirage hotels, and waited to be reunited with their luggage.

Almost two years later, the hotel reopened the charred floor offering 50 high-amenity studios and suites.

Carol Lombard Dies in Plane Crash

At the height of her fame at age 33, prominent actress Carol Lombard was returning to California from a war bond rally when TWA Flight #3, a DC-3, stopped for refueling in Las Vegas. On January 16, 1942 the plane took off and crashed into Mt. Potosi, 32 miles southwest of Las Vegas. Her husband, the legendary Clark Gable, was distraught with grief and awaited word in the Pioneer Saloon in nearby Goodsprings. Inconsolable, he immediately joined military service, and even though he remarried, was buried next to Lombard when he died.

Roy Mauled by Tiger

During an October 2003 production of "Siegfried & Roy," one of the most successful shows in Las Vegas history, performer Roy Horn was seriously injured when one of the show's animals, a white tiger named Montecore, bit him on the neck.

The 380-pound, seven-year-old white tiger sank its teeth into Horn's neck and dragged him off stage in front of a horrified audience at the Mirage show-

Siegfried and Roy *(photo courtesy Mirage Hotel & Casino)*

room. The animal damaged an artery carrying oxygen to the magician's brain and crushed his windpipe.

Critically injured, he still mouthed, "Don't shoot the cat," on the way to the hospital. Doctors removed one-quarter of his skull to relieve the pressure of his swelling brain during an operation known as a decompressive craniectomy. He was eventually transferred to UCLA Medical Center in Los Angeles for long-term recovery and rehabilitation. The mauling left Horn, 60, partially paralyzed and ended the long-running show. Federal investigators never did learn what set off the animal that Horn had trained since a cub. Montecore was not shot.

Luxor Explosion

The Luxor Hotel parking garage was the site of a vehicle explosion in May 2007, which killed one of its employees. Local authorities believe the victim, who worked in a business inside the hotel, was the specific target for this bombing. The hotel was not evacuated, and the parking structure where the explosion occurred suffered no damage. The explosion is believed to be caused by a homemade bomb, and the perpetrator was never caught.

New York New York Shooting

At about 12:45 a.m. on July 6, 2007, guests at the New York New York Hotel & Casino had to duck for their lives. A Las Vegas resident on a walkway high above the casino floor opened fire on them, sending five people to the hospital, all with non-life threatening injuries. One brave casino guest, Justin Lampert from North Dakota, tackled and subdued the gunman until security personnel arrived. The gunman, Steve Zegrean, 51, was found guilty on 49 accounts.

CityCenter Accidents

Six deaths occurred during the construction of CityCenter from February 6, 2007 to May 31, 2008. The sixth death prompted a construction walkout on June 3, 2008 to protest safety conditions at the project. The union demanded the general contractor take three steps before its workers would return to their jobs: agree to pay for additional safety training, allow union researchers to examine root causes of safety problems on the site, and allow union leaders full access to the work site. They agreed that day and work was resumed within 24 hours.

Fires and tragedies happen everywhere. In the case of the disastrous MGM Grand fire, the lessons learned saved lives in subsequent fires and prevented yet other fires from happening, not only in Las Vegas but in cities around the country.

Movies Made in Las Vegas
VEGAS GETS ITS DUE

Something about Las Vegas, the gambling, entertainment, glamour, and excitement, has a broad appeal. Film makers know that and have constantly brought those images to the movie-going public. There have been many movies about and/or filmed in the Las Vegas area over the years. In fact, the author compiled a comprehensive list of 149 movies made in the Las Vegas area from 1936 to 2010. It appears that there really is "something about Vegas."

One of the most popular was 1960's *Ocean's Eleven* starring Frank Sinatra, Dean Martin, and their pals. It was filmed mostly on location in Las Vegas and featured the elaborate heist of the Desert Inn, Flamingo, Sahara, Sands, and Riviera casinos.

A new generation of box office stars (George Clooney, Brad Pitt, Julia Roberts) starred in sequels: *Ocean's Eleven* (2001), *Ocean's Twelve* (2004), and *Ocean's Thirteen* (2007).

Other classics were 1963's *Viva Las Vegas* with Elvis Presley and Ann Margret, the 1971 James Bond flick *Diamonds Are Forever*, 1992's *Honeymoon in Vegas*, and 1995's *Leaving Las Vegas*. Movies about the Entertainment Capital of the World include scores of Hollywood's biggest names, and some lesser known ones. Whether about gambling, or entertainment, or mobsters, the movie-going public seems to enjoy identifying with Las Vegas.

TV Shows About Vegas
THE SMALL SCREEN

Television producers also have had a hard time resisting the Las Vegas lure. Along with the long-running ABC show "Vega$," starring Robert Urich (1978-1981), there have been numerous TV shows about Sin City.

Perhaps the most popular has been the NBC series "Las Vegas," which first aired in 2003. Starring Josh Duhamel, James Caan, James Lesure, and Vanessa Marcil, viewers got a nifty idea as to the inner workings of a casino.

Back in the 1960s, there was "Teenbeat Club," an interview and Dance Show Production; in the 1970s, a Vegas- based series called "Blansky's Beauties" aired on ABC, and NBC offered "Crime Story" in the 1980s.

There have been numerous shows since, including "Hearts Are Wild," "Caesar's Challenge," the CBS shows "Dr. Vegas," "CSI: Las Vegas," "Heroes" which featured a fictional Las Vegas casino, and "Las Vegas Law." Las Vegas-based reality shows have been real popular, including "The Casino," "The Real World: Las Vegas," "The Surreal Life", numerous episodes of "Fear Factor" and "Cops," and "America's Got Talent."

The current History Channel show *Pawn Shop* features the beefy black-shirted Harrison family wheeling and dealing. Nowadays there's often a line out front of the pawn shop on Las Vegas Blvd. just waiting to get in.

The initial television airing of Las Vegas poker tournaments created an insatiable demand and now there are so many poker shows on TV that the average "couch potato" knows about the "river" card, and going "all in."

Concerts, live entertainment, magic shows, telethons, cooking shows, and it seems every conceivable type of show has been filmed in Las Vegas for broad distribution. Regular TV game shows, from "The Today Show" to "Wheel of Fortune" have often broadcast "live" from the Entertainment Capital of the World.

Sporting events for every fan, from major boxing matches, tennis matches, golf tournaments, auto races, and much more have originated in Las Vegas for the small screen. The "Las Vegas Line" is considered the official odds for sports wagering worldwide.

Throw in a few travelogues and documentaries and it's obvious that the city of Las Vegas is better represented on the small screen than any other place in the world.

High Speed Trains to Vegas

Back To The Future

Trains are what got Las Vegas off to a start. The railroad people are the ones who changed "The Meadows" from a watering hole with a couple of ranches to a town. They created a major station, auctioned off lots, and laid out the town.

As the town grew and the decades flew by, the train began diminishing in importance. The highway from Los Angeles was improved, and Las Vegas McCarran International Airport began shuttling people from around the world.

In fact, McCarran has been ranked the fifteenth busiest in the world by the Airports Council International. McCarran serves 51 air carriers, averaging 980 flights a day. In 2010, both going and coming, 39,757,359 passengers passed though McCarran. This figure was close to the 40.5 million of 2009, but down from 43 million in 2008, and the 2006 and 2007 highs of 46 million. Over 1.2 million of those passengers were international.

Most visitors, however, arrive by ground (car/bus). In 2009, 58% arrived via ground transportation compared to the 42% who arrived by plane. The ground transportation numbers are growing (up from 54% in 2007). Generally about a third of all Las Vegas visitors are from California (31% in 2009).

Yet, nobody arrived by train. When Amtrak discontinued its Desert Wind service to Las Vegas on May 10, 1997, the train era ended. Now, two competing firms are hoping to change the way people get to Las Vegas. Both American Magline and Las Vegas-based DesertXpress are

Desert Wind train in Las Vegas (Peter VandenBossche photo, 1994)

pitching high-speed rail routes to provide the first train service between Los Angeles and Las Vegas. The timing is right as President Barack Obama has been pushing for high-speed rail transportation to counter the uncertain price of oil.

American Magline Group — Maglev

The Los Angeles based American Magline Group (AMG) wants to build the California-Nevada Interstate Maglev Project, a magnetic-levitation train that would hover slightly above the tracks with a top speed of more than 300 miles per hour on its route linking Las Vegas and Anaheim, California. The proposed $12 billion project would connect Southern Californians with Las Vegas in just 80 minutes.

The American Magline Group is a coalition of companies partnered to build the maglev for the nonprofit California-Nevada Super Speed Train Commission (CNSSTC). They are planning the construction of the 35-mile segment from Las Vegas to Primm as the first step of the full corridor. Construction is planned in three phases, with the timing dependent upon funding availability. It would be a publicly financed project.

The project will have six stations: the cities of Anaheim, Ontario, Victorville, and Barstow in Southern California, the town of Primm on the Nevada border, and the City of Las Vegas. The CNSSTC was formed in 1988 to promote the development of, and issue a franchise to build, the super-speed train system.

DesertXpress

A competing company, the privately-backed DesertXpress is proposing a steel-wheels-on-rail train from Las Vegas that can travel up to 150 miles per hour but would terminate in Victorville, California, because of the steep grades separating the high desert from the Los Angeles Basin. Builders of the $6 billion DesertXpress high-speed train received good news in April 2011 when the last of the five federal agencies involved approved the final environmental impact report. At the announcement presentation, Senator Harry Reid said DesertXpress would bring 35,000 jobs to Clark County alone.

The company hopes to break ground by early 2012 on the project between Las Vegas and Victorville, California, anticipating a five year completion date. Many people question the Victorville terminus, but according to developers costs at this time to go over the mountains would be prohibitive and it is only 85 miles from Los Angeles. It is planned to later connect with Palmdale, where it could tie in to a proposed high speed rail system between Los Angeles and San Francisco.

Alliance formed

An alliance of several Western transit agencies has been formed to help kick-start the projects and secure funding to bring the train passenger traffic back to Las Vegas.

However, Senate Majority Leader Harry Reid (D.-NV) got frustrated over the Maglev project's many years of delays, inability to raise sufficient funds, and failure to complete an environmental impact report. So he redirected

$45 million earmarked for the project to road improvements near Las Vegas' McCarran International Airport.

American Magline disputed Reid's statement, saying it has had the necessary funds, and blamed the delays on the Federal Railroad Administration for holding up completion of the environmental impact statement.

The American Magline Group said they will forge ahead with their plans even as the rival DesertXpress group appears to break ground first. Neil Cummings, president of the American Magline Group, said he thinks the public would be more supportive of his project, the 300 mile-an-hour, 80-minute travel between Las Vegas and Anaheim, versus the one hour and 40 minute trip only to Victorville. "Even if DesertXpress gets built, I'd have no problem building our train alongside it and put them out of business," he said.

Train Competition

Seems like what goes around comes around. Nothing like rival train companies to add a little excitement. Las Vegas got its start with the rival San Pedro, Los Angeles & Salt Lake Railroad battling the Union Pacific to be the first into Las Vegas.

Whatever train service ultimately wins the ongoing battle, hopefully it will be completed soon enough to make a difference. Other Western cities like Salt Lake City, Phoenix, and Denver could also connect with Las Vegas via high speed rail service.

Meanwhile, anyone from Southern California who has traveled the mind-numbing, heavily-clogged I-15 on a weekend knows that a high speed train to Las Vegas couldn't come soon enough.

It Stays in Vegas
CHASINQ THE TOURIST DOLLAR

At the south entrance to the Las Vegas Strip is the famous and iconic "Welcome to Las Vegas" sign.

These days that message is all-important to Las Vegas businesses, hotels, and casinos as they reel to counter the dwindling dollars caused by a tight worldwide market. During the recent tough economic times, some people, companies, and even the government, have decided to shun that welcome. President Barack Obama even made the comment, "When times are tough, you tighten your belts...You don't blow a bunch of cash on Vegas when you're trying to save for college."

Needless to say, that comment didn't sit too well with Nevadans. Rep. Shelley Berkley (D.-NV), whose district includes the Las Vegas Strip, led the contingent of politicians and the media to voice their disapproval.

Las Vegas, with over 36 million visitors each year, needs tourists, and needs them to bring and leave money to survive. While many budgets have been strained in recent years, the number of visitors has remained relatively constant. But Las Vegas has still felt the pinch. While Las Vegas tourism has roughly held its own in the total number of visitors (37.3 million in 2010, 36.4 million in 2009, and 37.4 in 2008), the amount they have spent is way down. The average time tourists spent in Las Vegas has also remained constant (2010–3.3 days, 2009–3.6 days, 2008–3.5 days). However, the Las Vegas Convention and Visitors Authority reported that visitors in 2009 and 2010 spent a lot less on gambling, food, casino shows, and shopping than they had in recent years.

Discounted lodging to attract the tourists has contributed to the lower dollar amounts they have left in Las Vegas. During 2009, tourists spent about 22% less for hotel rooms that they did in 2008. The actual cost for all hotel rooms averaged $92.93 in 2009, and $94.91 in 2010, down from $119.19 in 2008.

Visitors spent less on food and drink. In 2010 it was $256.82, up slightly from 2009's $250.32, but still down from $273.39 in 2008. Shopping expenditures dropped from an average $121.90 in 2008 to $101.97 in 2009.

The 80% of all visitors who gambled in 2010 was still a six-year low, down from 2009 (83%), and 2008 (85%). Gambling dollars dropped steadily too. Of those gambling, the average gambling budget of $466.20 in 2010 was less than the $481.57 in 2009, down from $531.98 in 2008, and well below the high of $651.94 in 2006.

Las Vegas is the fifth most popular vacation destination in the world for foreign travel and the number-one summer destination in the United States. Its economy revolves around tourists and needs them to survive.

Conventions

Back in 1970 there were 6.8 million visitors to Las Vegas. Within 35 years—by 2005—that number increased by 550%, aided by conventions. During 2010 there were 18,004 conventions hosting 4,473,134, or 12% of all visitors. That was down from 19,394 conventions hosting 4,492,275 in 2009, and way down from 2008 when 5,899,725 conventioneers attended 22,454 conventions. The original Las Vegas Convention Center, a 6,300-seat, silver-domed rotunda with an adjoining 90,000-square-foot exhibit hall that opened in 1959 was demolished in 1990 to make room for one of the largest single-level facilities in the world. The 3.2 million-square-foot Convention Center includes approximately two million square feet of exhibit space and 380,000 square feet of meeting rooms. The city not only wants conventions, it definitely has the framework in place.

While the overall economy has slowed things down for the past few years, many see recovery on the horizon. There are still a few bright spots, like New Year's Eve when over 300,000 revelers party along the blocked-off Strip and the Fremont Street Experience downtown. Super Bowl weekend is big in Las Vegas—Nevada being the only state where sports wagering is legal. Even getting only about 1.5% of all U.S. sports bets, it's still a considerable amount.

Challenges

There are a few challenges ahead that Las Vegas must weather. In recent decades, Las Vegas has realized it's not the only game in town. Indian casinos and riverboat casinos have sprung up all around the country. Ma and Pa Slot Puller can head for a casino a short drive away and no longer have to save up for a trip to Vegas.

Las Vegas has countered the neighborhood casinos by trying different things. They explored making the casinos kid-friendly. They have ratcheted up entertainment way beyond the high-caliber floor shows, and now offer sexier shows, high-energy nightclubs, fine dining, and more attractions than one would ever find in a neighborhood casino. As long as Las Vegas is able to adapt to a changing climate, Las Vegas will prevail.

Macau

Las Vegas is still the "Entertainment Capital of the World," but back in 2006 it lost its title of "The Gambling Capital of the World" to the Chinese city of Macau. The former Portuguese island colony now has 33 casinos and from January-November 2006 had taken in $6.485 billion from slots and table games, beating Vegas' $6.079 billion. In 2008, when Las Vegas reported annual revenues of $7.5 billion, Macau almost doubled that with $13.8 billion. Macau has continued to set records each month, and by March 2011 hit a one-month gambling revenue high of $2.5 billion, a 48% increase over March 2010. The Macau gamblers are generally different from those in Las Vegas. Most are from the Chinese mainland, most are men, and they stay for much shorter durations; they don't shop or see shows, and they spend about three times more money gambling.

Many Asians tend to have more of a reliance on luck, and that makes gambling not only popular but much more acceptable. The Chinese primarily don't go for fun; they see it as a serious business. The Macau casinos have been not only attracting Chinese gamblers, but gamblers from all over the world.

Three Las Vegas companies, Las Vegas Sands Corp., Wynn Resorts Ltd., and MGM Resorts International, are hedging their gambling revenue by operating casinos in Macau.

Vegas resorts may not be able to compete with the Macau's gambling dollar, but by offering more they can still rule the tourist dollar.

Internet Gambling

The big new alligator on the block that could affect Las Vegas is not half a world away, but within most homes. Out of a total $27 billion in Internet gambling wagered worldwide each year, about $6 billion of that is from Americans, even though it's technically illegal for them. In 2006, then-President Bush signed the Unlawful Internet Gaming Enforcement Act (UIGEA), a controversial de facto ban on Internet wagering because it forbids credit card companies from processing transactions from online gambling sites, and puts the onus on them to recognize where payments are going. In effect it is a backdoor ban on Internet gambling. After delays and extensions, the bill went into effect on June 1, 2010.

Meanwhile, Rep. Barney Frank (D.-MA), as chairman of the House Financial Services Committee, introduced a bill (H.R.2267) to allow U.S. residents to gamble on their computers, bypassing the country's casinos, and raising approximately $42 billion in taxes over 10 years. Frank's bill attracted 66 co-signers. One of them, Rep. Jim McDermott (D.-WA), introduced legislation that spelled out the collection of license fees and taxes. His bill also offered states the right to refuse participation, but they would lose any tax revenues generated. The bills overwhelmingly passed the House, and Nevada Senator Harry Reid picked up the banner with the Internet Poker Act of 2010, but the new Congress, by tacking the bills on a tax relief act, assured their demise.

Undaunted, on March 17, 2011 Congressman Frank, this time with Congressman John Campbell (R.-CA) and others, reintroduced an anti-UIGEA bill, similar legislation to his previous HR 2267.

In 2011, the government began to enforce the UIGEA law and indicted 11 people from three popular overseas-based Internet poker sites, charging fraud and illegal gambling. Seems they used circuitous means to trick U.S. financial institutions into processing payments. The American Gaming Association (most of the nation's casino operators) said it was open to the concept of legalized Internet gaming, as long as a regulatory structure was in place to protect consumers and the game's integrity.

William Eadington, professor of economics and director of the Institute for the Study of Gambling and Commercial Gaming at the University of Nevada, Reno, said, "It's better to legalize and regulate gambling than fight a losing battle against it. Technology can keep a record of gambling activity, restrict the hours and expenditures, and block access to offshore sites."

Las Vegas casinos are a bit divided on whether or not to support the legislation. MGM Mirage, back in 2001, ran an Internet gambling site licensed on the Isle of Man. They refused wagers from Americans, and abandoned the project after 21 months. Both MGM Mirage and Caesars Entertainment, which owns the World Series of Poker, support legalizing and taxing Internet gaming. Caesars senior vice president Jan Jones, speaking at a panel of casino executives in May 2011, emphasized, "You're not going to stop the Internet. You can regulate it. You can put in protections, but it's going to exist." Panel members, who estimate legal U.S. Internet gambling revenue at nearly $80 billion, concurred. Several panel members felt that a few states would legalize the action before the federal government gets on board.

Nevada, it would seem, should have the jump on other states. They have the experience, existing technologies, and control systems in place to investigate, validate, and license proposed Internet companies. It appears that legalized gambling will need trustworthy and branded sites, and Nevada is definitely ahead there.

But other states, like California, are lurking in the wings. By July 2011, lawmakers from the Golden State were already planning internet gambling legislation. In April 2011, Washington D.C. set the precedent by legalizing Internet gambling to those making bets from within the district. They are counting on loopholes in the 2006 UIGEA. In New Jersey, the governor recently vetoed a bill that would have permitted it there, saying the voters should decide, so it's going on the ballot.

There are revenue benefits in allowing licensed online operators to offer gambling to Americans. Online businesses would pay up-front fees and be taxed at the same rate as brick and mortar casinos, currently 6.75%. Would gamblers forego casinos and trips to Las Vegas to gamble legally at home? Definitely some who are not already doing it illegally would, but the biggest benefit to Las Vegas would be the fees and taxation, as well as the profits the Las Vegas gaming companies astute enough to get in on the ground floor would realize.

Vegas is Resilient

Las Vegas, though it's weathered a few tough years, is resilient. Las Vegas, the city that never sleeps, thrives on its excesses, its reputation, whether viewed as incredibly fantastic, or sordid and sullied. Las Vegas, with all its imperfections, bounces back.

In a private April 2010 interview, longtime Vegas entertainer Wayne Newton mentioned that despite the economic downturn, he felt Las Vegas has greater years ahead. "What we've seen is just the tip of the iceberg," he said.

Jonathan Galaviz of Globalysis Ltd., a private tourism and leisure sector strategy consultancy, also offered a positive outlook: "Anybody who bets against Las Vegas in the long run will be placing a losing bet." That "Welcome to Las Vegas" sign at the edge of town has never meant as much as it has lately. The "happenings" in Vegas that are supposed to "stay in Vegas" are the visitors having a good time—and spending money while doing it.

Bibliography

Albert, Alexia. *Brothel: Mustang Ranch and Its Women*. New York: Ballentine Books, 2001

Automobile Club of Southern California. *Las Vegas and Laughlin*. Costa Mesa, California: Travel Information Products, 2008.

Axelrad, Josh. *Repeat Until Rich*. New York: Penguin Press, 2010.

Berman, Susan. *Easy Street: The True Story of a Gangster's Daughter*. New York: Bantam Books, 1983.

Binkley, Christina. *Winner Takes All: Steve Wynn, Kirk Kerkorian, Gary Loveman and the Race to Own Las Vegas*. New York: Hyperion, 2008

Clarke, Norm. *Vegas Confidential: Sinsational Celebrity Tales*. Las Vegas: Stephens Press, 2009

Cunningham, Katie. *Nicotine Dreams: A Story of Compulsive Gambling*. College Station, TX: Virtualbookworm Publications, 2005

Fischer, Steve. *When The Mob Ran Vegas*. Omaha: Berkline Press, 2005

Fleeman, Michael. *If I Die…* New York: St. Martin's Press, 2002

Friedman, Bill. *Designing Casinos To Dominate The Competition*. Reno: Institute for Study of Gambling and Commercial Gaming. University of Nevada, Reno, 2000

German, Jeff. *Murder in Sin City*. New York: Avon Books, 2001

Gollehon, John. *What Casinos Don't Want You To Know*. Grand Rapids, MI: Gollehon Press, 1999

Gollehon, John. *Casino Gambling: How To Play To Win*. Grand Rapids, MI: Gollehon Press, 2004

Griffin, Dennis N. *The Battle for Las Vegas*. Las Vegas: Huntington Press, 2006

Gros, Roger. *How To Win At Casino Gambling*. New York: Barnes and Noble Books, 2000

Hopkins, A. D., and Evans, K. J. *The First 100: Portraits of the Men and Women Who Shaped Las Vegas*. Las Vegas: Huntington Press, 1999

Karlins, Dr. Marvin. *The Book Casino Managers Fear The Most*. Grand Rapids, MI: Gollehon Press, 1998

Kelley, Kitty. *His Way: The Unauthorized Biography of Frank Sinatra*. New York: Bantam Books, 1986

Lancelot, Marilyn, *Gripped by Gambling*. Tucson, AZ: Wheatmark Publications, 2007

Macdonald, Ross. *Black Money*. New York: Alfred A. Knopf, 1966

Marg, Susan. *Las Vegas Weddings*. New York: Harper Collins Publishers, 2004

Martin, Don and Betty. *Las Vegas: The Best of Glitter City*. Las Vegas: Discover Guides, 2003

Mezrich, Ben. *Bringing Down The House*. New York: Simon & Schuster, 2002

Mezrich, Ben. *Busting Vegas*. New York: Morrow/Harper Collins, 2005

Moehring, Eugene P. *Las Vegas: A Centennial History*. Las Vegas: University of Nevada Press, 2005

Moehring, Eugene P. *Resort City in the Sunbelt: Las Vegas, 1930-2000*. Las Vegas: University of Nevada Press, 2000

Moore, Terry. *The Passions of Howard Hughes*. Los Angeles: General Publishing Group, 1996

Munchkin, Richard. *Gambling Wizards*. Las Vegas: Huntington Press. 2003

Newton, Michael. *Mr. Mob: The Life and Crimes of Moe Dalitz*. Jefferson, NC: McFarland, 2009

Newton, Wayne. *Once Before I Go*. New York: William Morrow & Co. 1989

O'Brien, Matthew. *Beneath the Neon: Life and Death in the Tunnels of Las Vegas*. Las Vegas: Huntington Press, 2007

Pileggi, Nicholas. *Casino*. New York: Simon & Schuster, 1995

Puit, Glenn. *Witch: The True Story of Las Vegas' Most Notorious Female Killer*. New York: Berkeley Books, 2005

Puit, Glenn. *Fire In The Desert*. Las Vegas: Stephens Press, 2007

Reid, Ed and Ovid Demaris. *The Green Felt Jungle*. New York: Trident Press, 1963

Reid, Harry. *Searchlight: The Camp That Didn't Fail*. Las Vegas: University of Nevada Press, 1998

Reid, Sen. Harry. *The Good Fight*. New York: G.P. Putnam's Sons, 2008

Revere, Lawrence. *Playing Blackjack As A Business*. New Jersey: Carol Publishing Group, 1971

Shaner, Lora. *Madam: Chronicles of a Nevada Cathouse*. Las Vegas: Huntington Press, 1999

Sheehan, Jack. *The Players: The Men Who Made Las Vegas*. Reno: University of Nevada Press, 1997

Smith, John L. *Sharks in the Desert: The Founding Fathers and Current Kings of Las Vegas*. Fort Lee, New Jersey: Barricade Books, 2005

Smith, John L. *Of Rats and Men*. Las Vegas: Huntington Press, 2003

Schumacher, Geoff. *Sun, Sin and Suburbia: An Essential History of Modern Las Vegas*. Las Vegas: Stephens Press. 2005

Sparks, Richard. *Diary of a Mad Poker Player*. Milford, CT: Russell Enterprises, 2005

Tepperman, Lorne. *Betting Their Lives: The Close Relationship of Problem Gamblers*. Oxford University Press. 2009

Thorp, Dr. Edward O. *Beat the Dealer: A Winning Strategy for the Game of Twenty-One*. New York: Vintage Press, 1962

Periodicals/Magazines

Where Las Vegas. Morris Visitor Publications, Las Vegas

What's On: The Las Vegas Guide. Kellogg Media Group, Las Vegas

Las Vegas Magazine/VEGAS 2 Go. The Las Vegas Sun, Las Vegas

The Las Vegas Age, Las Vegas Gaming and Wagering Business

Websites

www.vegas.com
www.earlyvegas.com
www.lvol.com
www.lasvegassun.com
www.classiclasvegas.com
www.wikipedia.com
www.harrahs.com
http://gaming.nv.gov/index.htm
http://www.visitlasvegas.com/vegas/index.jsp
http://www.public-domain-photos.com/travel/las-vegas
www.lasvegas.com
www.lasvegasweekly.com
http://www.lasvegassands.com/
http://www.mgmmirage.com/
www.wynnlasvegas.com
www.lasvegasnevada.gov/

Index

Charo................................... 202
Cheetah 169, 189
Cheetahs........................ 158
Chemehuevi 24
Cher 136
Cherry Patch Ranch............ 196
Chessan, Ray 21, 27
Chicago Bulls 203
Chicago Joey 92
Chicago University 187
Chicken Ranch.................... 196
Chippendale's 208
Chopin 138-139
Christ Episcopal Church....... 20
CIA 89
CineVegas Film 235
Circus Circus Enterprises....227,
231
Circus Circus Hotel.........80, 85,
92, 114-115, 127-128, 137-
138, 166, 207-209, 226-227,
231-232, 238, 249
Cirqué du Soleil...........129, 137,
191, 240
CityCenter............... 2, 206, 219,
238-242, 277
Civella, Nick.....................86, 95
Civil War 22, 31, 272
Civilian Conservation Corps258
Clark County Museum........ 251
Clark County School..........3, 20
Clark County School Board .. 20
Clark County Sheriff......89, 159
Clark, Ed 40, 46
Clark, J. Ross ...32-33, 35-36, 38
Clark, Wilbur 55, 59, 78, 83
Clark, William Andrews........20,
31-33, 35-37, 40, 157
Classic Las Vegas 43, 81,
114, 140
Cleveland Clinic................. 225
Clooney, George 277
Clooney, Rosemary.........78, 136
Club Paradise 190
CNN 249
CNSSTC............................. 280
Coast Casinos...............115, 123
Cocopah 24
Cohen, Carl...................... 160

Cohen, Mickey 72
Cold War 243, 246
Cole, Lewis............................ 14
Cole, Nat King 106
Collins, Bill........................... 21
Collins, Jackie 192
Collins, Joan 201
Colorado.................. 14, 22-23,
25-26, 44-46, 231, 235, 255,
258-259, 262-265
Colorado Belle..............231, 255
Colorado River 14, 22-23,
25-26, 44-46, 255, 258-259,
262-265
Colorado River Compact....... 45
Colton, George Frederick.... 254
Comcast.............................. 242
COMDEX 233
Commission, Colorado
River 45-46
Conde Naste Traveler 241
Conforte, Joe 158
Conger, Darva 203
Congo Room 78
Conte, Richard 140
Continental Press Service 71
Convention Center,
Las Vegas...... 129, 211, 228,
233, 237, 282
Coolidge, Calvin................... 45
Copa Room 139
Copacabana Club 139
Copperfield, David 137
Coppola, Mike...................... 95
Cornero, Tony....... 56, 69-70, 83
Costa Bella 204
Costello, Frank 68, 70, 89
Costner, Kevin 24
Cottontail Ranch................ 196
Cottonwood Island............... 25
Court TV 166
Cox, Courtney 24
Coyote Ugly 146
Cragin, Ernie............. 51, 81-82,
103-104
Crane, Philip 275
Cravings Buffet................... 207
Crawford, Joan.................... 202
Crazy Girls 188

Crazy Horse III.................... 190
Crazy Horse Paris................ 191
Crazy Larry 93
Creative Commons ShareAlike
License 136
Creech Air Force Base......... 246
Creel, Clarence 157
Cronkite, Walter................. 245
Crowe, Frank............ 46-47, 252
Crozier, Oscar..................... 108
Crystal, Stephen 123
CSI 278
Cuba..................................... 76
Cugat, Xavier...................... 202
Culinary Workers Union 61,
160, 171
Cullotta, Frank 93-94, 97
Cunningham, Katie 215
Curtis, Tony......................... 201

D

Dalitz, Moe 65, 69, 78,
83-85, 97, 117, 153
Dallas Cowboys 161
Damon, Matt...................... 177
Dancing Waters 208-209
Daniels, Billy 60, 135
Davis Dam 22, 46
Davis, Arthur Powell 46
Davis, Sammy Jr..............60, 79,
105-106, 135, 140
Dead Hooker Story............. 149
Death Row Records 160
Death Valley 196, 259
Death Valley Junction.......... 196
Death Valley National Park.. 259
Déjà Vu 190
Delano Hotel....................... 237
Demaris, Ovid 105
Dempsey, Jack...................... 53
DeNiro, Robert..................... 91
Denver................... 96, 110, 281
Desert Tortoise Conservation
Center 259
DesertWind 279
DesertXpress 279-281
Desperado Roller Coaster.... 253
DeStefano, Sam..................... 94

L

M

X

Y

Z

W

GREG NIEMANN

Author Greg Niemann is a fourth-generation Californian who has been visiting Las Vegas regularly since Fremont Street was the biggest show in town and the Strip was mostly vacant lots. He's also romped all over the southern Nevada deserts and became especially familiar with the Eldorado Canyon area. He is a member of the Las Vegas/Clark County Library District Foundation, and the Friends of Classic Las Vegas.

Since retiring from UPS where he edited company publications, Niemann has authored several books, including: *Baja Fever, Baja Legends, Palm Springs Legends*, and *Big Brown: The Untold Story of UPS*.

The memoirs brought out in *Baja Fever* created a loyal following of Baja fans. *Baja Legends*, which focuses on the characters, events, and locations that put Baja California on the map, won an award from the Outdoor Writers Association of California (OWAC), and is in its third printing. *Palm Springs Legends* is also in its third printing, and *Big Brown* has been selling worldwide, in both English and foreign versions.

Niemann enjoys fishing and other outdoor activities, and occasionally hits the casinos to play a little blackjack. He has served on the board of directors of the Outdoor Writers Association of California. He and his wife reside in Southern California and travel as much as possible.

www.gregniemann.com

Sunbelt's Southwest Bookshelf

Incorporated in 1988, with roots in publishing since 1973, Sunbelt Publications produces and distributes natural science and outdoor guidebooks, regional histories and pictorials, and stories that celebrate the land and its people.

Sunbelt books help to discover and conserve natural, historical, and cultural heritage of unique regions on the frontiers of adventure and learning. Our books guide readers into distinctive communities and special places, both natural and man-made.

We carry hundreds of books on the southwest!
Visit us online at:

www.sunbeltbooks.com

Las Vegas Area Directory

Information and Assistance

City of Las Vegas
City Hall, 400 Stewart Ave.
Las Vegas, NV 89101
http://www.lasvegasnevada.gov

Las Vegas Chamber of Commerce
6671 Las Vegas Blvd. So. Suite 300
Las Vegas, NV 89119
http://www.lvchamber.com

Clark County
500 S. Grand Central Pkwy. 6th Floor
Las Vegas, NV 89155-1111
http://www.clarkcountynv.gov

City of Henderson
http://www.visithenderson.com

City of Boulder City
http://www.visitbouldercity.com

Las Vegas Convention and Visitors Authority
3150 Paradise Rd.
Las Vegas, NV 89109
http://www.lvcva.com/index.jsp

Nevada Commission on Tourism
http://travelnevada.com

Nevada Resort Association
http://www.nevadaresorts.org

Peeking Into The Past

Nevada Historical Society; Nevada State Museum, Las Vegas; Lost City Museum, Overton; Nevada State Railroad Museum, Boulder City
http://museums.nevadaculture.org

Nevada State Museum, Las Vegas
700 Twin Lakes Drive
Las Vegas, NV 89107
http://museums.nevadaculture.org

Las Vegas Natural History Museum
900 Las Vegas Blvd. No.
Las Vegas NV 89101
http://www.lvnhm.org

Museums of Southern Nevada
http://museums.travelnevada.com

Clark County Museum, Henderson
http://www.clarkcountynv.gov/Depts/parks

Boulder City/Hoover Dam Museum
http://www.bcmha.org

Atomic Testing Museum
http://www.atomictestingmuseum.org

Red Rock Canyon National Conservation Area
Interpretive Association/Visitors Center
Las Vegas, NV 89161
http://www.redrockcanyonlv.org/index.html

Gamblers General Store
www.gamblersgeneralstore.com

University of Nevada, Las Vegas
http://go.unlv.edu

University of Nevada, Reno
http://www.unr.edu

Eldorado Canyon Mine Tours
http://eldoradocanyonminetours.com

Vegas Online and Print Media

AccessVegas.com
http://accessvegas.com/

Vegas.com (Entertainment)
http://www.vegas.com

ONE (Online Nevada Encyclopedia)
http://www.onlinenevada.org

Classic Las Vegas, As We Knew It
http://www.classiclasvegas.com

Las Vegas Magazine
Greenspun Media Group
http://lasvegasmagazine.com

What's On, The Las Vegas Guide
http://www.whats-on.com

Desert Companion
Published by Nevada Public Radio
http://desertcompanion.com